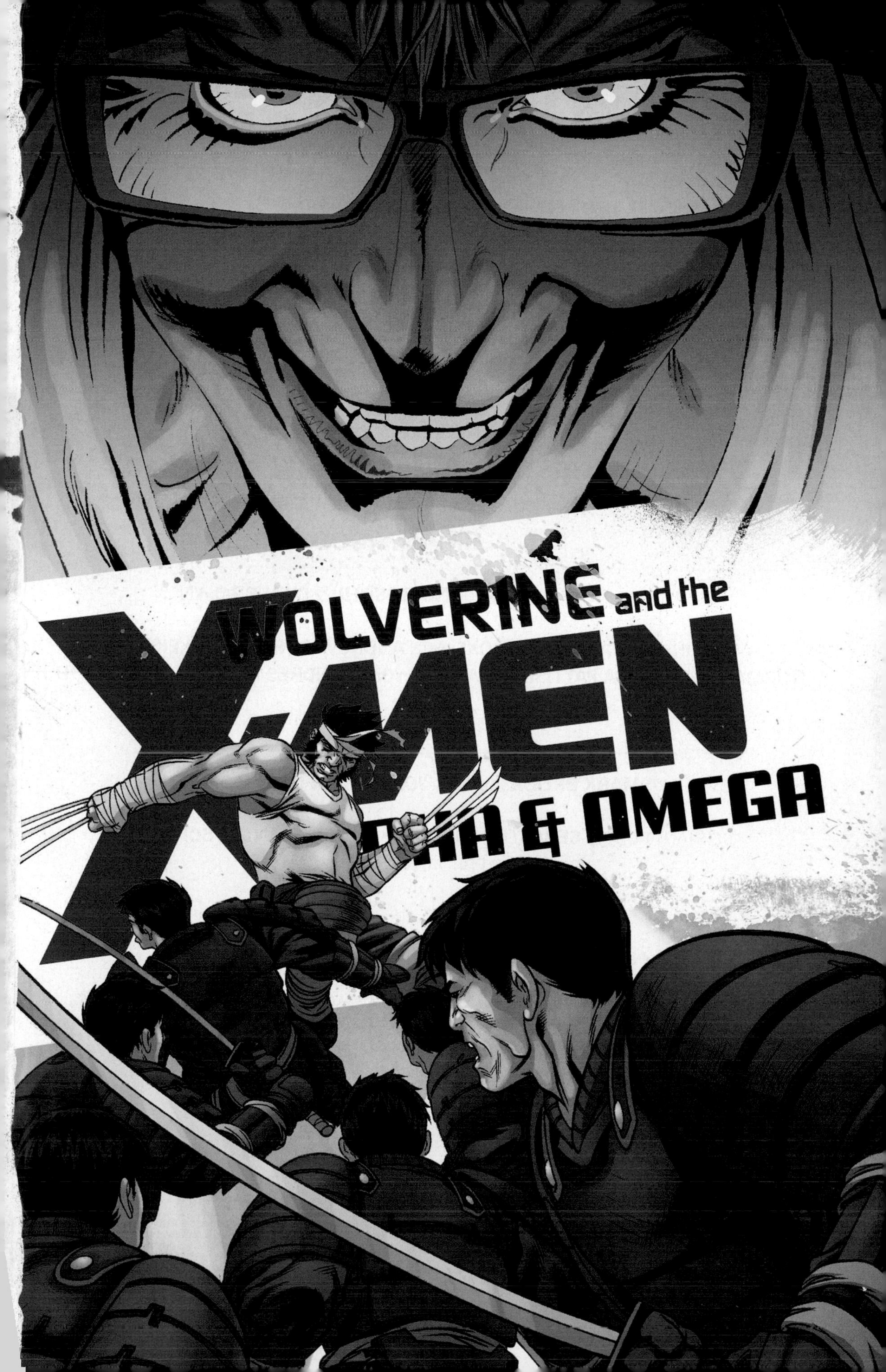
WOLVERINE and the
X-MEN
ALPHA & OMEGA

WOLVERINE and the X-MEN
ALPHA & OMEGA

WRITER: **BRIAN WOOD**

ART (WESTCHESTER): **ROLAND BOSCHI** & **DAN BROWN**

ART (CONSTRUCT): **MARK BROOKS** WITH **ANDREW CURRIE, JAY LEISTEN, NORMAN LEE, RONDA PATTISON, WALDEN WONG, ANDRES MOSSA** & **CAM SMITH**

LETTERER: **VC'S JOE SABINO**

COVER ART: **MARK BROOKS** (#1-2) & **JOHN TYLER CHRISTOPHER** (#3-4)

ASSISTANT EDITOR: **SEBASTIAN GIRNER** • EDITOR: **JEANINE SCHAEFER**

GROUP EDITOR: **NICK LOWE**

COLLECTION EDITOR: **JENNIFER GRÜNWALD**
ASSISTANT EDITORS:
ALEX STARBUCK & **NELSON RIBEIRO**
EDITOR, SPECIAL PROJECTS: **MARK D. BEAZLEY**
SENIOR EDITOR, SPECIAL PROJECTS:
JEFF YOUNGQUIST
SENIOR VICE PRESIDENT OF SALES: **DAVID GABRIEL**
SVP OF BRAND PLANNING & COMMUNICATIONS:
MICHAEL PASCIULLO
BOOK DESIGN: **RODOLFO MURAGUCHI** & **JEFF POWELL**

EDITOR IN CHIEF:
AXEL ALONSO
CHIEF CREATIVE OFFICER:
JOE QUESADA
PUBLISHER:
DAN BUCKLEY
EXECUTIVE PRODUCER:
ALAN FINE

WOLVERINE & THE X-MEN: ALPHA & OMEGA. Contains material originally published in magazine form as WOLVERINE & THE X-MEN: ALPHA & OMEGA #1-5. First printing 2012. Hardcover ISBN# 978-0-7851-6400-5. Softcover ISBN# 978-0-7851-6401-2. Published by MARVEL WORLDWIDE, INC., a subsidiary of MARVEL ENTERTAINMENT, LLC. OFFICE OF PUBLICATION: 135 West 50th Street, New York, NY 10020.

Hardcover: $24.99 per copy in the U.S. and $27.99 in Canada (GST #R127032852). Softcover: $19.99 per copy in the U.S. and $21.99 in Canada (GST #R127032852). Canadian Agreement #40668537. All characters featured in this issue and the distinctive names and likenesses thereof, and all related indicia are trademarks of Marvel Characters, Inc. No similarity between any of the names, characters, persons, and/or institutions in this magazine with those of any living or dead person or institution is intended, and any such similarity which may exist is purely coincidental. **Printed in the U.S.A.** ALAN FINE, EVP - Office of the President, Marvel Worldwide, Inc. and EVP & CMO Marvel Characters B.V.; DAN BUCKLEY, Publisher & President - Print, Animation & Digital Divisions; JOE QUESADA, Chief Creative Officer; TOM BREVOORT, SVP of Publishing; DAVID BOGART, SVP of Operations & Procurement, Publishing; RUWAN JAYATILLEKE, SVP & Associate Publisher, Publishing; C.B. CEBULSKI, SVP of Creator & Content Development; DAVID GABRIEL, SVP of Publishing Sales & Circulation; MICHAEL PASCIULLO, SVP of Brand Planning & Communications; JIM O'KEEFE, VP of Operations & Logistics; DAN CARR, Executive Director of Publishing Technology; SUSAN CRESPI, Editorial Operations Manager; ALEX MORALES, Publishing Operations Manager; STAN LEE, Chairman Emeritus. For information regarding advertising in Marvel Comics or on Marvel.com, please contact Niza Disla, Director of Marvel Partnerships, at ndisla@marvel.com. For Marvel subscription inquiries, please call 800-217-9158. **Manufactured between 5/28/2012 and 6/25/2012 (hardcover), and 5/28/2012 and 12/17/2012 (softcover), by R.R. DONNELLEY, INC., SALEM, VA, USA.**

10 9 8 7 6 5 4 3 2 1

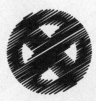

1

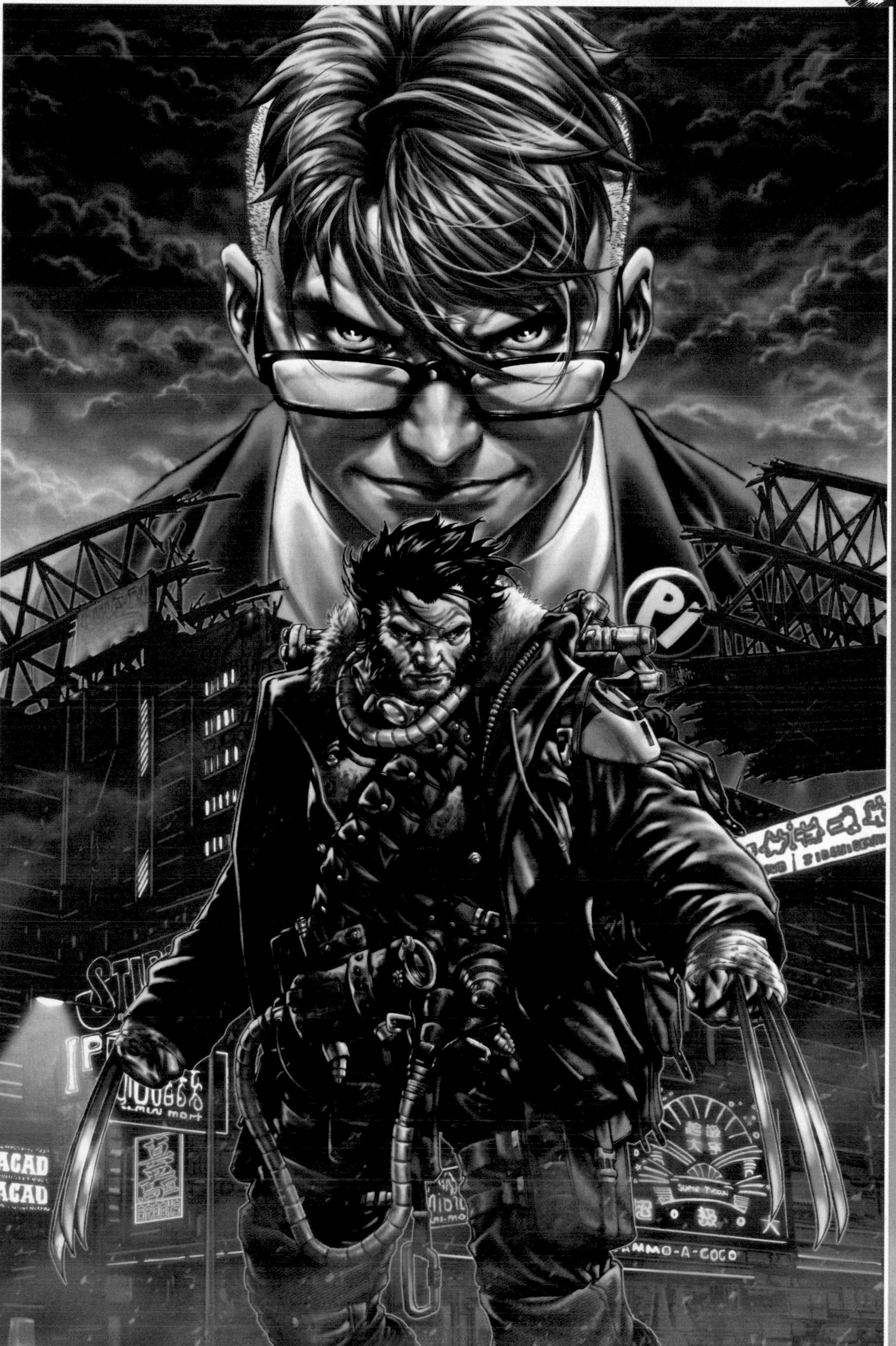
AMMO-A-GOGO

If you were born different with mutant powers, the Jean Grey School for Higher Learning is the school for you. Founded by Wolverine and staffed by experienced X-Men, you will learn everything you need to survive in a world that hates and fears you.

WOLVERINE and the X-MEN
ALPHA & OMEGA

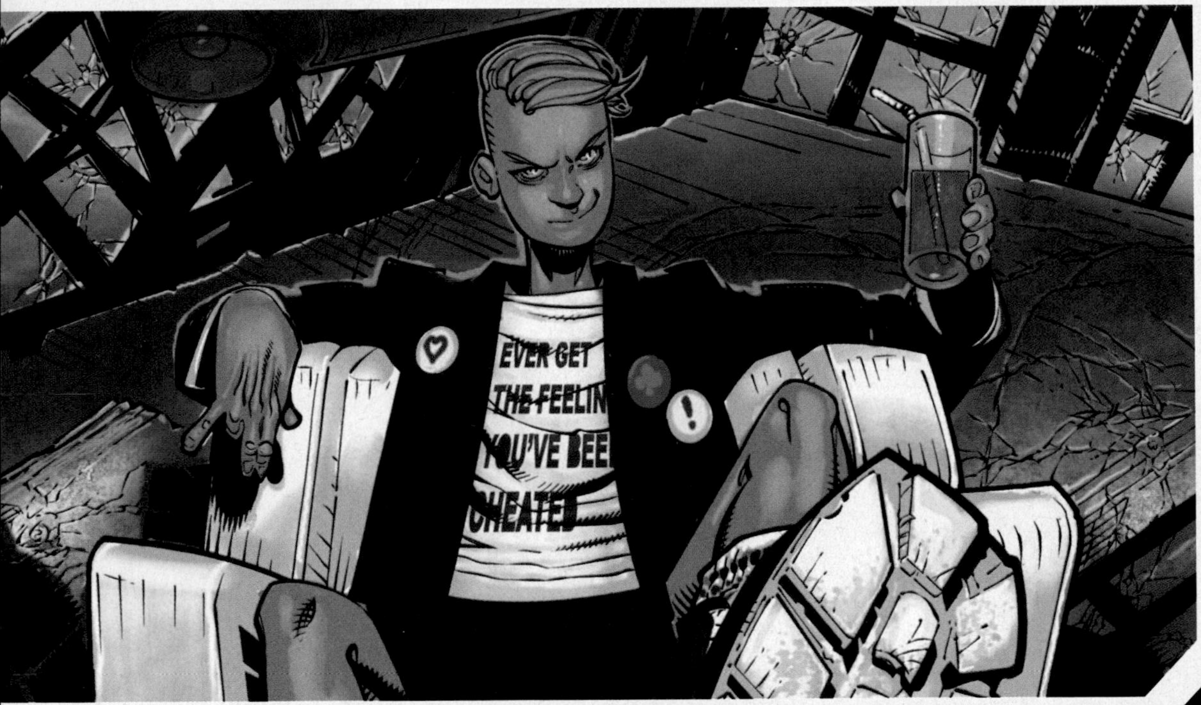
EVER GET
THE FEELIN
YOU'VE BEE
CHEATED

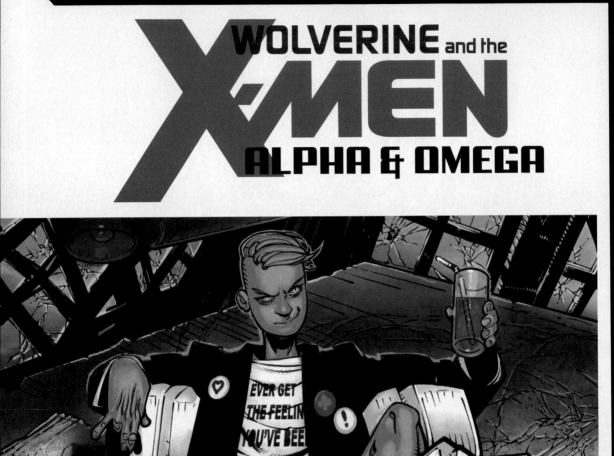

Born with incredible telepathic powers and a rebellious nature, Quentin Quire has caused no small amount of trouble for a teenage boy, from inciting riots to declaring a full-on war on humanity. His most recent antics have caused Wolverine to attempt to set him straight by forcefully enrolling him in the recently reopened mutant school in Westchester. But Quentin despises Wolverine and has vowed revenge...

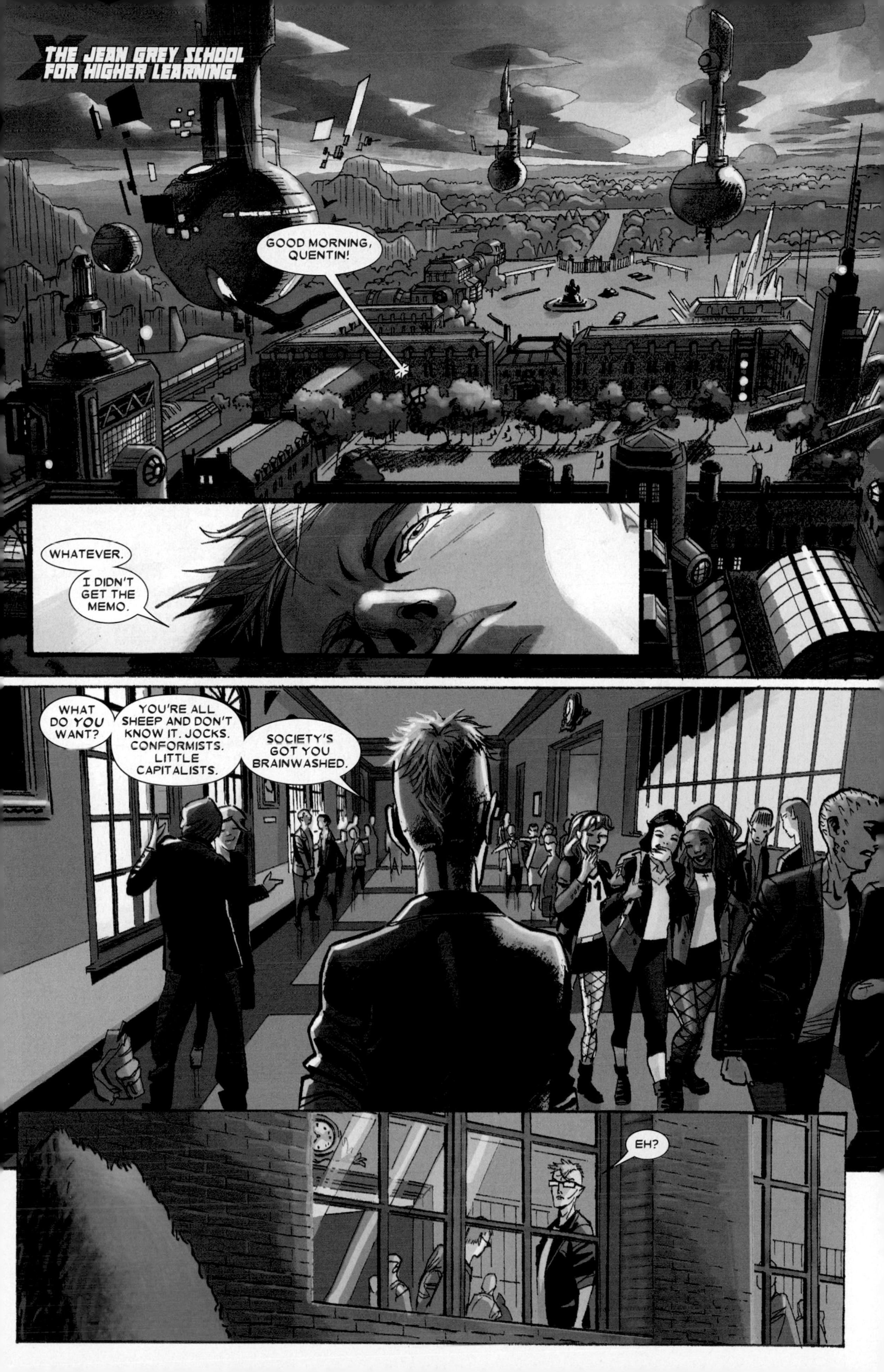
THE JEAN GREY SCHOOL FOR HIGHER LEARNING.
GOOD MORNING, QUENTIN!
WHATEVER.
I DIDN'T GET THE MEMO.
WHAT DO YOU WANT?
YOU'RE ALL SHEEP AND DON'T KNOW IT. JOCKS. CONFORMISTS. LITTLE CAPITALISTS.
SOCIETY'S GOT YOU BRAINWASHED.
EH?

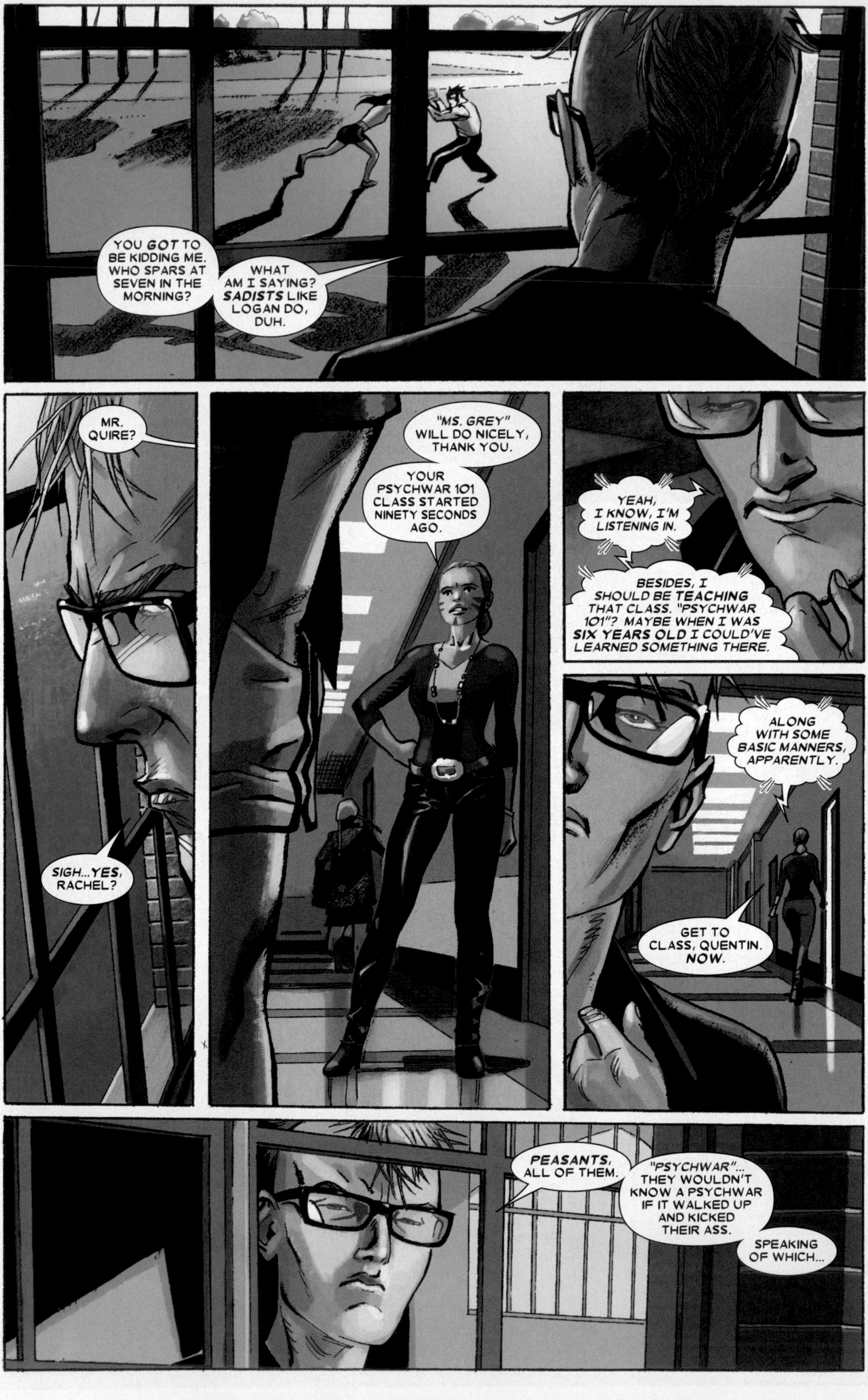
YOU GOT TO BE KIDDING ME. WHO SPARS AT SEVEN IN THE MORNING?
WHAT AM I SAYING? SADISTS LIKE LOGAN DO, DUH.
MR. QUIRE?
SIGH...YES, RACHEL?
"MS. GREY" WILL DO NICELY, THANK YOU.
YOUR PSYCHWAR 101 CLASS STARTED NINETY SECONDS AGO.
YEAH, I KNOW, I'M LISTENING IN.
BESIDES, I SHOULD BE TEACHING THAT CLASS. "PSYCHWAR 101"? MAYBE WHEN I WAS SIX YEARS OLD I COULD'VE LEARNED SOMETHING THERE.
ALONG WITH SOME BASIC MANNERS, APPARENTLY.
GET TO CLASS, QUENTIN. NOW.
PEASANTS, ALL OF THEM.
"PSYCHWAR"... THEY WOULDN'T KNOW A PSYCHWAR IF IT WALKED UP AND KICKED THEIR ASS.
SPEAKING OF WHICH...

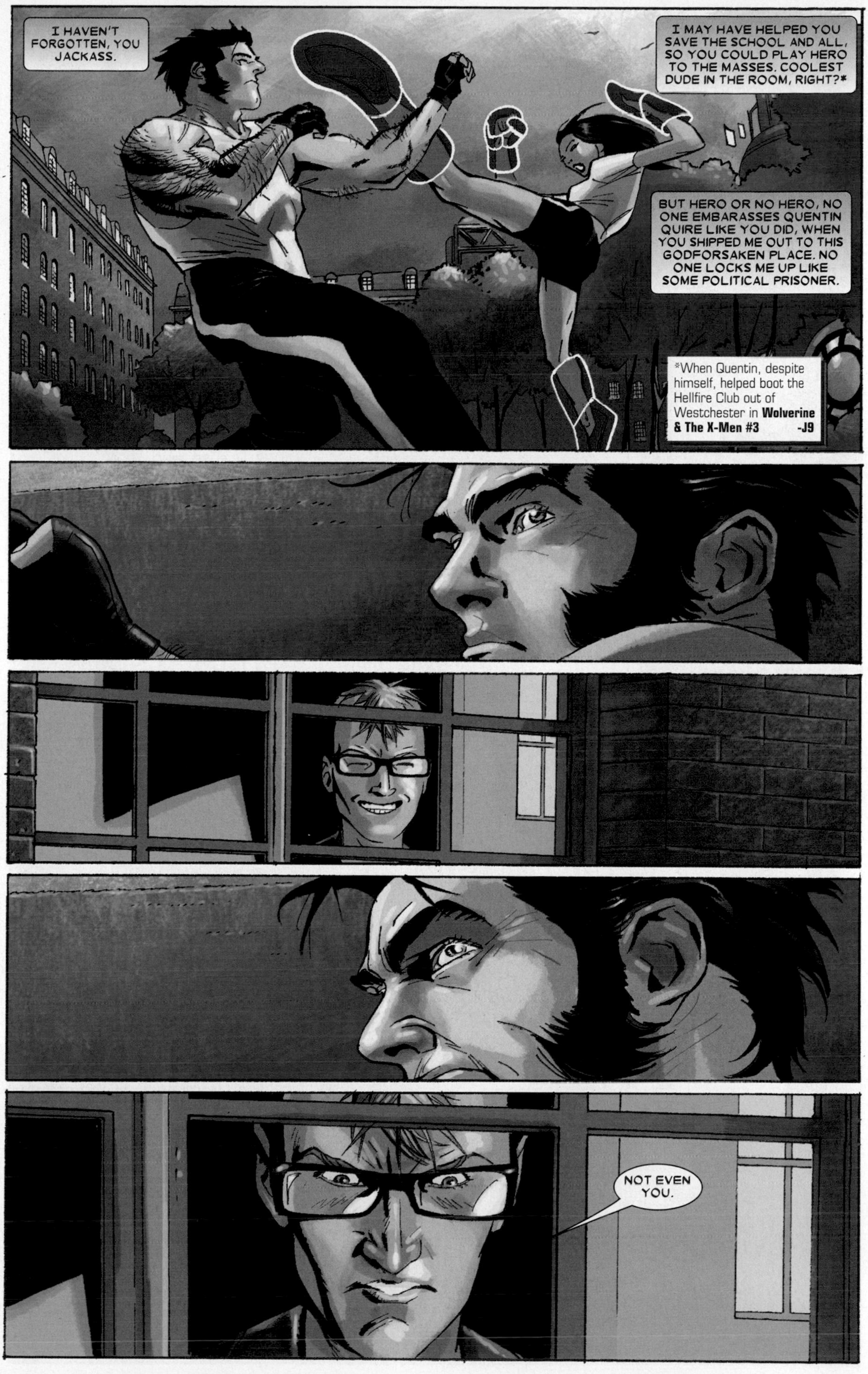
I HAVEN'T FORGOTTEN, YOU JACKASS.
I MAY HAVE HELPED YOU SAVE THE SCHOOL AND ALL, SO YOU COULD PLAY HERO TO THE MASSES. COOLEST DUDE IN THE ROOM, RIGHT?*
BUT HERO OR NO HERO, NO ONE EMBARASSES QUENTIN QUIRE LIKE YOU DID, WHEN YOU SHIPPED ME OUT TO THIS GODFORSAKEN PLACE. NO ONE LOCKS ME UP LIKE SOME POLITICAL PRISONER.
*When Quentin, despite himself, helped boot the Hellfire Club out of Westchester in **Wolverine & The X-Men #3** -J9
NOT EVEN YOU.

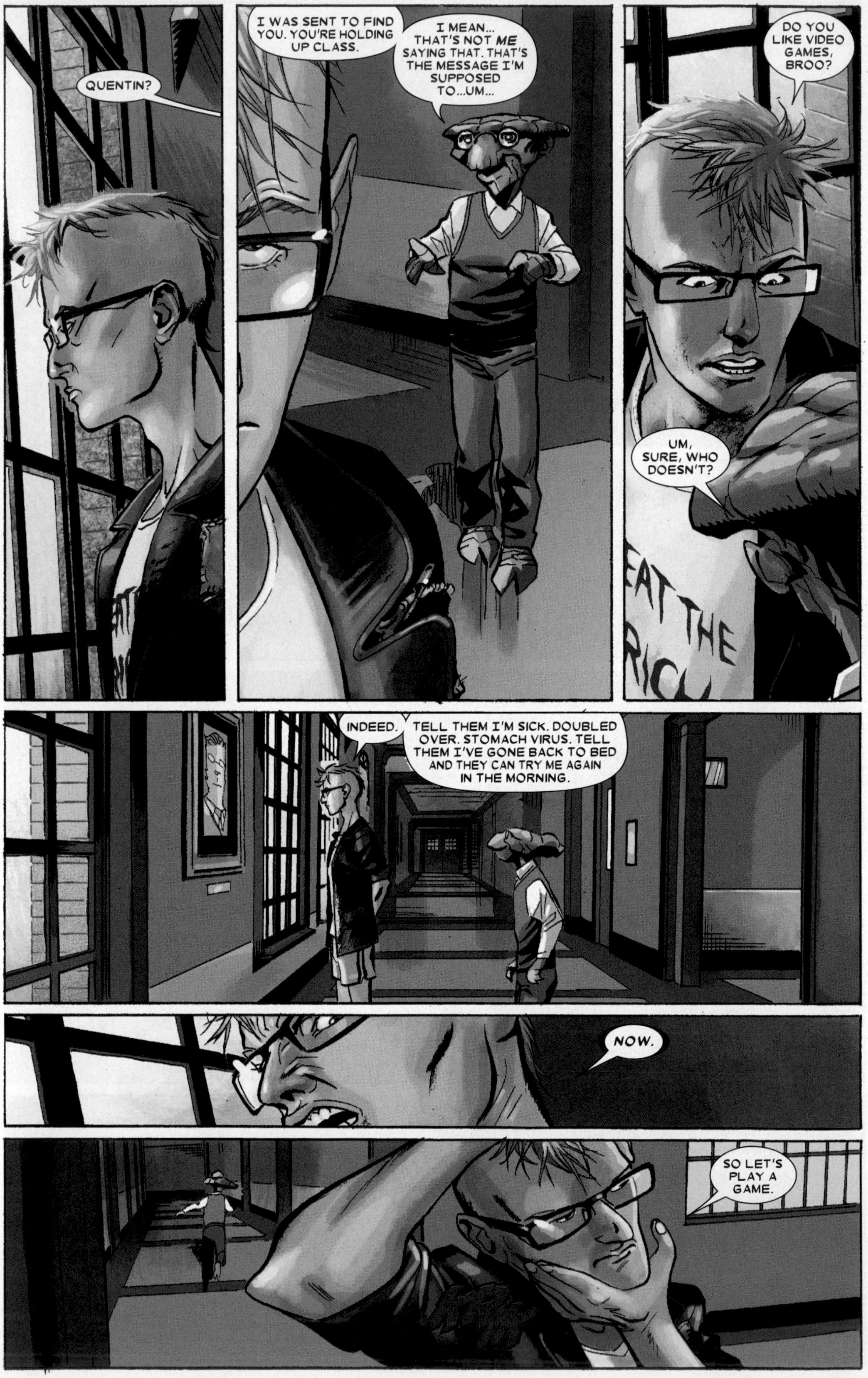
QUENTIN?
I WAS SENT TO FIND YOU. YOU'RE HOLDING UP CLASS.
I MEAN... THAT'S NOT ME SAYING THAT. THAT'S THE MESSAGE I'M SUPPOSED TO...UM...
DO YOU LIKE VIDEO GAMES, BROO?
UM, SURE, WHO DOESN'T?
EAT THE RICH
INDEED.
TELL THEM I'M SICK. DOUBLED OVER. STOMACH VIRUS. TELL THEM I'VE GONE BACK TO BED AND THEY CAN TRY ME AGAIN IN THE MORNING.
NOW.
SO LET'S PLAY A GAME.

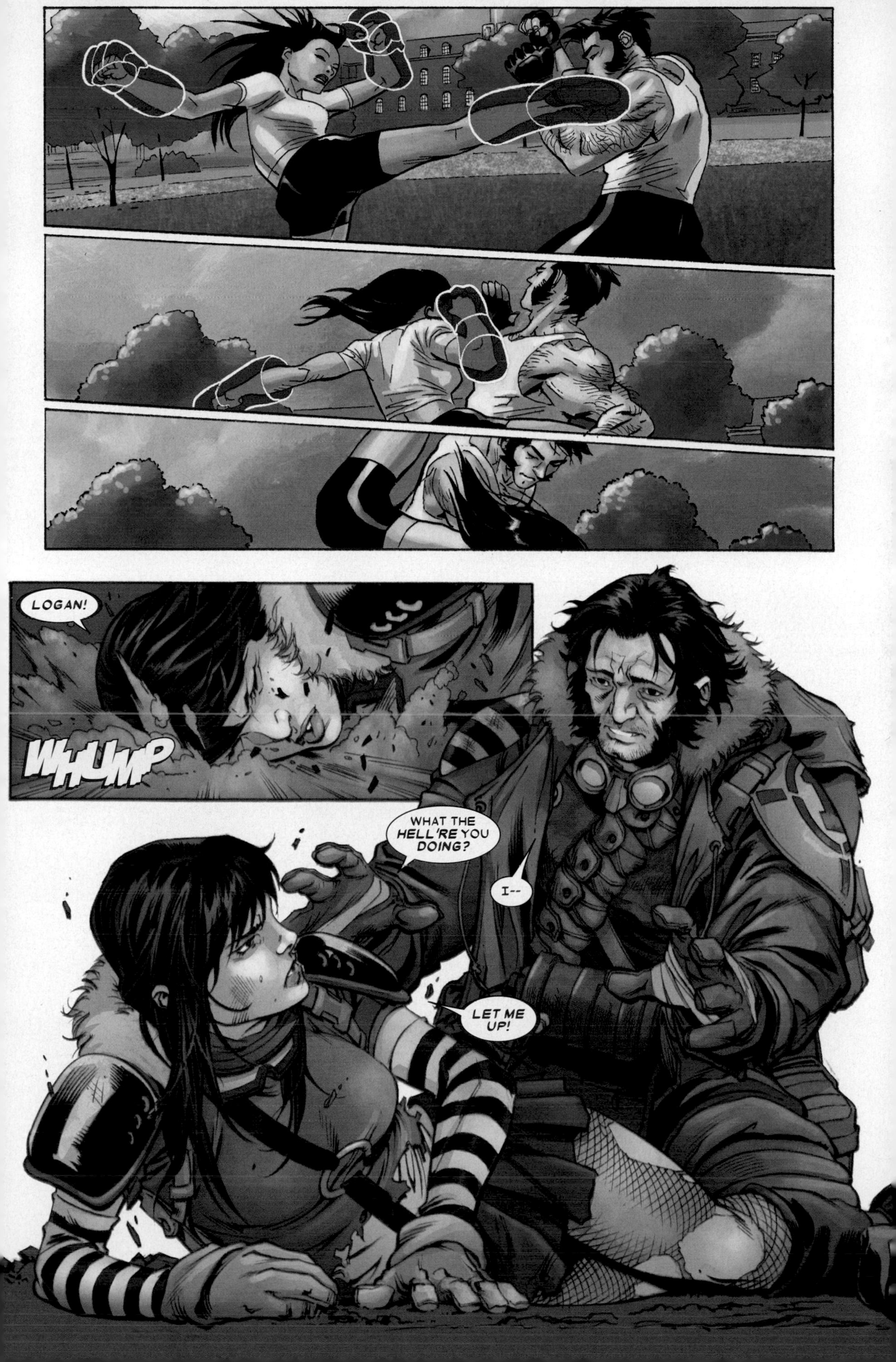

LOGAN!
WHUMP
WHAT THE HELL'RE YOU DOING?
I--
LET ME UP!

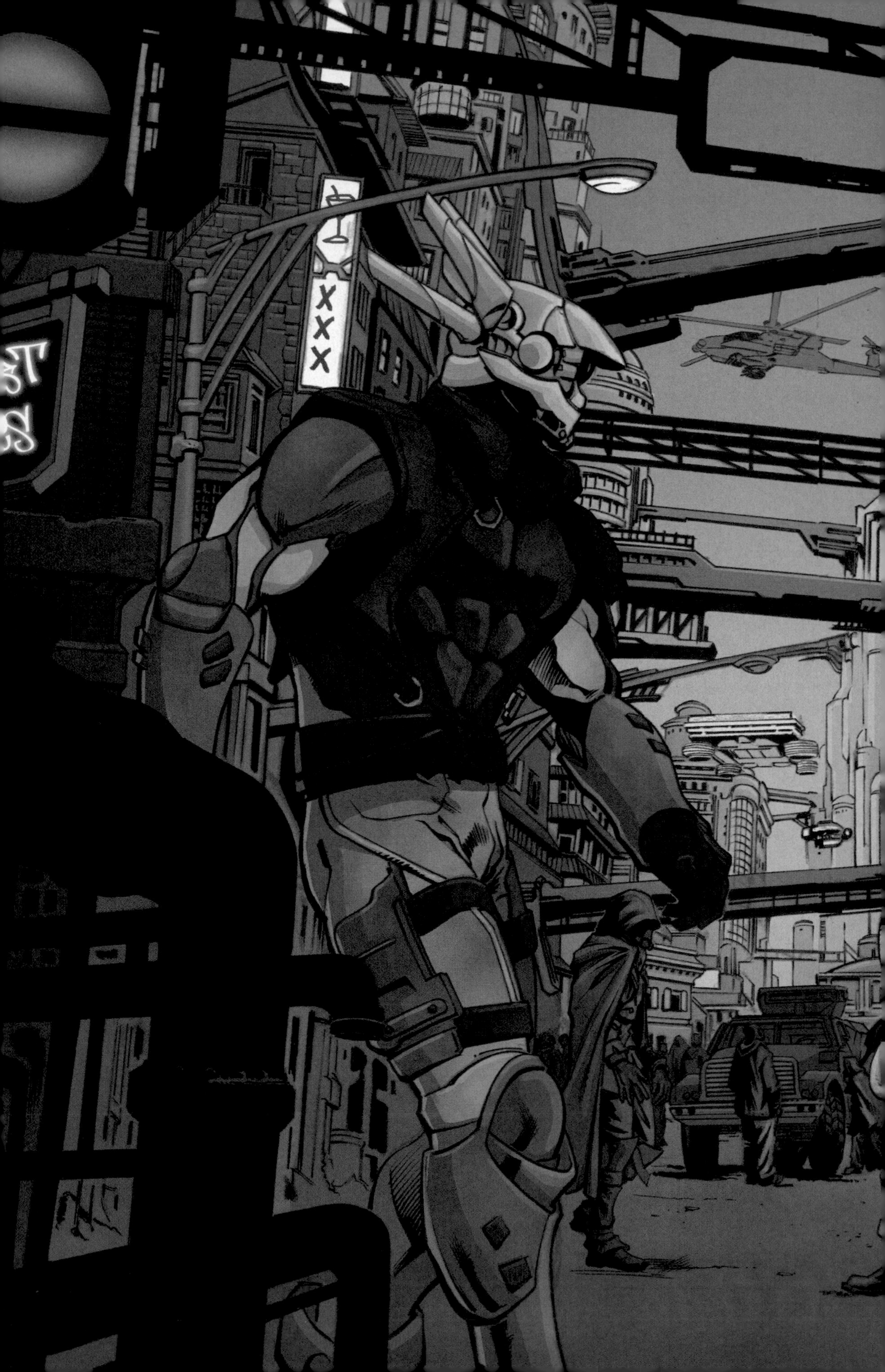
XXX

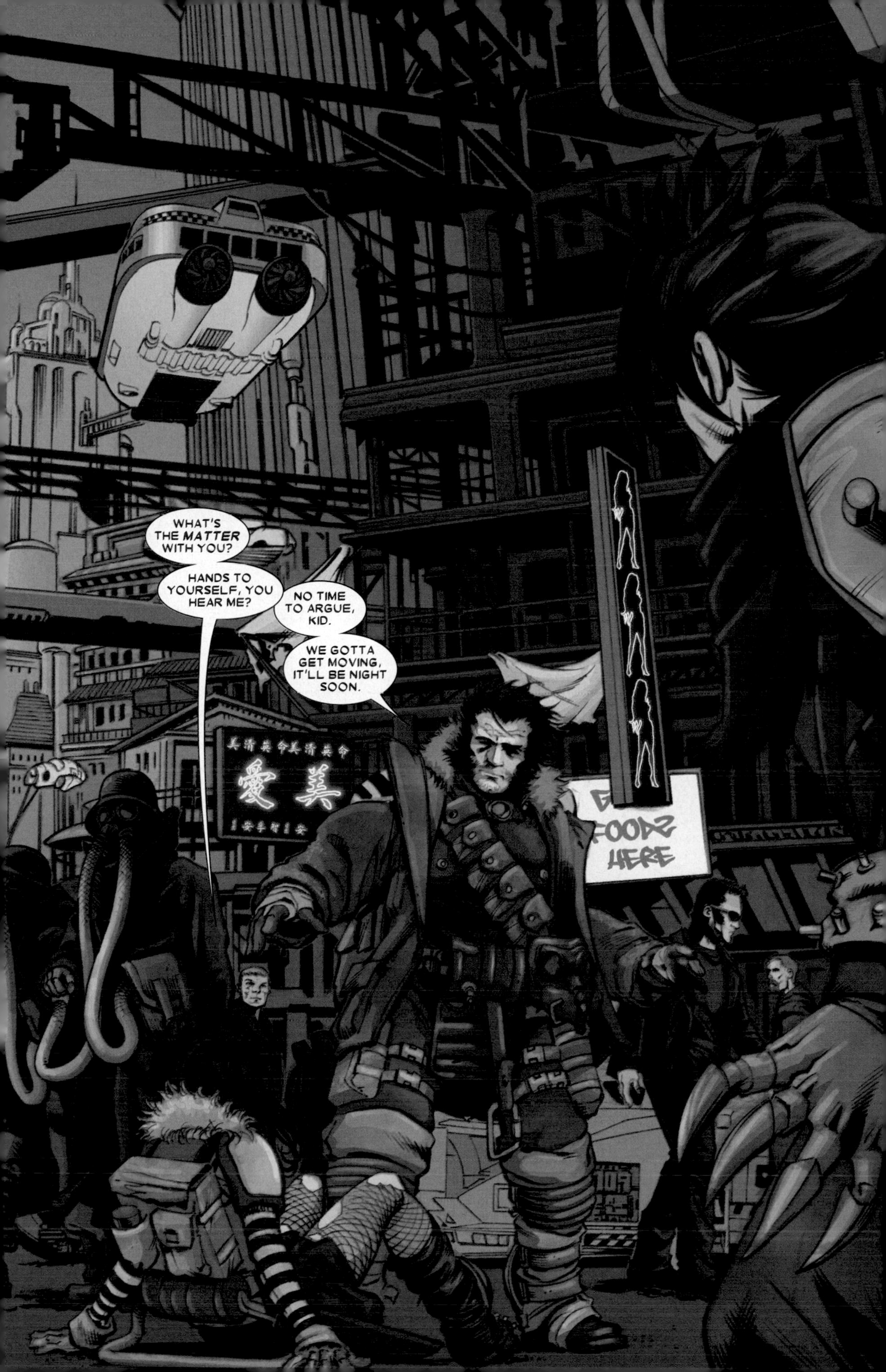
WHAT'S THE *MATTER* WITH YOU?
HANDS TO YOURSELF, YOU HEAR ME?
NO TIME TO ARGUE, KID.
WE GOTTA GET MOVING, IT'LL BE NIGHT SOON.
愛 美
FOODZ HERE

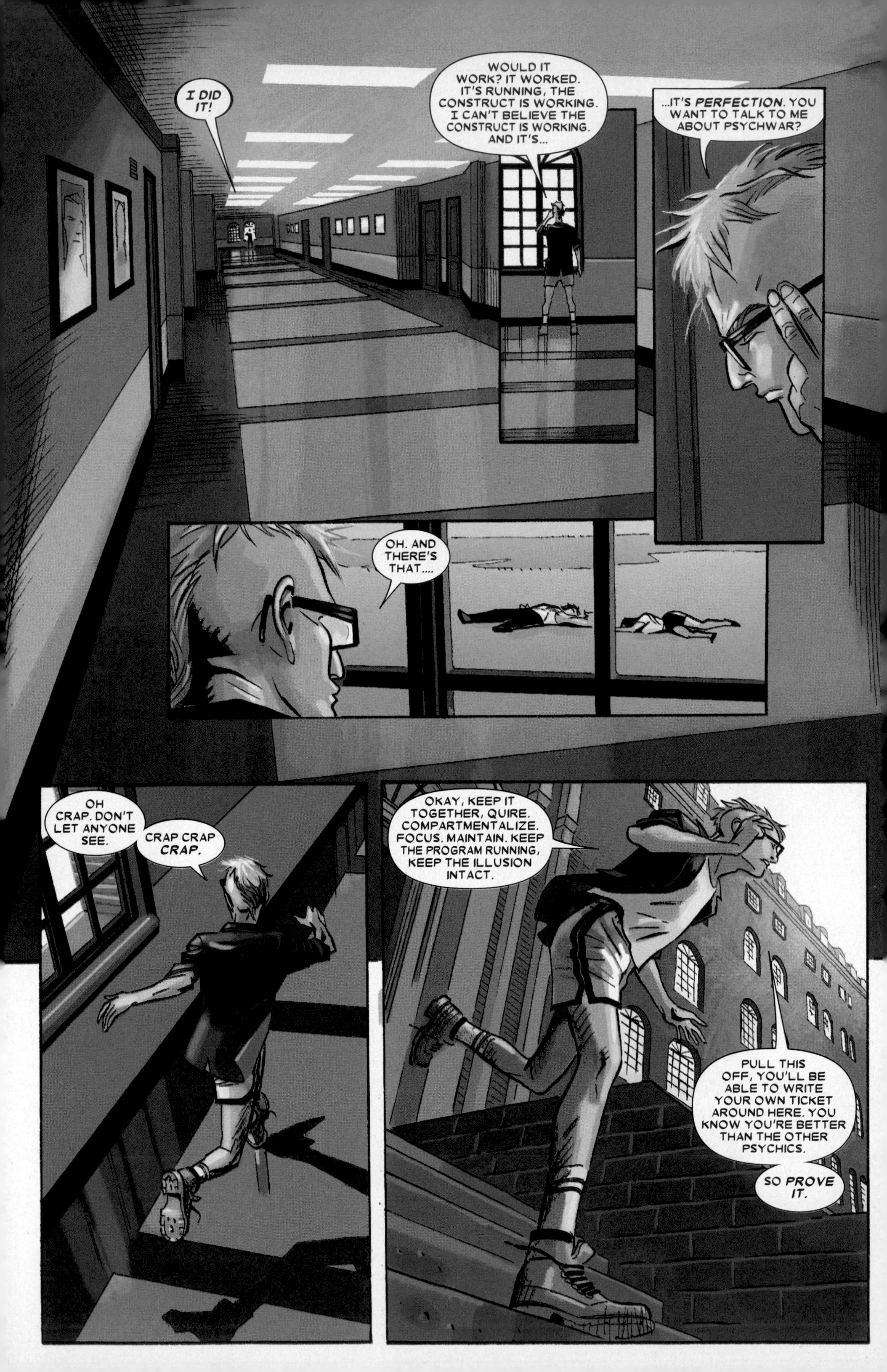
I DID IT!
WOULD IT WORK? IT WORKED. IT'S RUNNING, THE CONSTRUCT IS WORKING. I CAN'T BELIEVE THE CONSTRUCT IS WORKING. AND IT'S...
...IT'S PERFECTION. YOU WANT TO TALK TO ME ABOUT PSYCHWAR?
OH. AND THERE'S THAT....
OH CRAP. DON'T LET ANYONE SEE.
CRAP CRAP CRAP.
OKAY, KEEP IT TOGETHER, QUIRE. COMPARTMENTALIZE. FOCUS. MAINTAIN. KEEP THE PROGRAM RUNNING, KEEP THE ILLUSION INTACT.
PULL THIS OFF, YOU'LL BE ABLE TO WRITE YOUR OWN TICKET AROUND HERE. YOU KNOW YOU'RE BETTER THAN THE OTHER PSYCHICS.
SO PROVE IT.

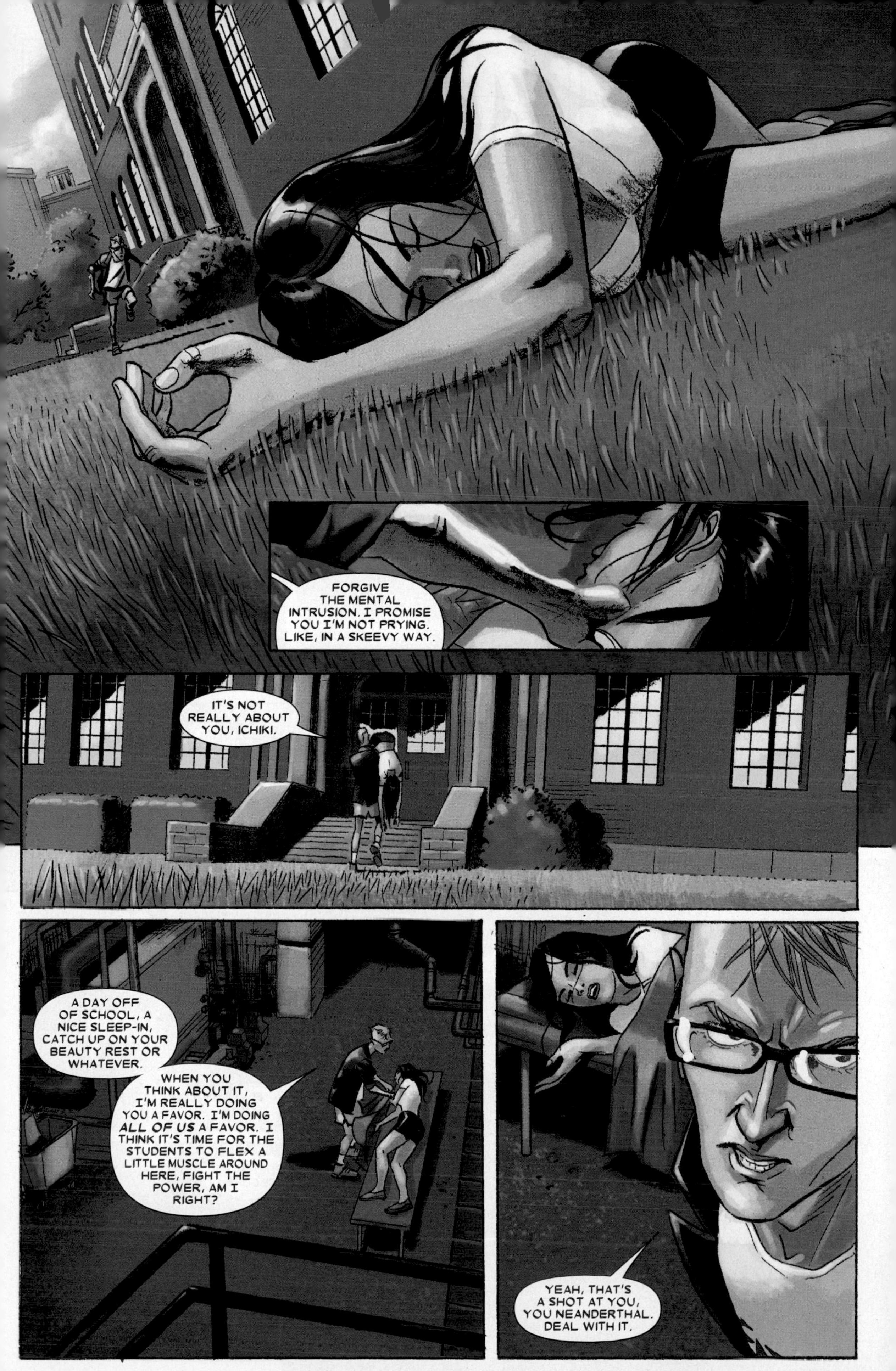
FORGIVE THE MENTAL INTRUSION. I PROMISE YOU I'M NOT PRYING. LIKE, IN A SKEEVY WAY.
IT'S NOT REALLY ABOUT YOU, ICHIKI.
A DAY OFF OF SCHOOL, A NICE SLEEP-IN, CATCH UP ON YOUR BEAUTY REST OR WHATEVER.
WHEN YOU THINK ABOUT IT, I'M REALLY DOING YOU A FAVOR. I'M DOING ALL OF US A FAVOR. I THINK IT'S TIME FOR THE STUDENTS TO FLEX A LITTLE MUSCLE AROUND HERE, FIGHT THE POWER, AM I RIGHT?
YEAH, THAT'S A SHOT AT YOU, YOU NEANDERTHAL. DEAL WITH IT.

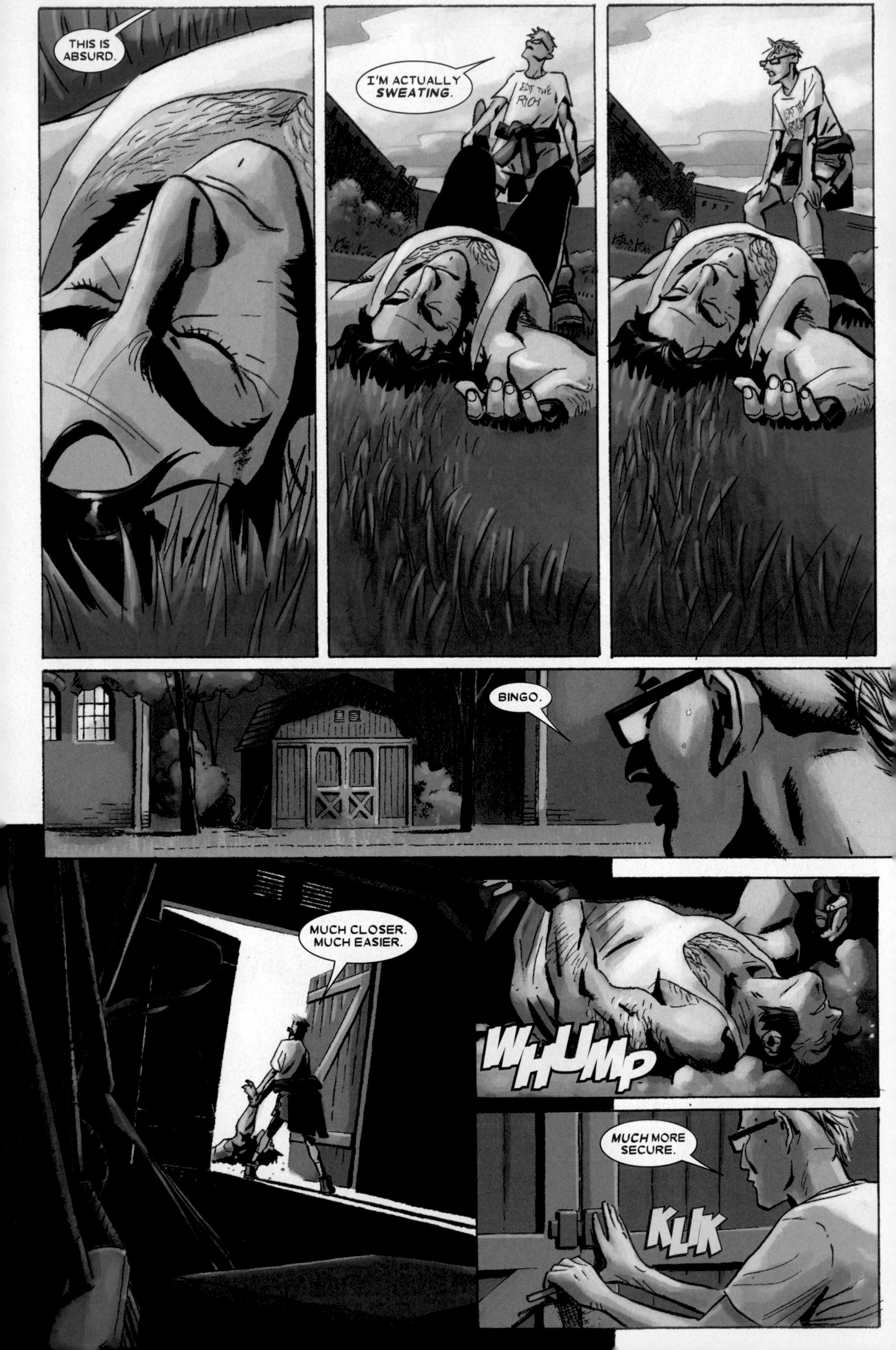
THIS IS ABSURD.
I'M ACTUALLY SWEATING.
EAT THE RICH
BINGO.
MUCH CLOSER. MUCH EASIER.
WHUMP
MUCH MORE SECURE.
KLIK

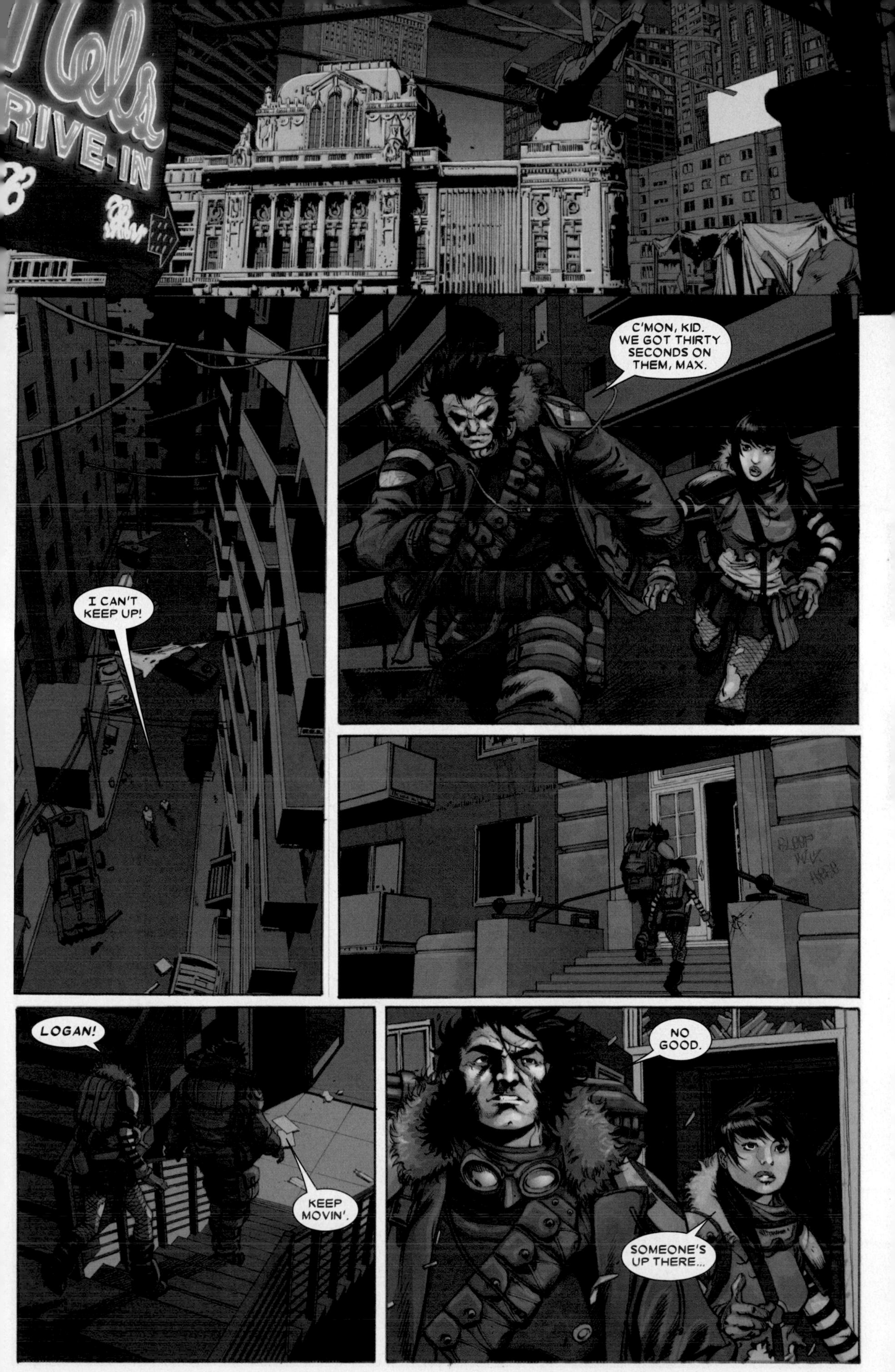

RIVE-IN
C'MON, KID. WE GOT THIRTY SECONDS ON THEM, MAX.
I CAN'T KEEP UP!
LOGAN!
KEEP MOVIN'.
NO GOOD.
SOMEONE'S UP THERE...

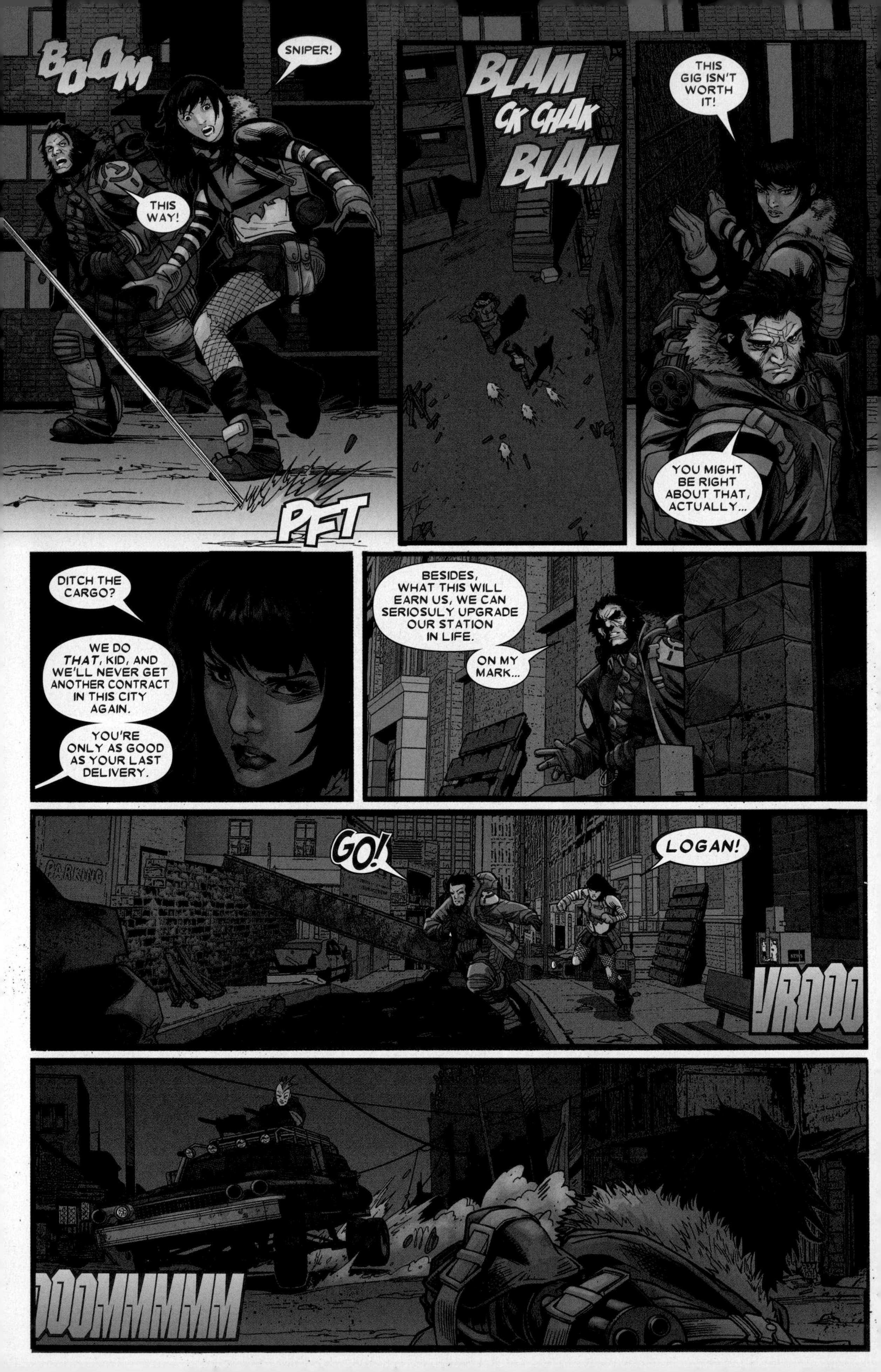
BOOM
SNIPER!
THIS WAY!
PFT
BLAM
CK CHAK
BLAM
THIS GIG ISN'T WORTH IT!
YOU MIGHT BE RIGHT ABOUT THAT, ACTUALLY...
DITCH THE CARGO?
WE DO *THAT*, KID, AND WE'LL NEVER GET ANOTHER CONTRACT IN THIS CITY AGAIN.
YOU'RE ONLY AS GOOD AS YOUR LAST DELIVERY.
BESIDES, WHAT THIS WILL EARN US, WE CAN SERIOSULY UPGRADE OUR STATION IN LIFE.
ON MY MARK...
PARKING
GO!
LOGAN!
VROOO
OOOMMMMMM

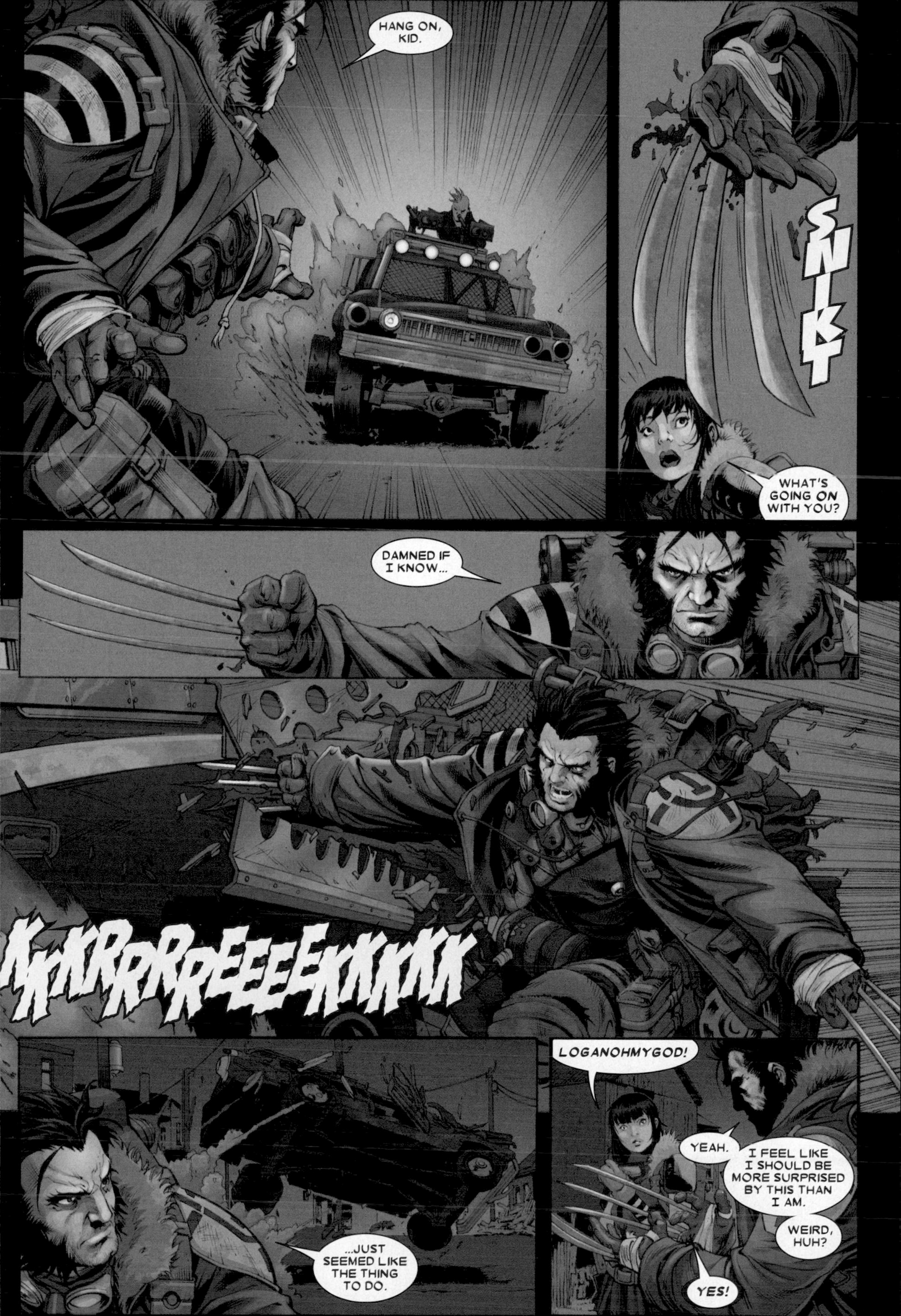
HANG ON, KID.
SNIKT
WHAT'S GOING ON WITH YOU?
DAMNED IF I KNOW...
KKKRRRRREEEEEKKKKK
...JUST SEEMED LIKE THE THING TO DO.
LOGANOHMYGOD!
YEAH.
I FEEL LIKE I SHOULD BE MORE SURPRISED BY THIS THAN I AM.
WEIRD, HUH?
YES!

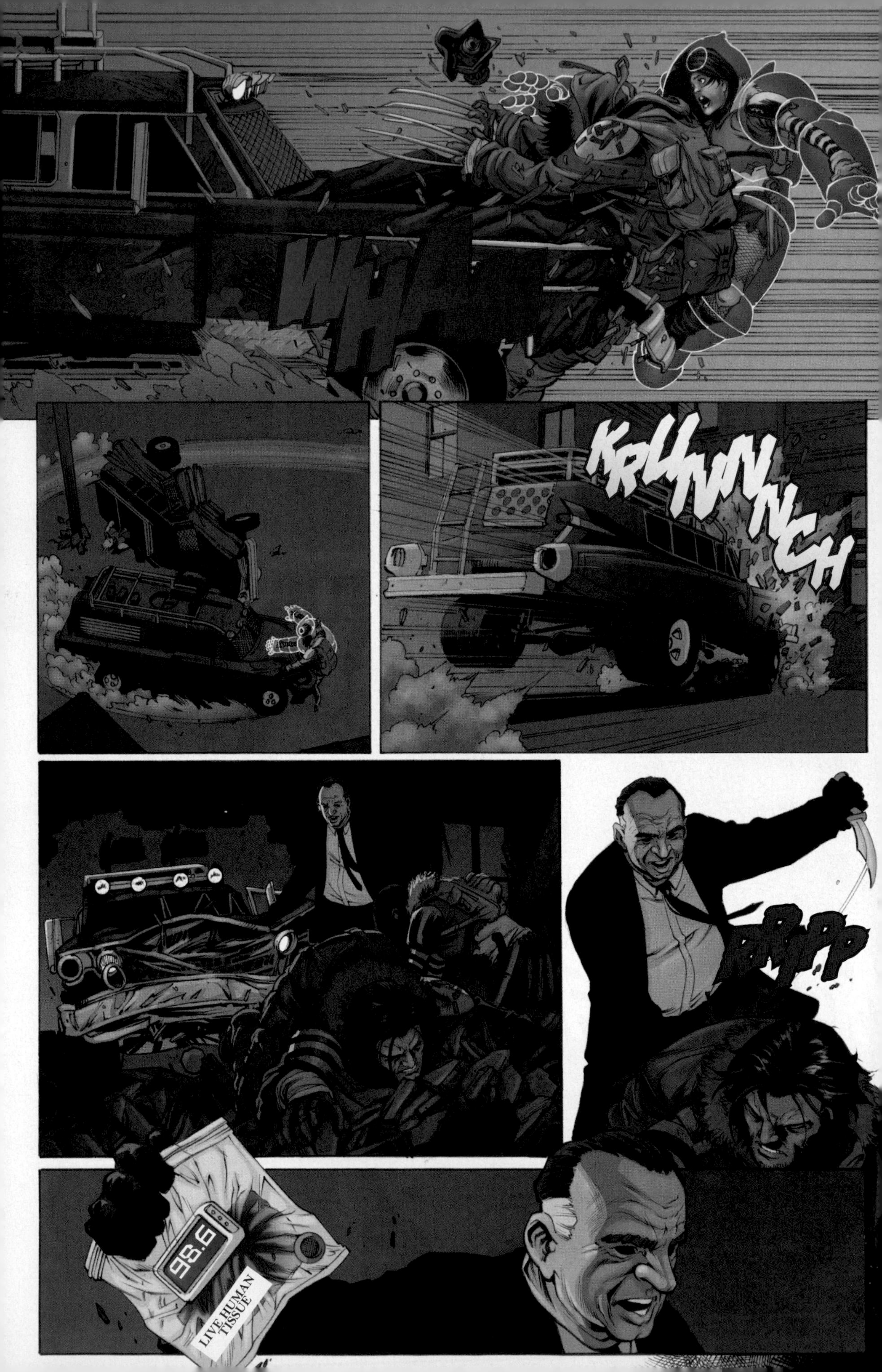
KRUNNNCH
98.6
LIVE HUMAN TISSUE

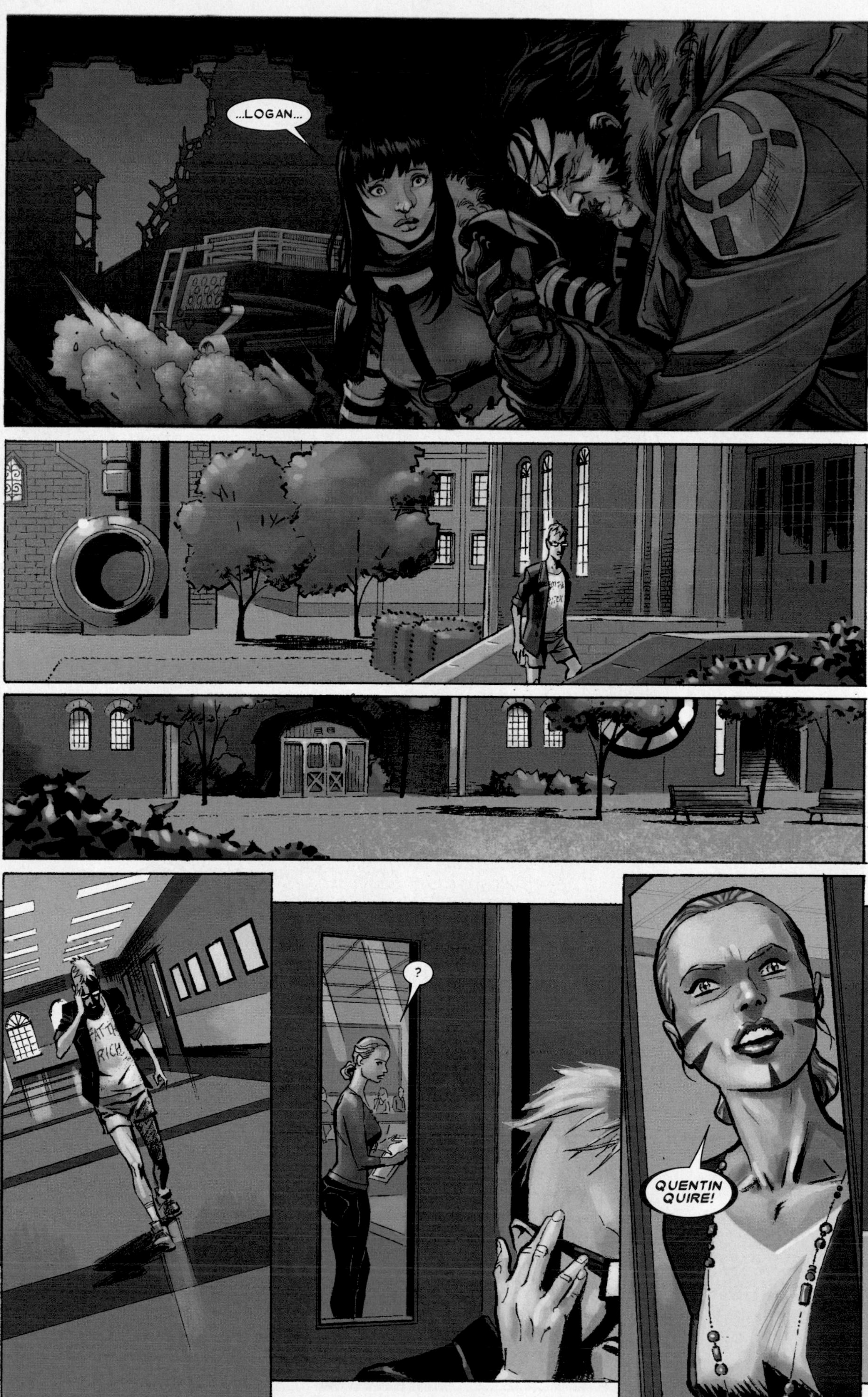
...LOGAN...
?
QUENTIN QUIRE!

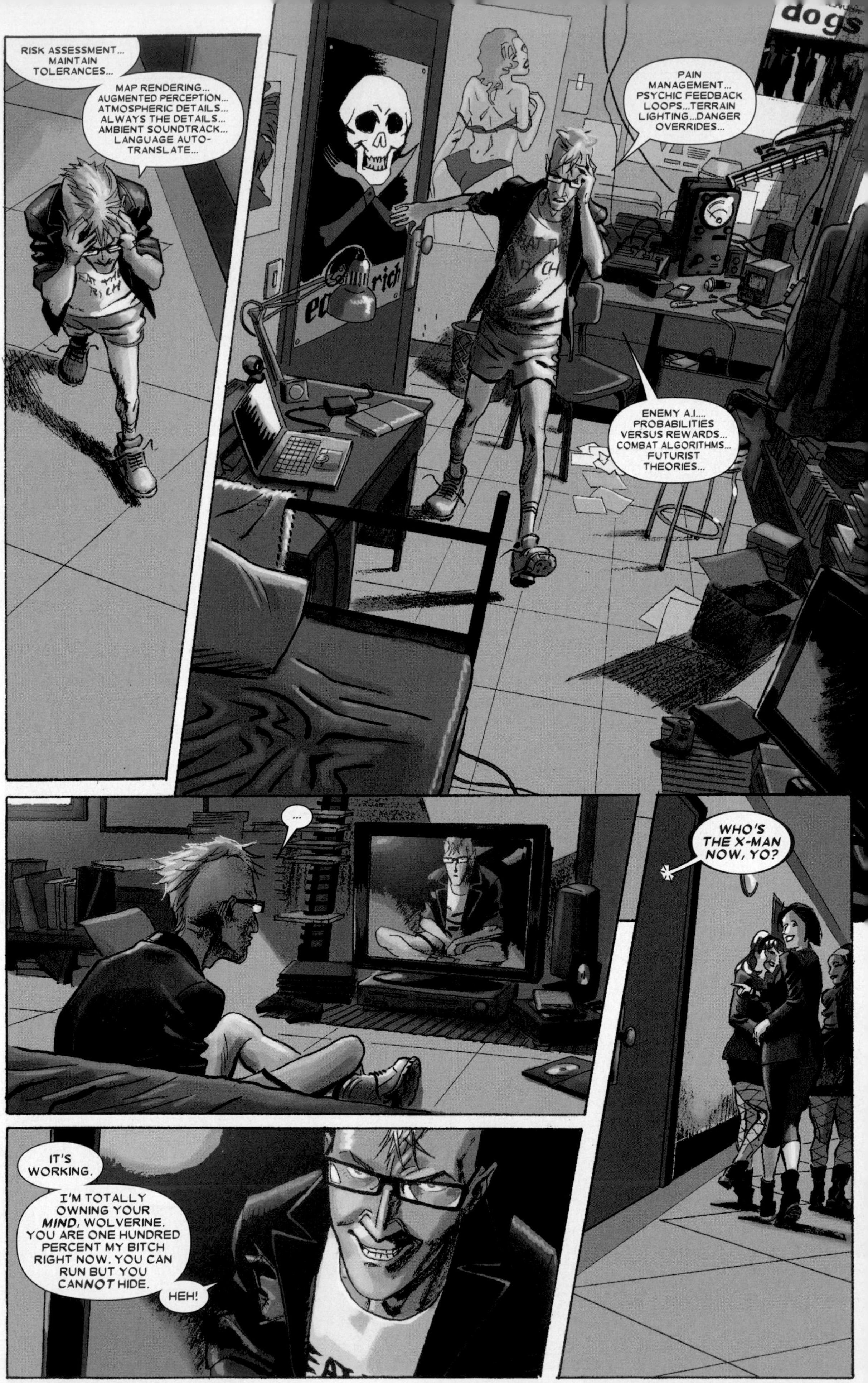

RISK ASSESSMENT... MAINTAIN TOLERANCES...
MAP RENDERING... AUGMENTED PERCEPTION... ATMOSPHERIC DETAILS... ALWAYS THE DETAILS... AMBIENT SOUNDTRACK... LANGUAGE AUTO-TRANSLATE...
PAIN MANAGEMENT... PSYCHIC FEEDBACK LOOPS...TERRAIN LIGHTING...DANGER OVERRIDES...
ENEMY A.I.... PROBABILITIES VERSUS REWARDS... COMBAT ALGORITHMS... FUTURIST THEORIES...
dogs
...
WHO'S THE X-MAN NOW, YO?
IT'S WORKING.
I'M TOTALLY OWNING YOUR *MIND*, WOLVERINE. YOU ARE ONE HUNDRED PERCENT MY BITCH RIGHT NOW. YOU CAN RUN BUT YOU CAN*NOT* HIDE.
HEH!

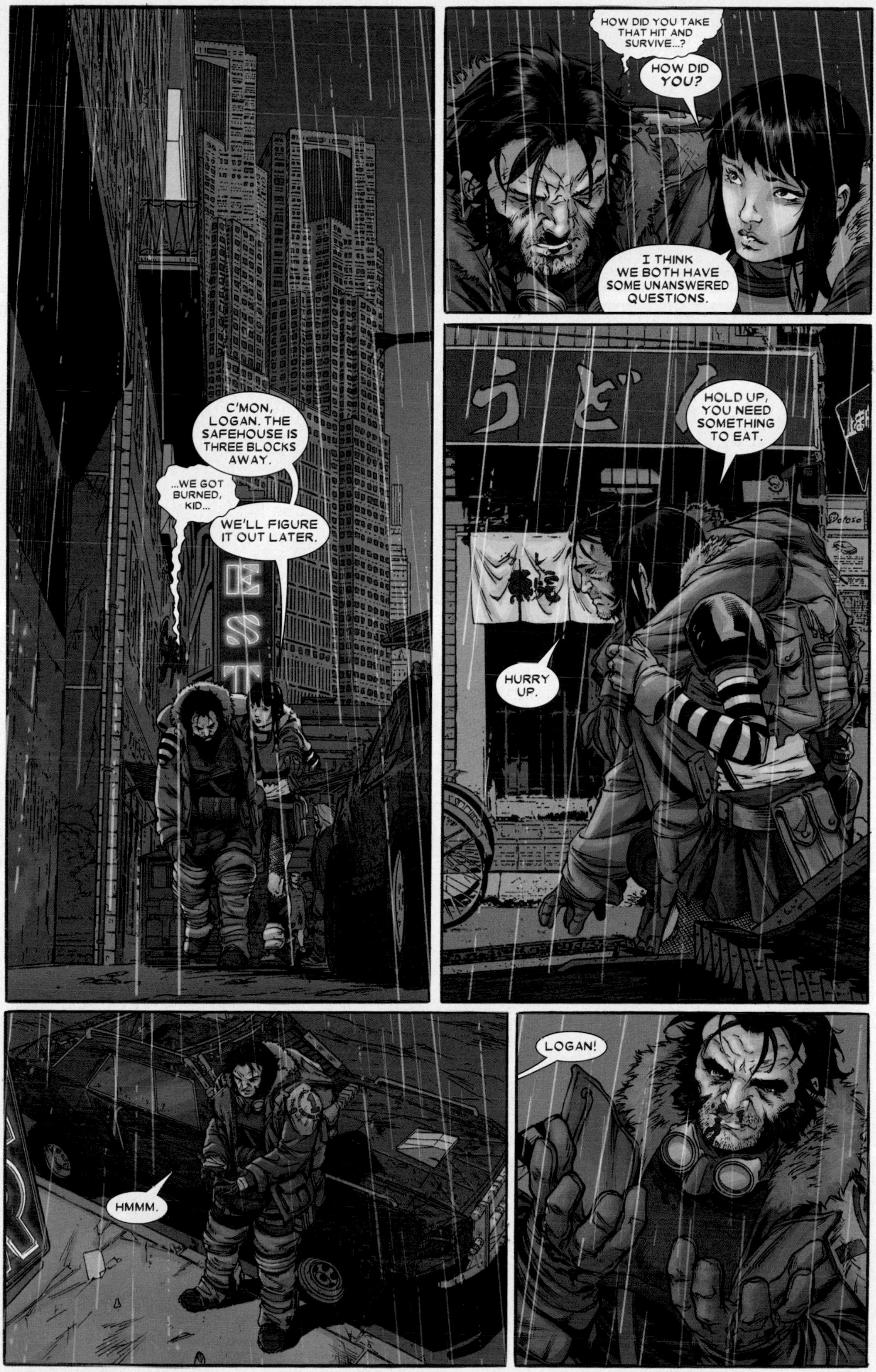
C'MON, LOGAN. THE SAFEHOUSE IS THREE BLOCKS AWAY.
...WE GOT BURNED, KID...
WE'LL FIGURE IT OUT LATER.
HOW DID YOU TAKE THAT HIT AND SURVIVE...?
HOW DID YOU?
I THINK WE BOTH HAVE SOME UNANSWERED QUESTIONS.
HOLD UP, YOU NEED SOMETHING TO EAT.
HURRY UP.
HMMM.
LOGAN!

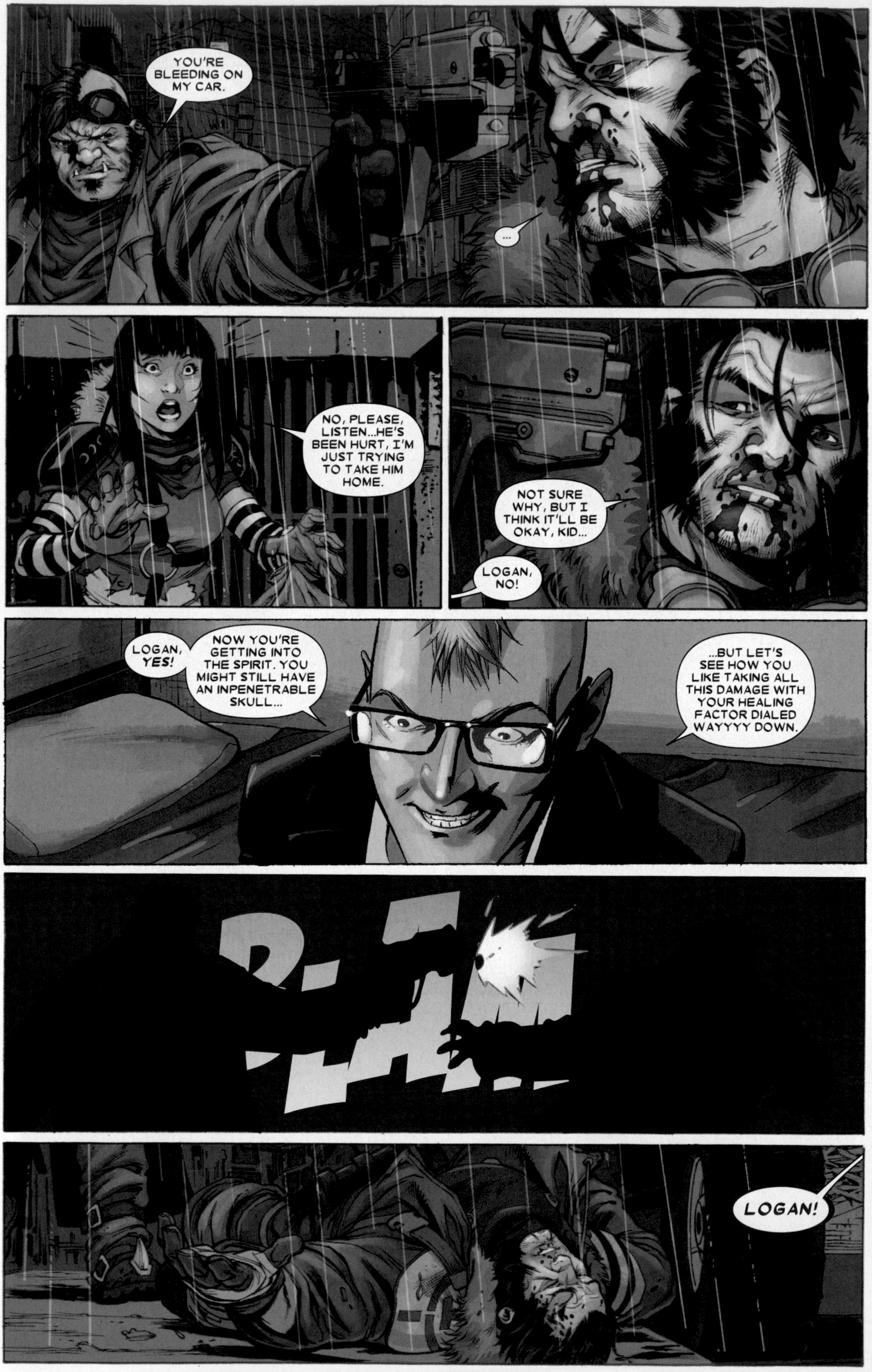
YOU'RE BLEEDING ON MY CAR.
...
NO, PLEASE, LISTEN...HE'S BEEN HURT, I'M JUST TRYING TO TAKE HIM HOME.
NOT SURE WHY, BUT I THINK IT'LL BE OKAY, KID...
LOGAN, NO!
LOGAN, YES!
NOW YOU'RE GETTING INTO THE SPIRIT. YOU MIGHT STILL HAVE AN INPENETRABLE SKULL...
...BUT LET'S SEE HOW YOU LIKE TAKING ALL THIS DAMAGE WITH YOUR HEALING FACTOR DIALED WAYYYY DOWN.
LOGAN!

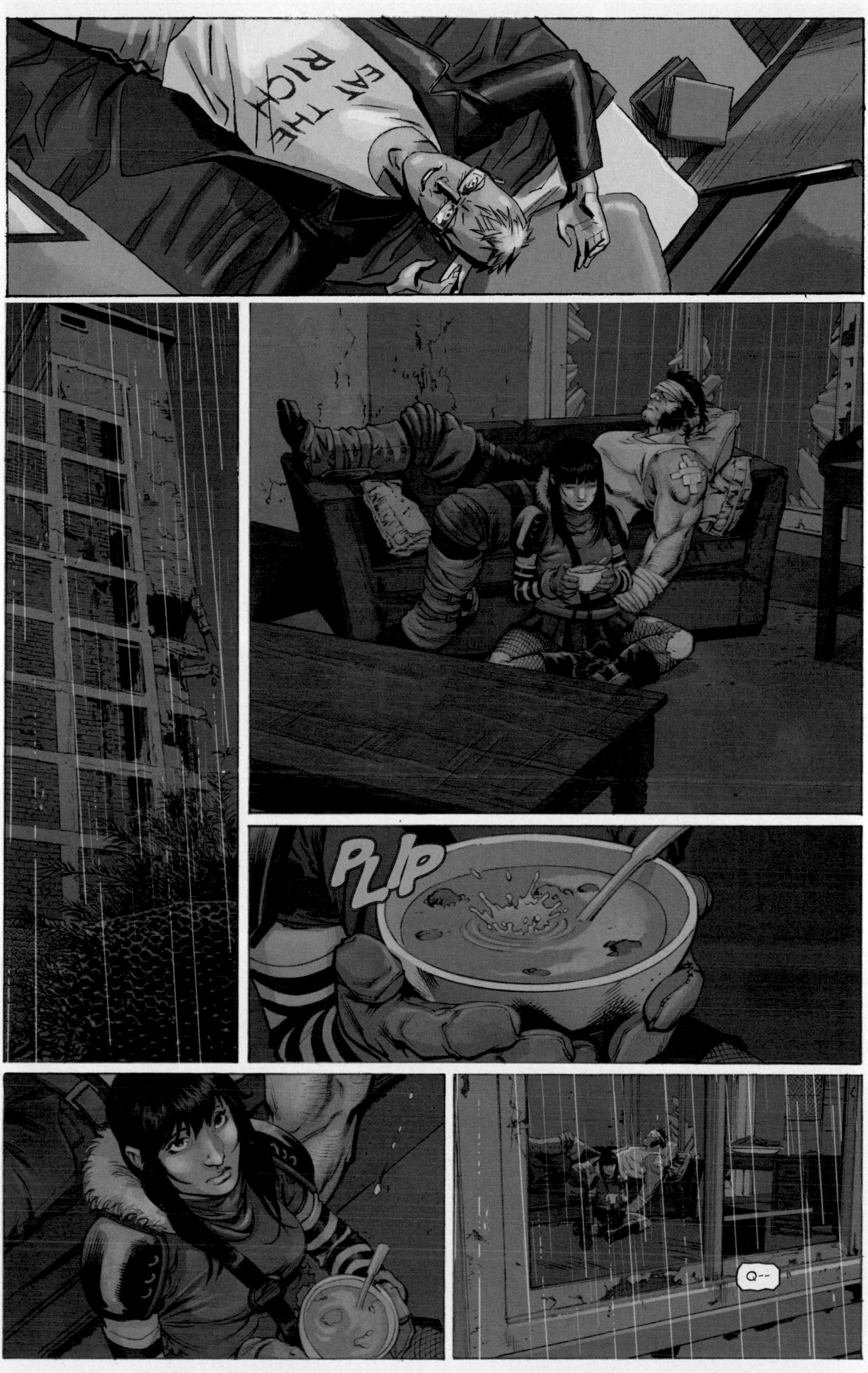
EAT THE RICH
PLIP
Q--

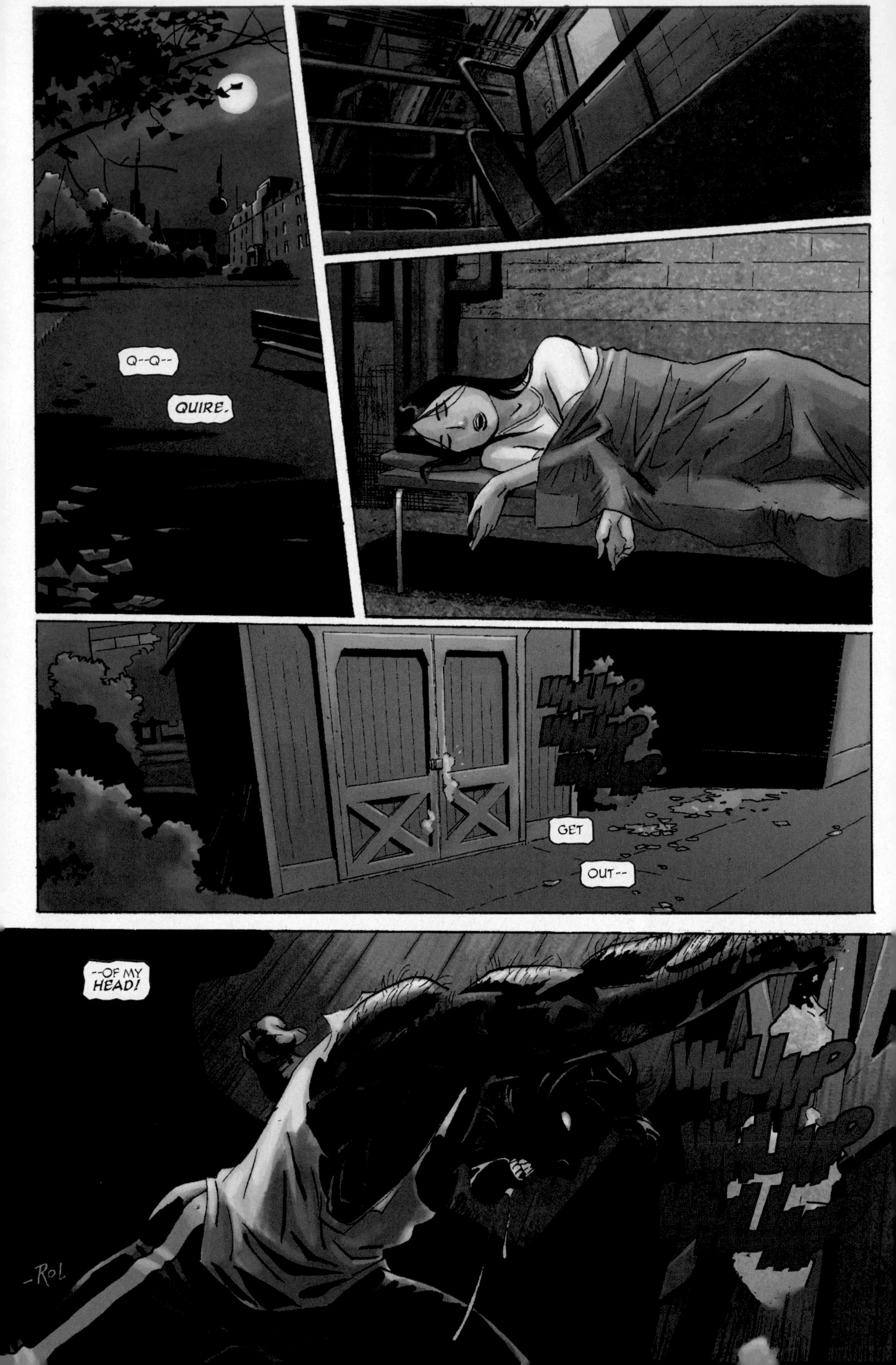
Q--Q--
QUIRE.
WHUMP WHUMP WHUMP
GET
OUT--
--OF MY HEAD!
WHUMP
-ROL

2

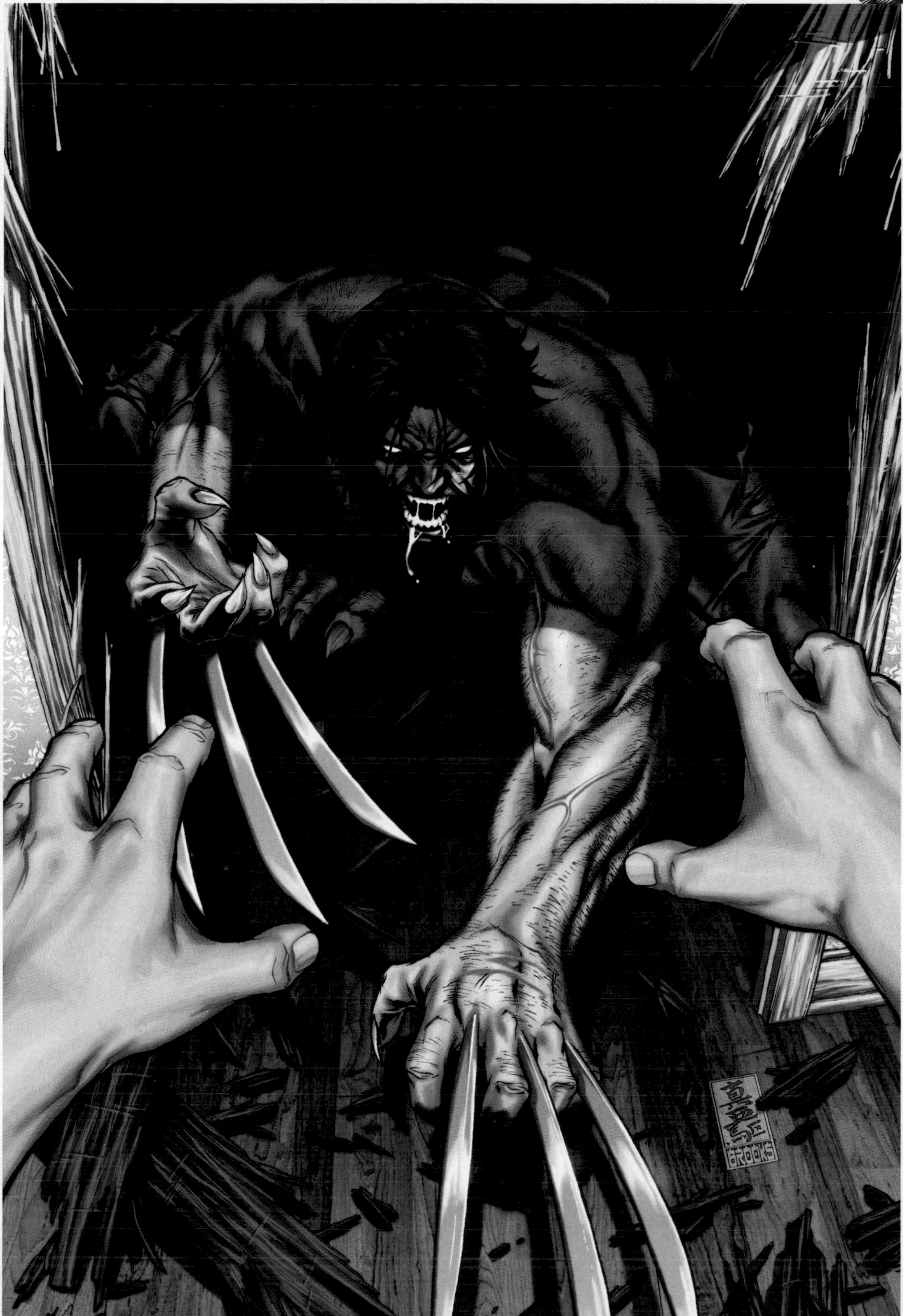

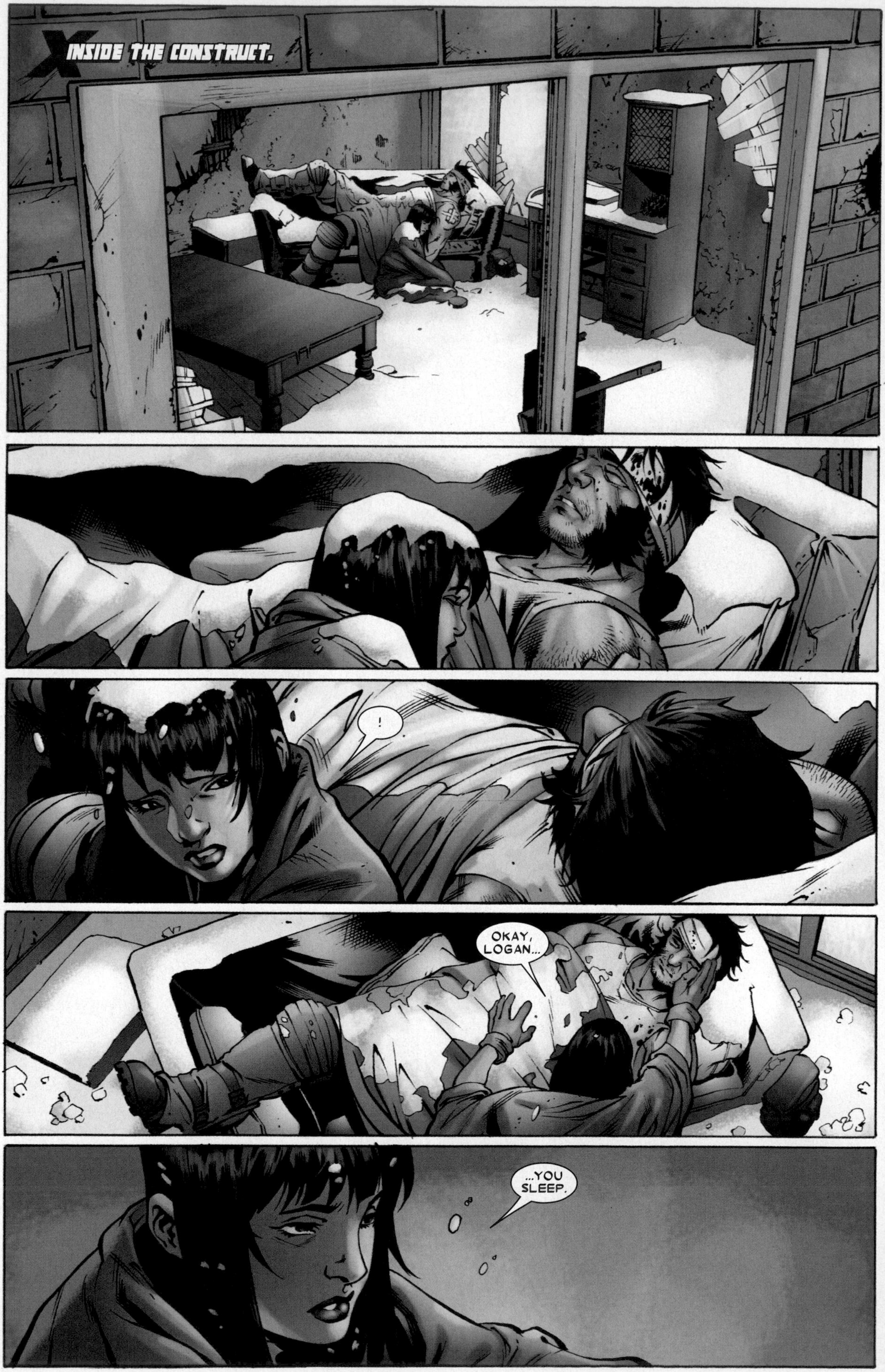
INSIDE THE CONSTRUCT.
!
OKAY, LOGAN...
...YOU SLEEP.

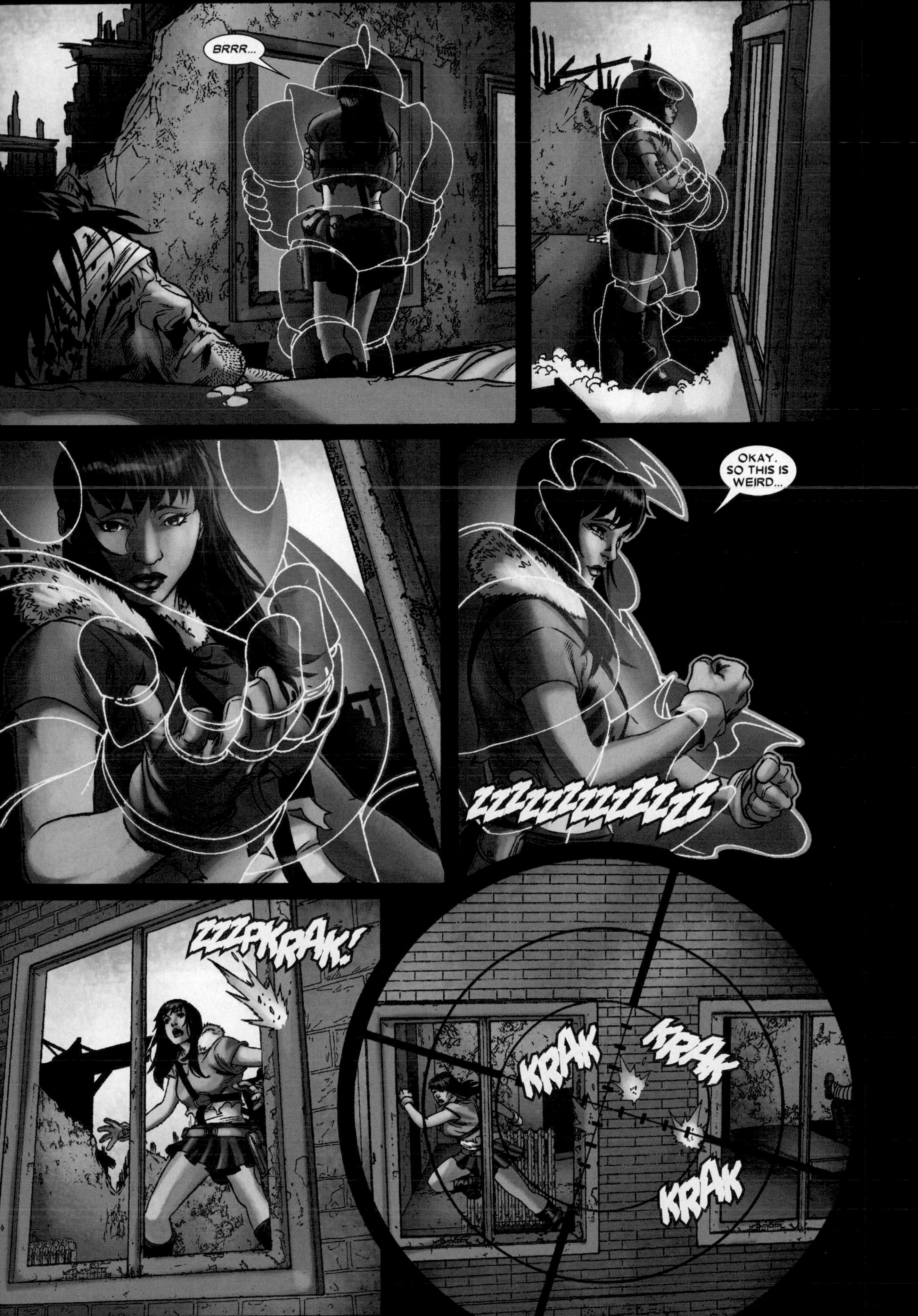
BRRR...
OKAY. SO THIS IS WEIRD...
ZZZZZZZZZZZZZZZZ
ZZZPKRAK!
KRAK
KRAK
KRAK

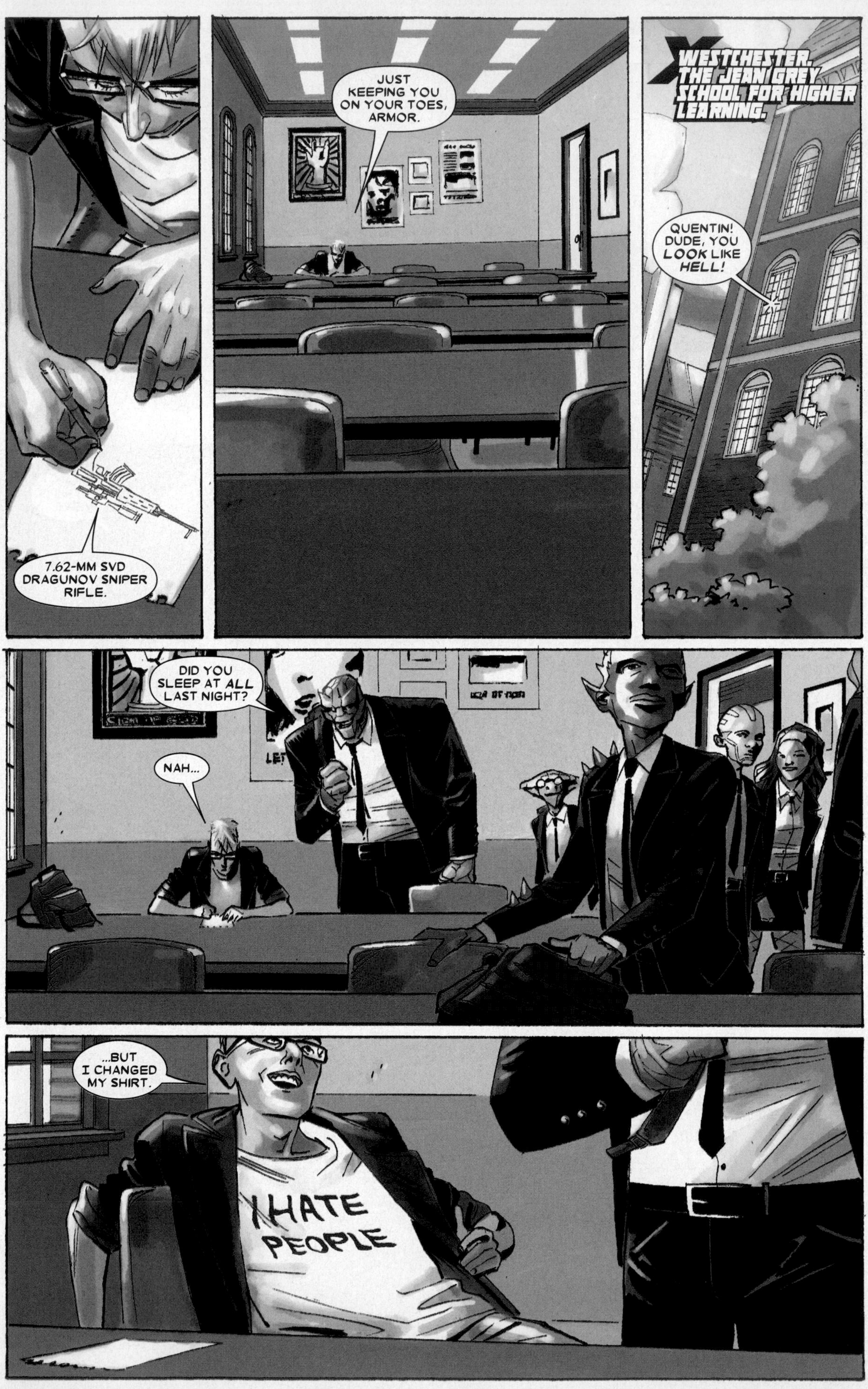
7.62-MM SVD DRAGUNOV SNIPER RIFLE.
JUST KEEPING YOU ON YOUR TOES, ARMOR.
WESTCHESTER. THE JEAN GREY SCHOOL FOR HIGHER LEARNING.
QUENTIN! DUDE, YOU LOOK LIKE HELL!
DID YOU SLEEP AT ALL LAST NIGHT?
NAH...
...BUT I CHANGED MY SHIRT.
I HATE PEOPLE

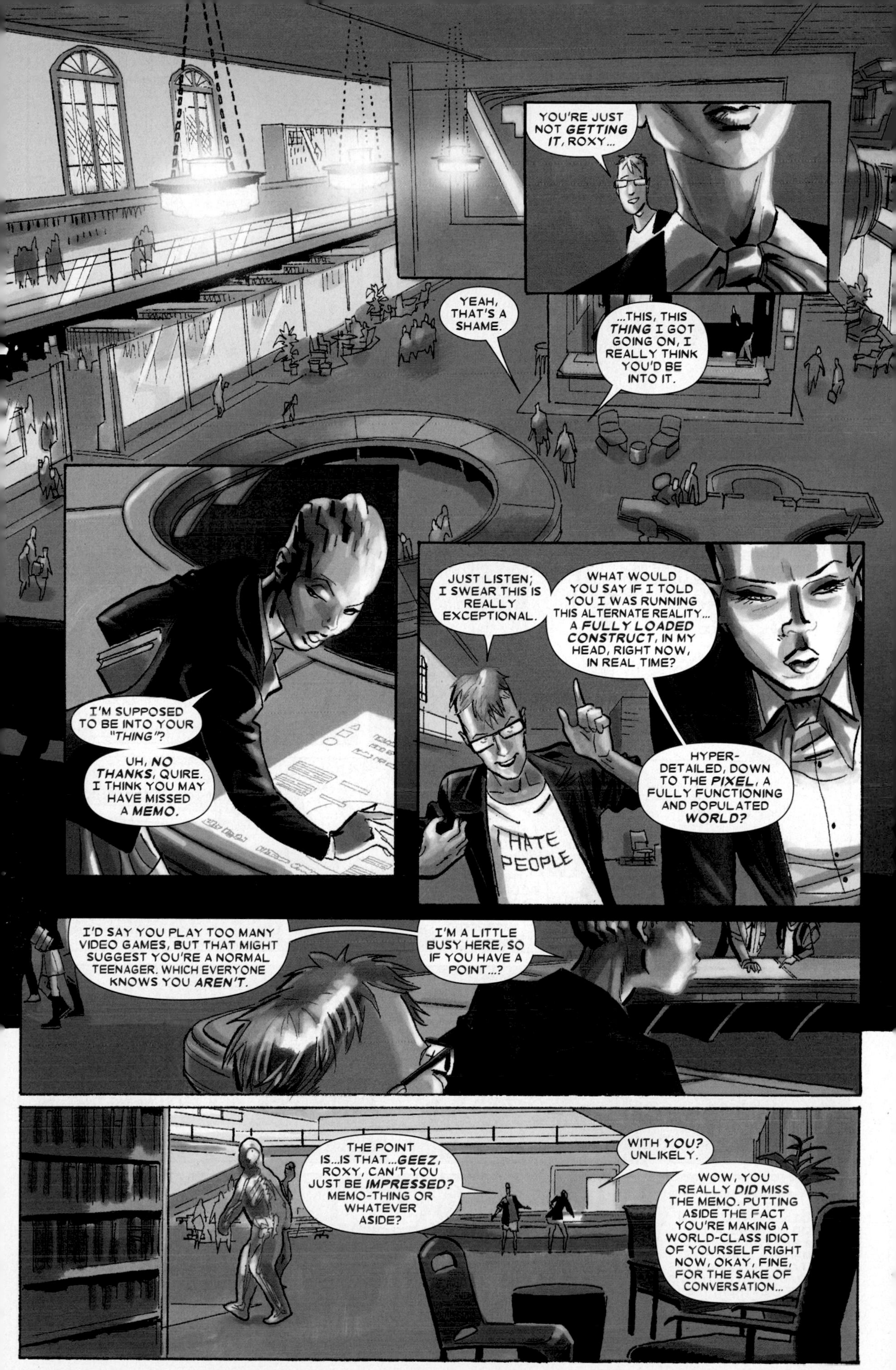
YOU'RE JUST NOT GETTING IT, ROXY...
YEAH, THAT'S A SHAME.
...THIS, THIS THING I GOT GOING ON, I REALLY THINK YOU'D BE INTO IT.
I'M SUPPOSED TO BE INTO YOUR "THING"?
UH, NO THANKS, QUIRE. I THINK YOU MAY HAVE MISSED A MEMO.
JUST LISTEN; I SWEAR THIS IS REALLY EXCEPTIONAL.
WHAT WOULD YOU SAY IF I TOLD YOU I WAS RUNNING THIS ALTERNATE REALITY... A FULLY LOADED CONSTRUCT, IN MY HEAD, RIGHT NOW, IN REAL TIME?
HYPER-DETAILED, DOWN TO THE PIXEL, A FULLY FUNCTIONING AND POPULATED WORLD?
I HATE PEOPLE
I'D SAY YOU PLAY TOO MANY VIDEO GAMES, BUT THAT MIGHT SUGGEST YOU'RE A NORMAL TEENAGER. WHICH EVERYONE KNOWS YOU AREN'T.
I'M A LITTLE BUSY HERE, SO IF YOU HAVE A POINT...?
THE POINT IS...IS THAT...GEEZ, ROXY, CAN'T YOU JUST BE IMPRESSED? MEMO-THING OR WHATEVER ASIDE?
WITH YOU? UNLIKELY.
WOW, YOU REALLY DID MISS THE MEMO. PUTTING ASIDE THE FACT YOU'RE MAKING A WORLD-CLASS IDIOT OF YOURSELF RIGHT NOW, OKAY, FINE, FOR THE SAKE OF CONVERSATION...

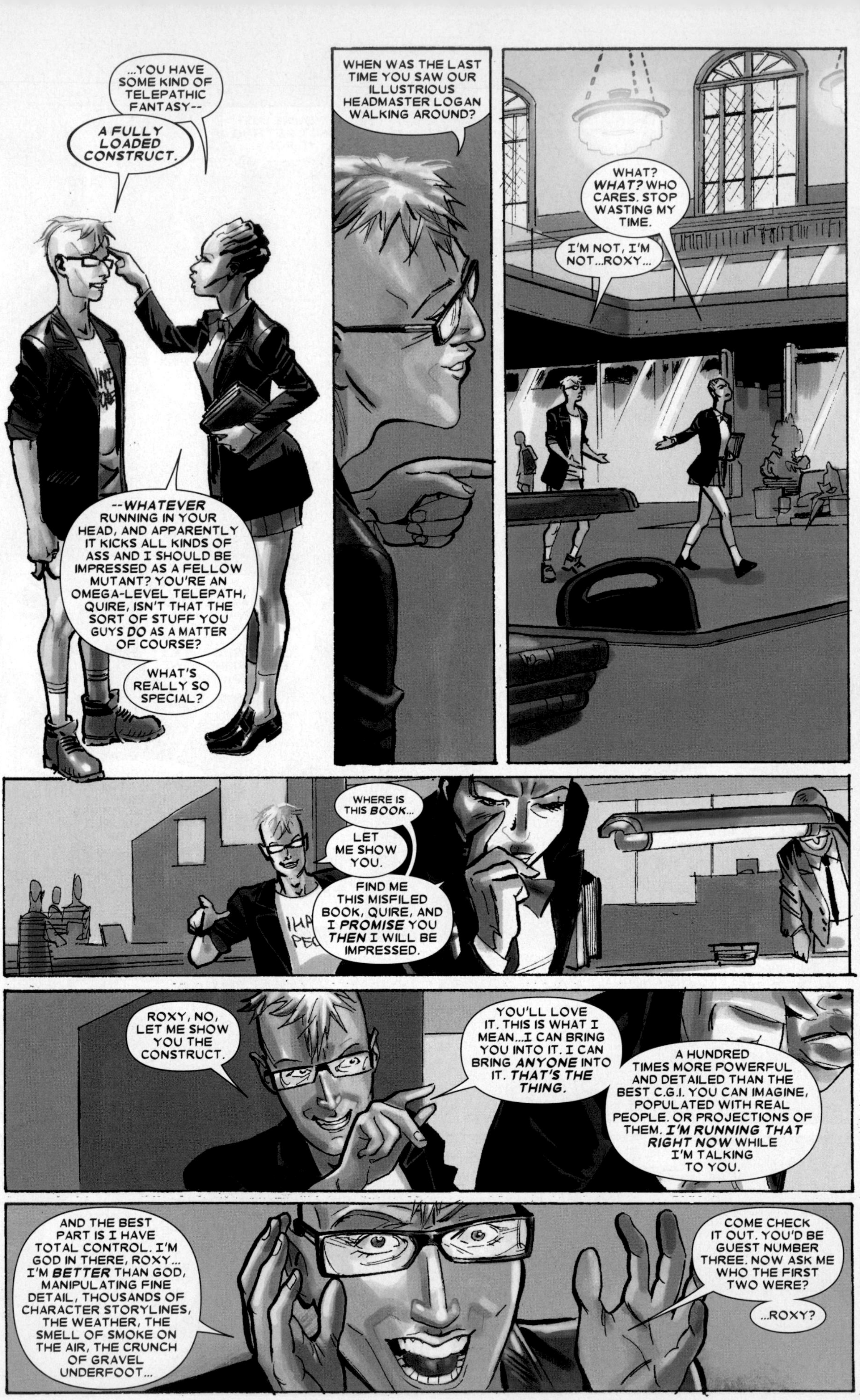
...YOU HAVE SOME KIND OF TELEPATHIC FANTASY--
A FULLY LOADED CONSTRUCT.
--WHATEVER RUNNING IN YOUR HEAD, AND APPARENTLY IT KICKS ALL KINDS OF ASS AND I SHOULD BE IMPRESSED AS A FELLOW MUTANT? YOU'RE AN OMEGA-LEVEL TELEPATH, QUIRE, ISN'T THAT THE SORT OF STUFF YOU GUYS DO AS A MATTER OF COURSE?
WHAT'S REALLY SO SPECIAL?
WHEN WAS THE LAST TIME YOU SAW OUR ILLUSTRIOUS HEADMASTER LOGAN WALKING AROUND?
WHAT? WHAT? WHO CARES. STOP WASTING MY TIME.
I'M NOT, I'M NOT...ROXY...
WHERE IS THIS BOOK...
LET ME SHOW YOU.
FIND ME THIS MISFILED BOOK, QUIRE, AND I PROMISE YOU THEN I WILL BE IMPRESSED.
ROXY, NO, LET ME SHOW YOU THE CONSTRUCT.
YOU'LL LOVE IT. THIS IS WHAT I MEAN...I CAN BRING YOU INTO IT. I CAN BRING ANYONE INTO IT. THAT'S THE THING.
A HUNDRED TIMES MORE POWERFUL AND DETAILED THAN THE BEST C.G.I. YOU CAN IMAGINE, POPULATED WITH REAL PEOPLE. OR PROJECTIONS OF THEM. I'M RUNNING THAT RIGHT NOW WHILE I'M TALKING TO YOU.
AND THE BEST PART IS I HAVE TOTAL CONTROL. I'M GOD IN THERE, ROXY... I'M BETTER THAN GOD, MANIPULATING FINE DETAIL, THOUSANDS OF CHARACTER STORYLINES, THE WEATHER, THE SMELL OF SMOKE ON THE AIR, THE CRUNCH OF GRAVEL UNDERFOOT...
COME CHECK IT OUT. YOU'D BE GUEST NUMBER THREE. NOW ASK ME WHO THE FIRST TWO WERE?
...ROXY?

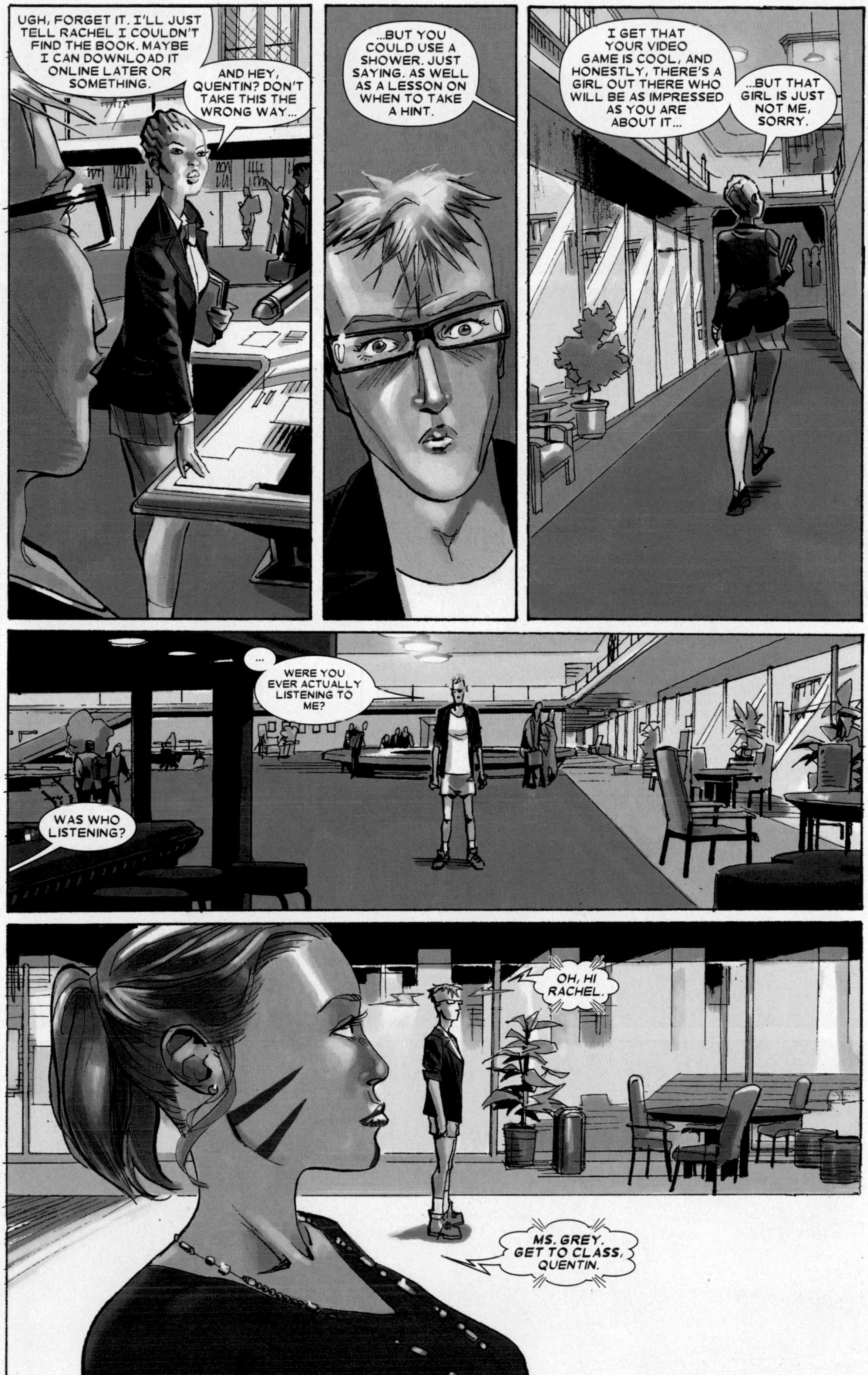
UGH, FORGET IT. I'LL JUST TELL RACHEL I COULDN'T FIND THE BOOK. MAYBE I CAN DOWNLOAD IT ONLINE LATER OR SOMETHING.
AND HEY, QUENTIN? DON'T TAKE THIS THE WRONG WAY...
...BUT YOU COULD USE A SHOWER. JUST SAYING. AS WELL AS A LESSON ON WHEN TO TAKE A HINT.
I GET THAT YOUR VIDEO GAME IS COOL, AND HONESTLY, THERE'S A GIRL OUT THERE WHO WILL BE AS IMPRESSED AS YOU ARE ABOUT IT...
...BUT THAT GIRL IS JUST NOT ME, SORRY.
...
WERE YOU EVER ACTUALLY LISTENING TO ME?
WAS WHO LISTENING?
OH, HI RACHEL.
MS. GREY. GET TO CLASS, QUENTIN.

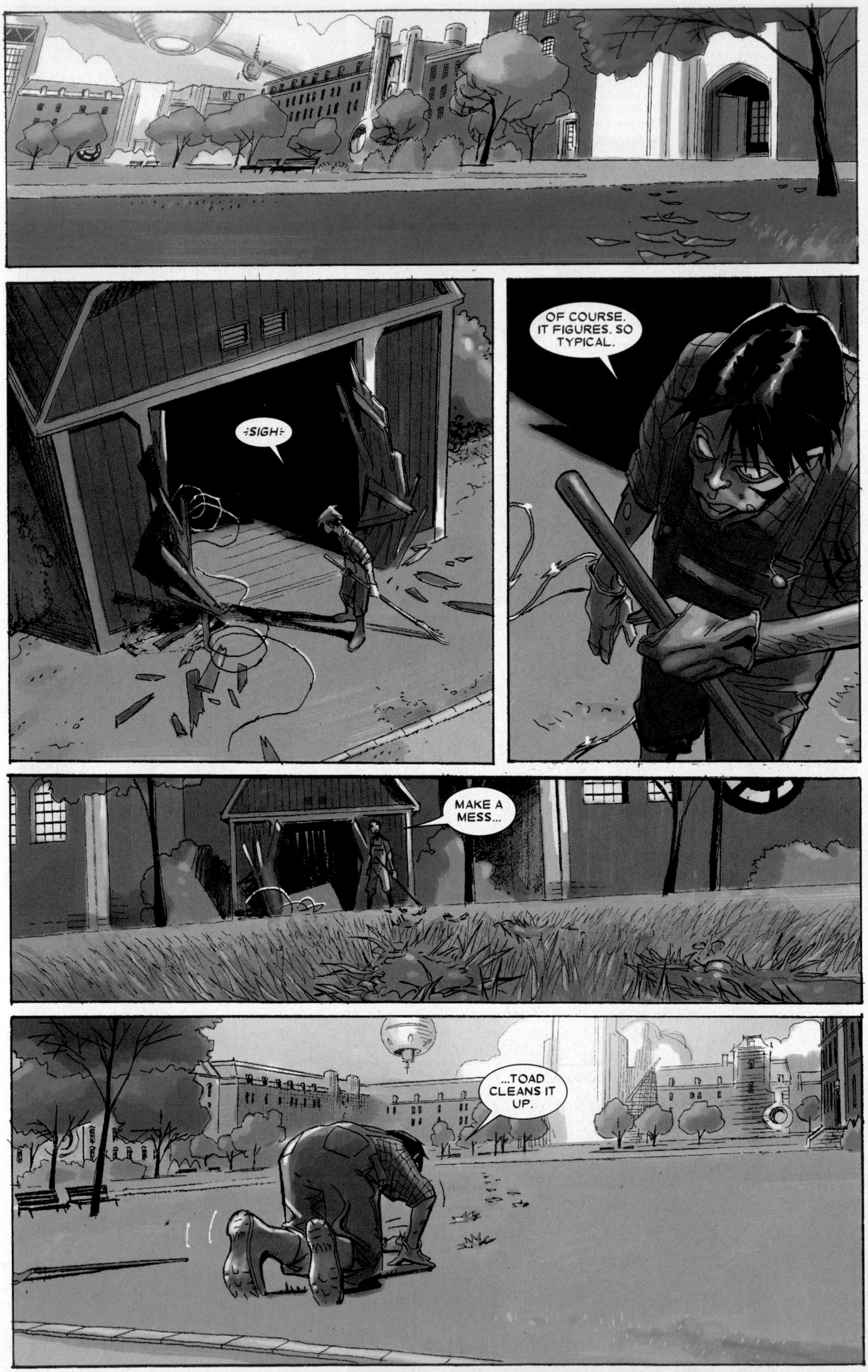

-SIGH-
OF COURSE. IT FIGURES. SO TYPICAL.
MAKE A MESS...
...TOAD CLEANS IT UP.

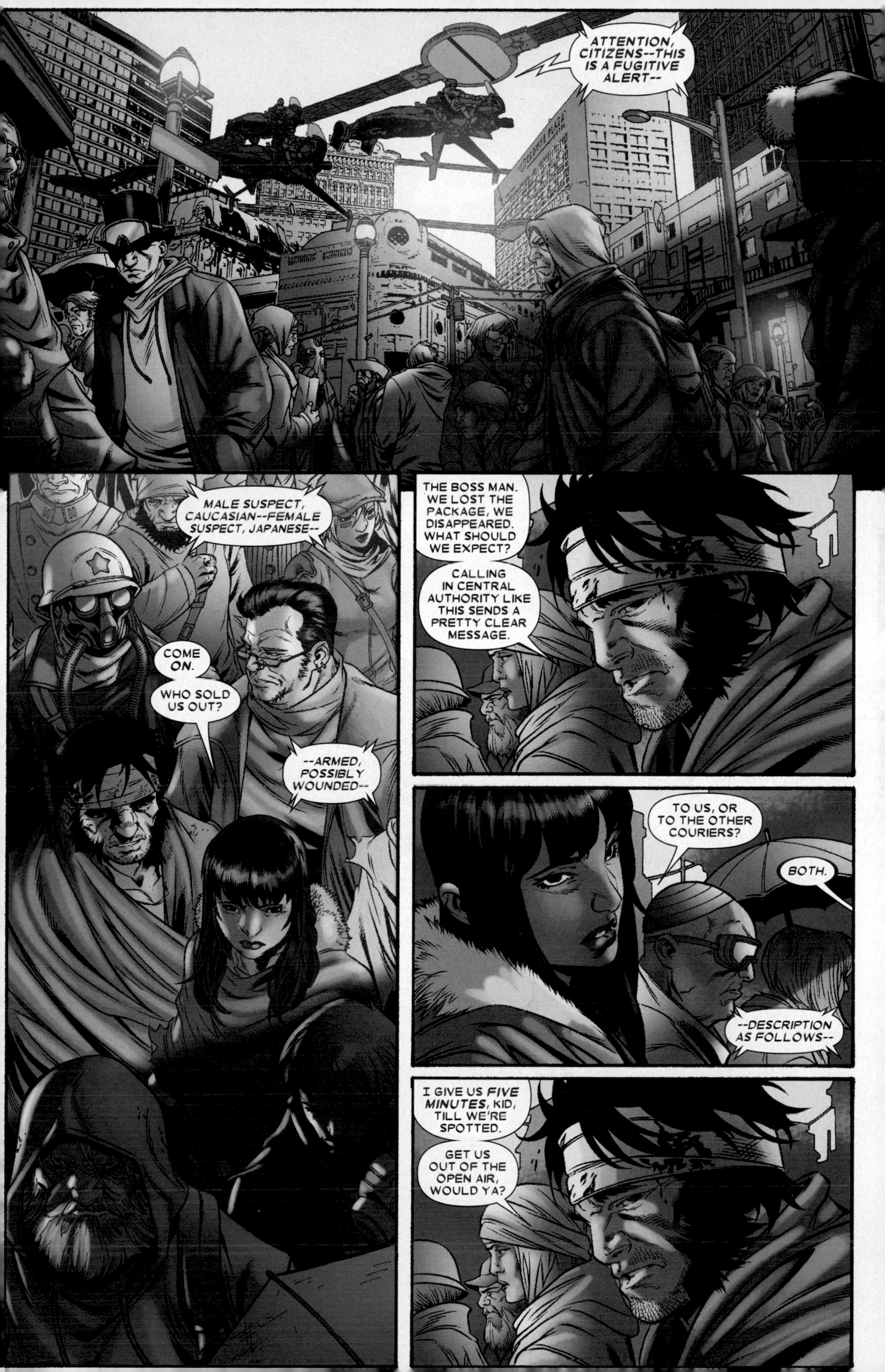
ATTENTION, CITIZENS--THIS IS A FUGITIVE ALERT--
MALE SUSPECT, CAUCASIAN--FEMALE SUSPECT, JAPANESE--
COME ON.
WHO SOLD US OUT?
--ARMED, POSSIBLY WOUNDED--
THE BOSS MAN. WE LOST THE PACKAGE, WE DISAPPEARED. WHAT SHOULD WE EXPECT?
CALLING IN CENTRAL AUTHORITY LIKE THIS SENDS A PRETTY CLEAR MESSAGE.
TO US, OR TO THE OTHER COURIERS?
BOTH.
--DESCRIPTION AS FOLLOWS--
I GIVE US FIVE MINUTES, KID, TILL WE'RE SPOTTED.
GET US OUT OF THE OPEN AIR, WOULD YA?

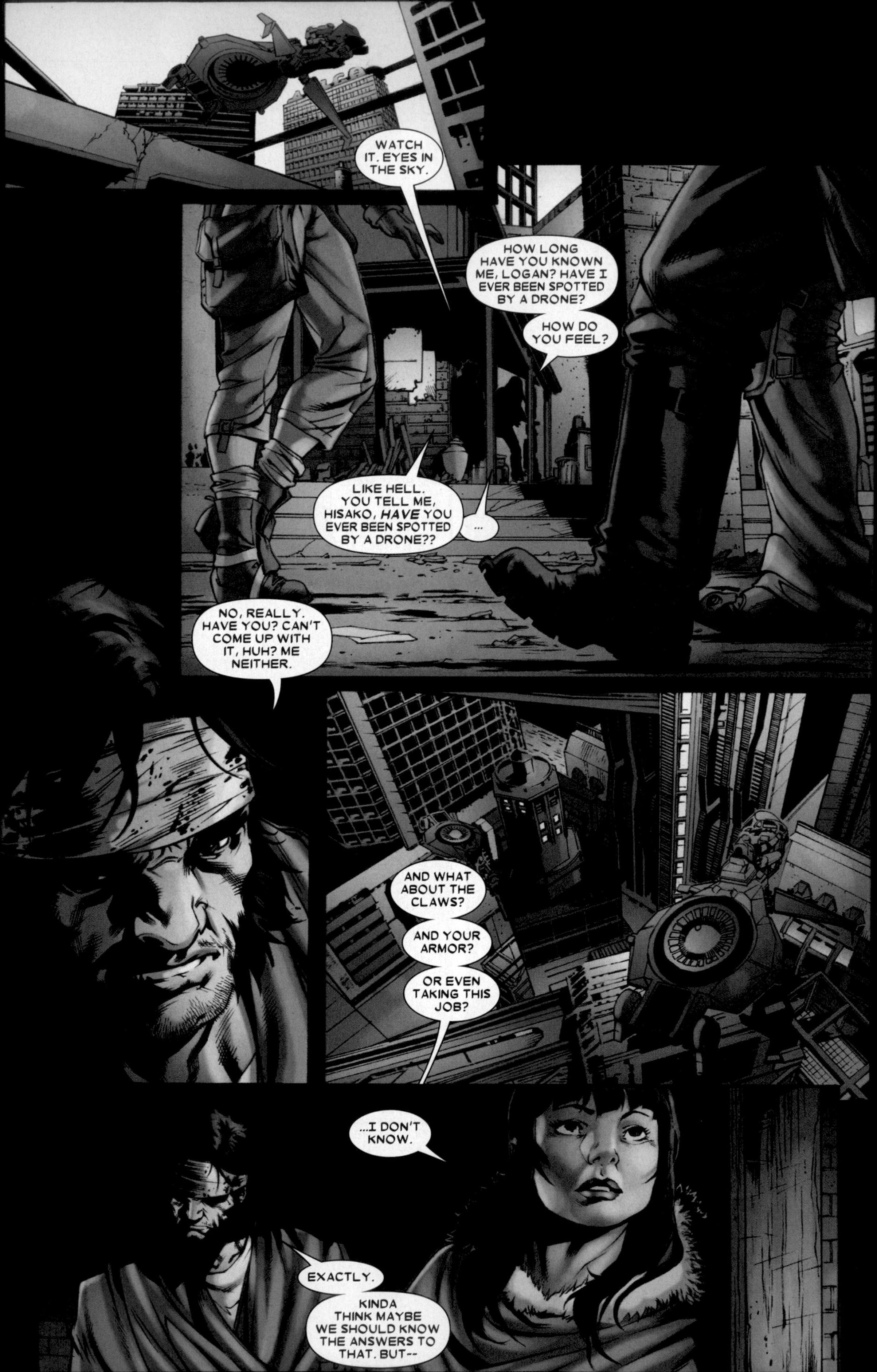
WATCH IT. EYES IN THE SKY.
HOW LONG HAVE YOU KNOWN ME, LOGAN? HAVE I EVER BEEN SPOTTED BY A DRONE?
HOW DO YOU FEEL?
LIKE HELL. YOU TELL ME, HISAKO, *HAVE* YOU EVER BEEN SPOTTED BY A DRONE??
...
NO, REALLY. HAVE YOU? CAN'T COME UP WITH IT, HUH? ME NEITHER.
AND WHAT ABOUT THE CLAWS?
AND YOUR ARMOR?
OR EVEN TAKING THIS JOB?
...I DON'T KNOW.
EXACTLY.
KINDA THINK MAYBE WE SHOULD KNOW THE ANSWERS TO THAT. BUT--

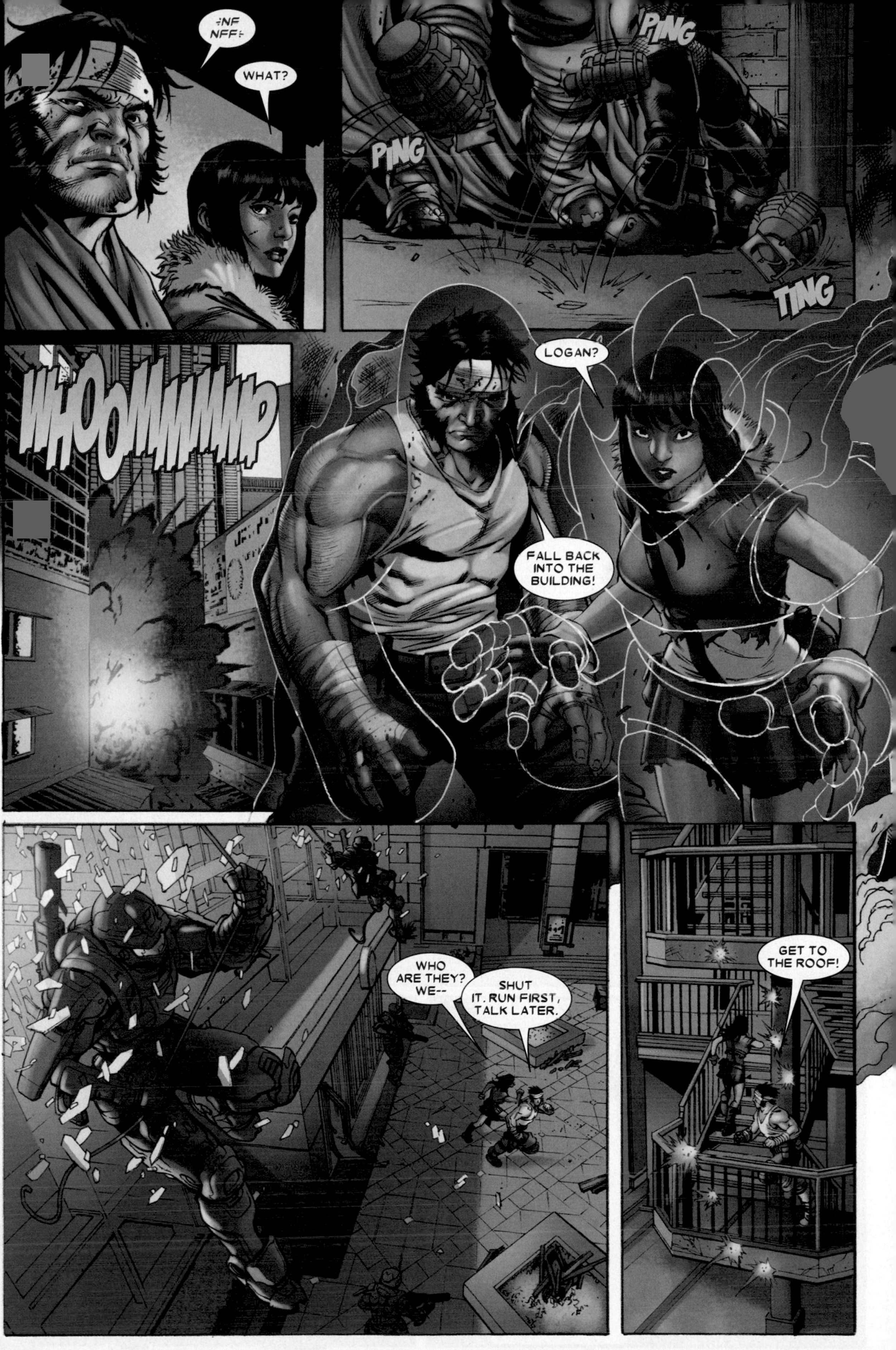

NF NFF
WHAT?
PING
PING
TING
WHOOMMMMMP
LOGAN?
FALL BACK INTO THE BUILDING!
WHO ARE THEY? WE--
SHUT IT. RUN FIRST, TALK LATER.
GET TO THE ROOF!

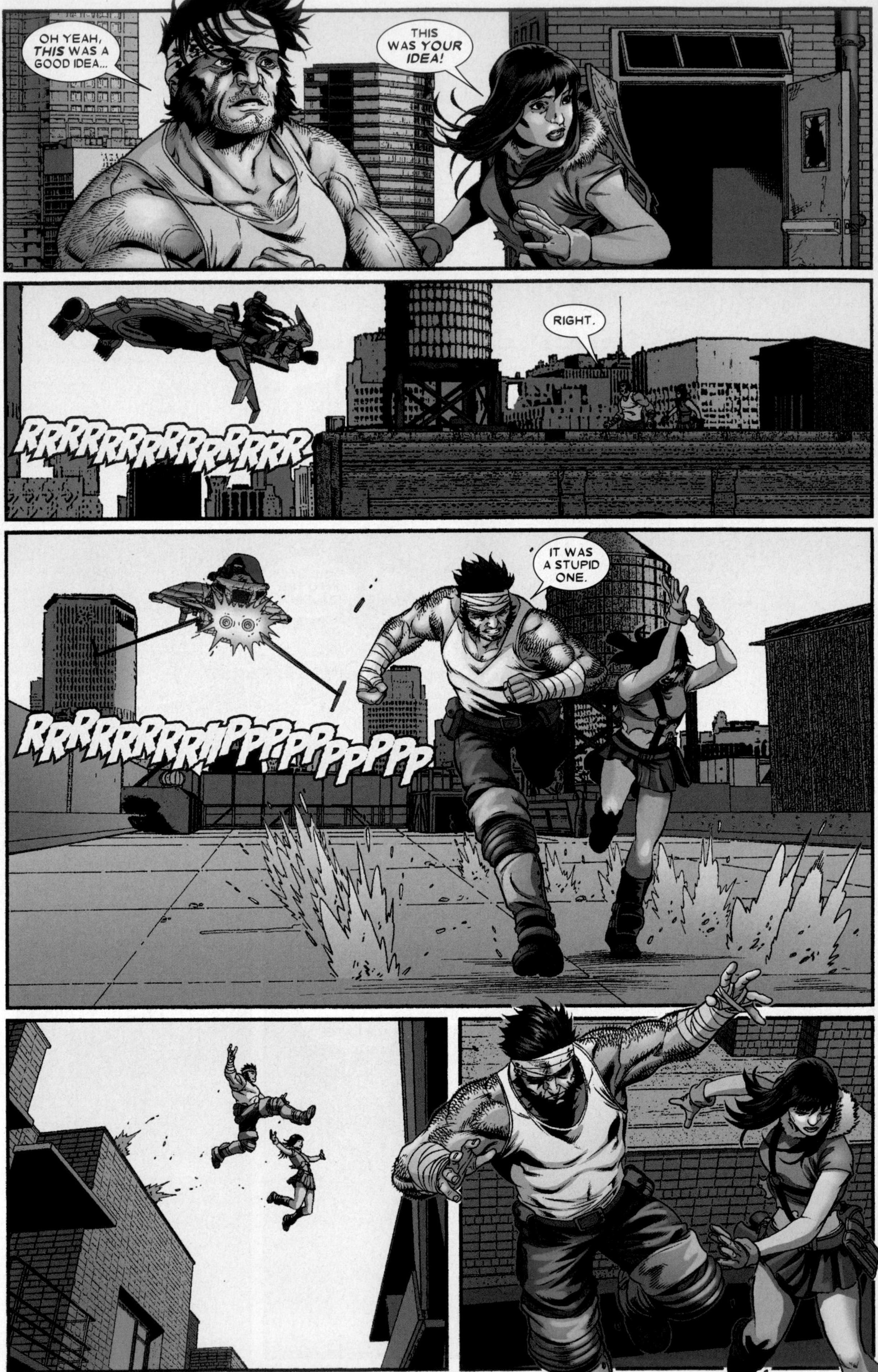

OH YEAH, THIS WAS A GOOD IDEA...
THIS WAS YOUR IDEA!
RRRRRRRRRRRRRRRR
RIGHT.
RRRRRRRRRMPPPPPPPPPPP
IT WAS A STUPID ONE.

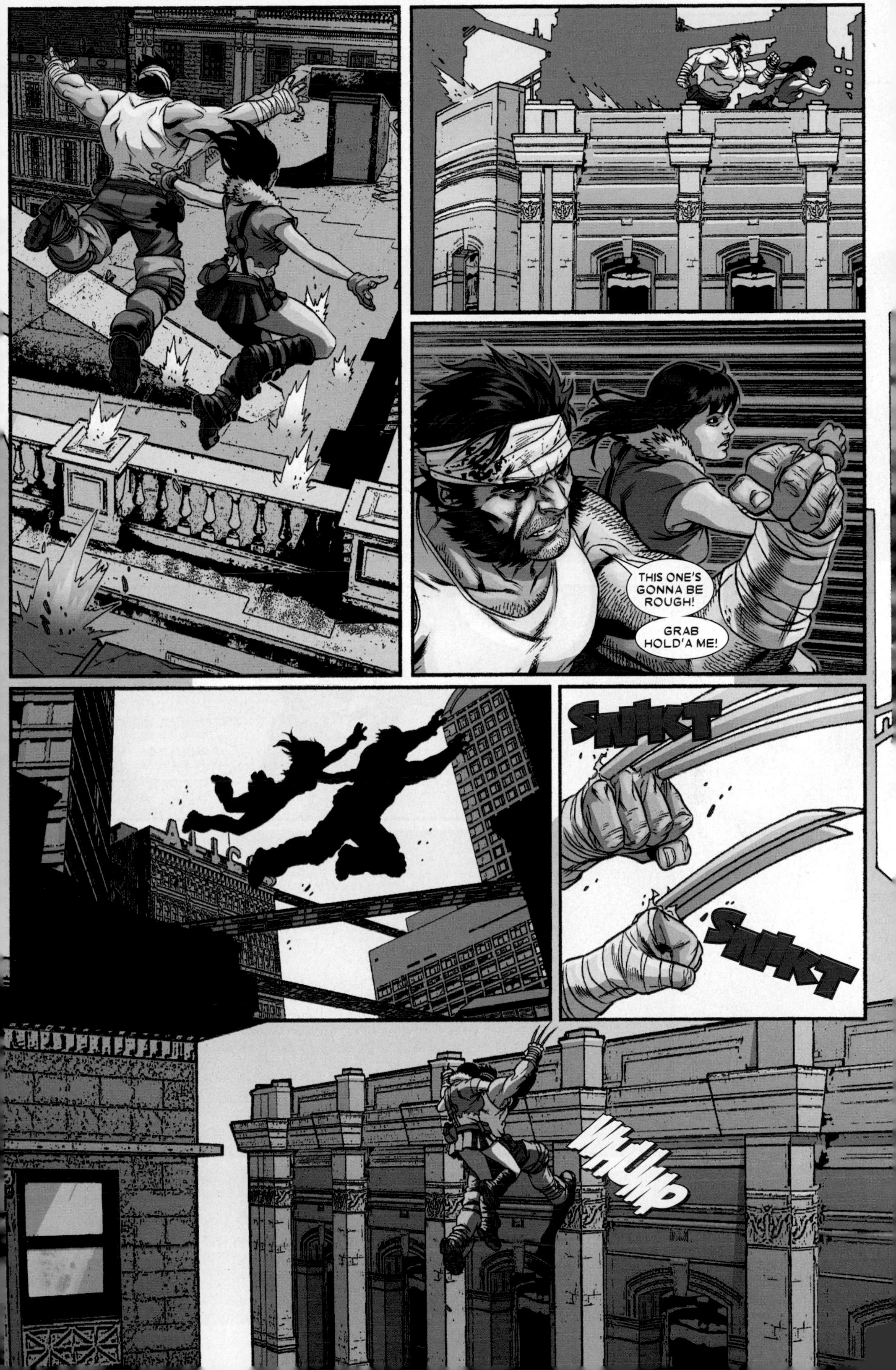
THIS ONE'S GONNA BE ROUGH!
GRAB HOLD'A ME!
SNIKT
SNIKT
WHUMP

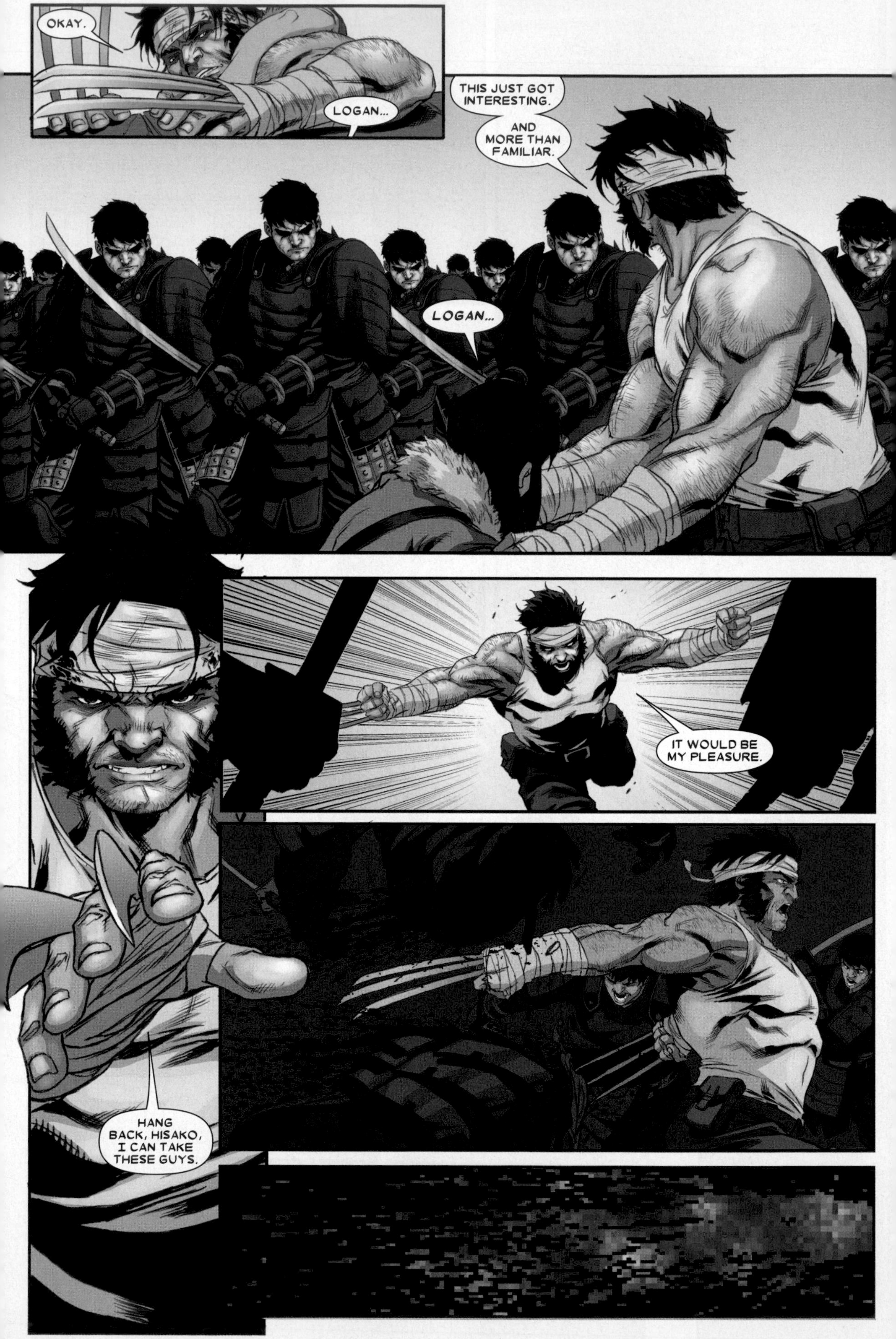
OKAY.
LOGAN...
THIS JUST GOT INTERESTING.
AND MORE THAN FAMILIAR.
LOGAN...
HANG BACK, HISAKO, I CAN TAKE THESE GUYS.
IT WOULD BE MY PLEASURE.

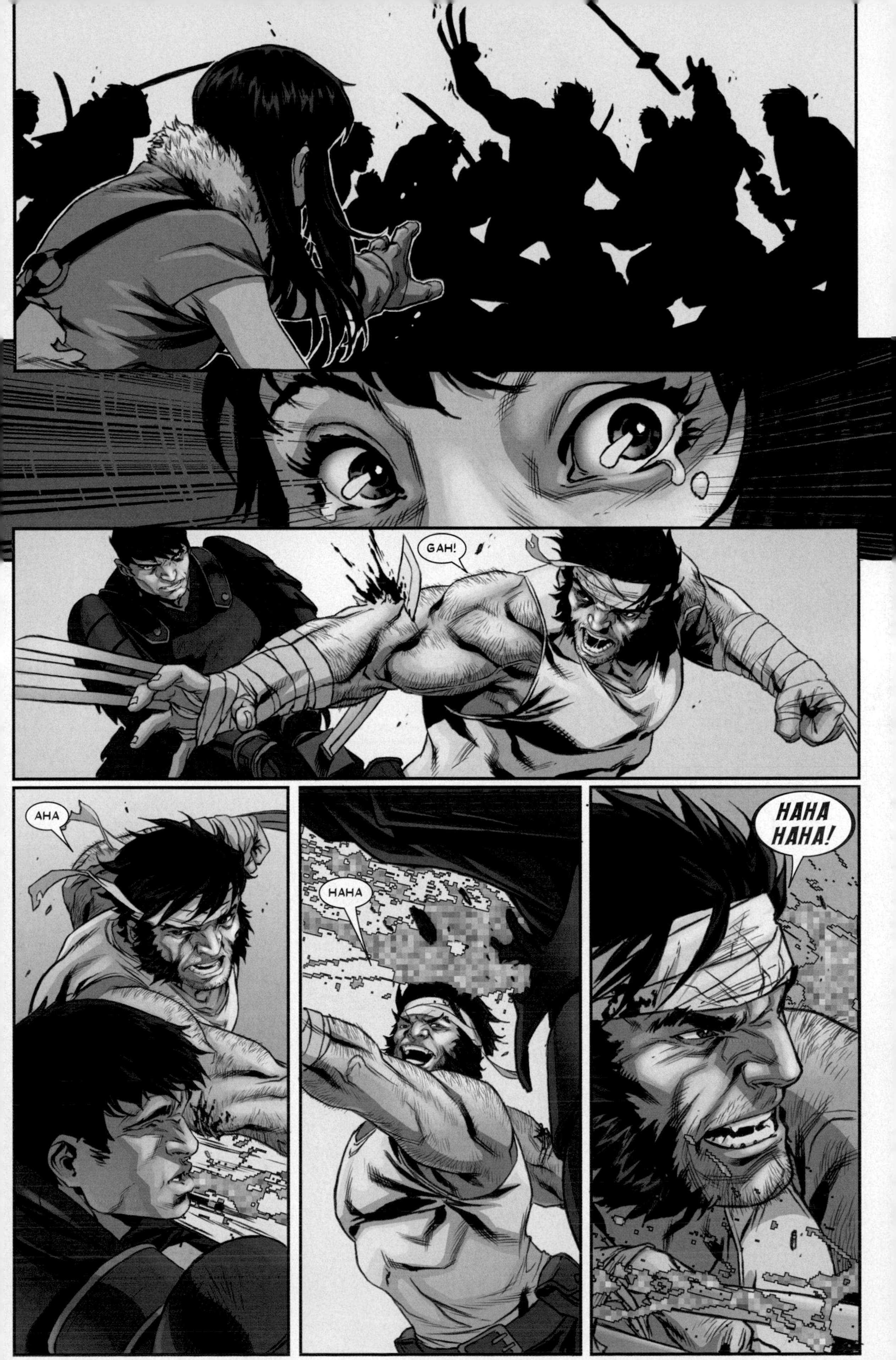
GAH!
AHA
HAHA
HAHA
HAHA!

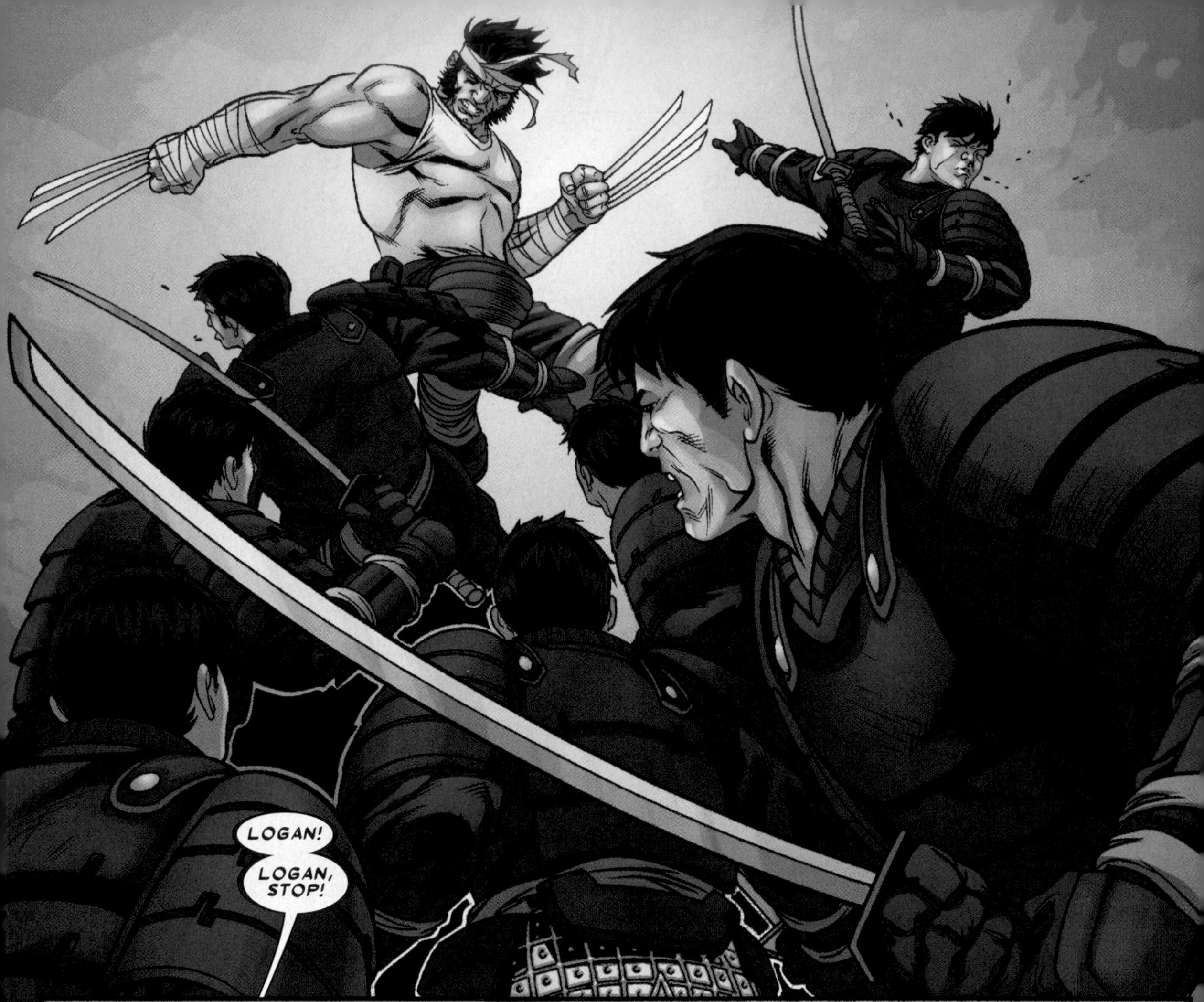
LOGAN!
LOGAN, STOP!

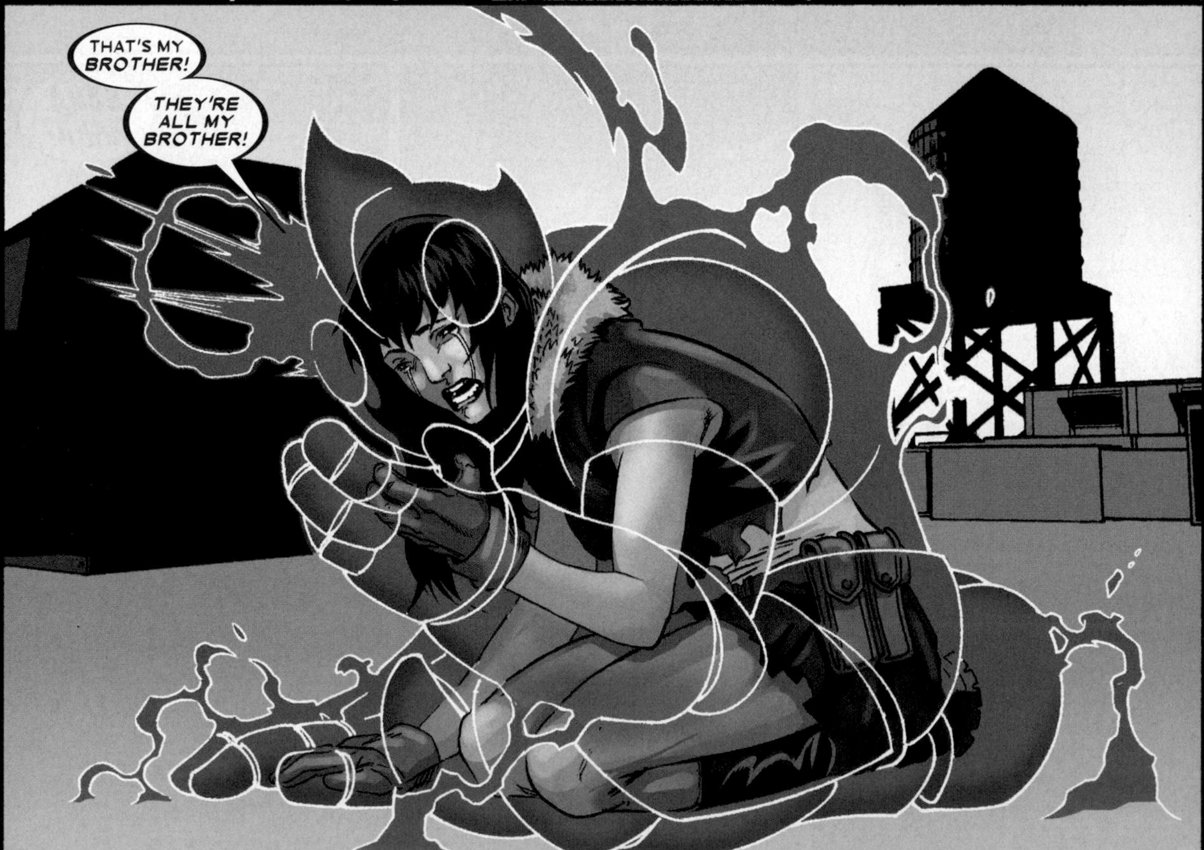
THAT'S MY BROTHER!
THEY'RE ALL MY BROTHER!

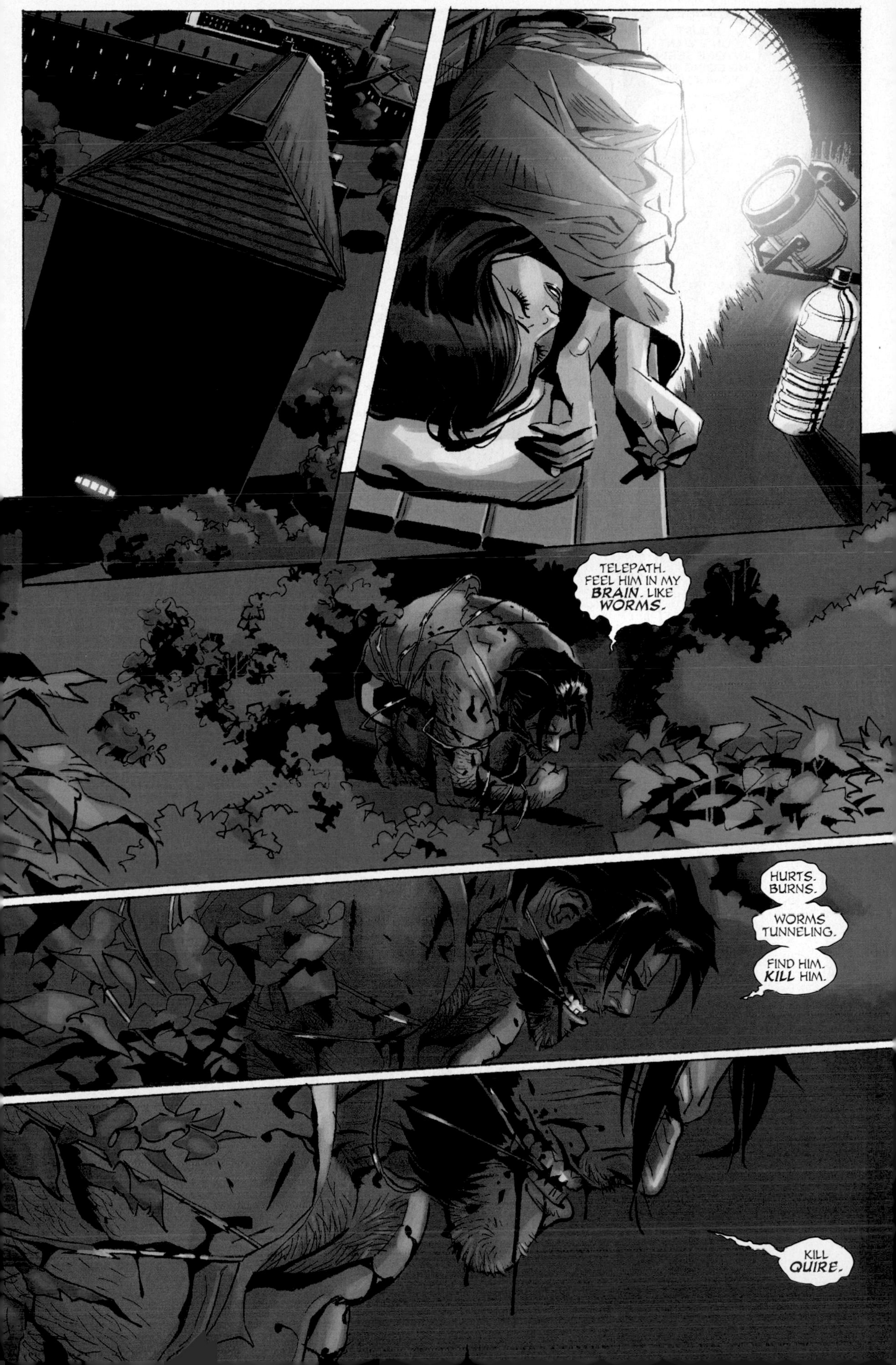
TELEPATH. FEEL HIM IN MY **BRAIN**. LIKE **WORMS**.
HURTS. BURNS.
WORMS TUNNELING.
FIND HIM. **KILL** HIM.
KILL **QUIRE**.

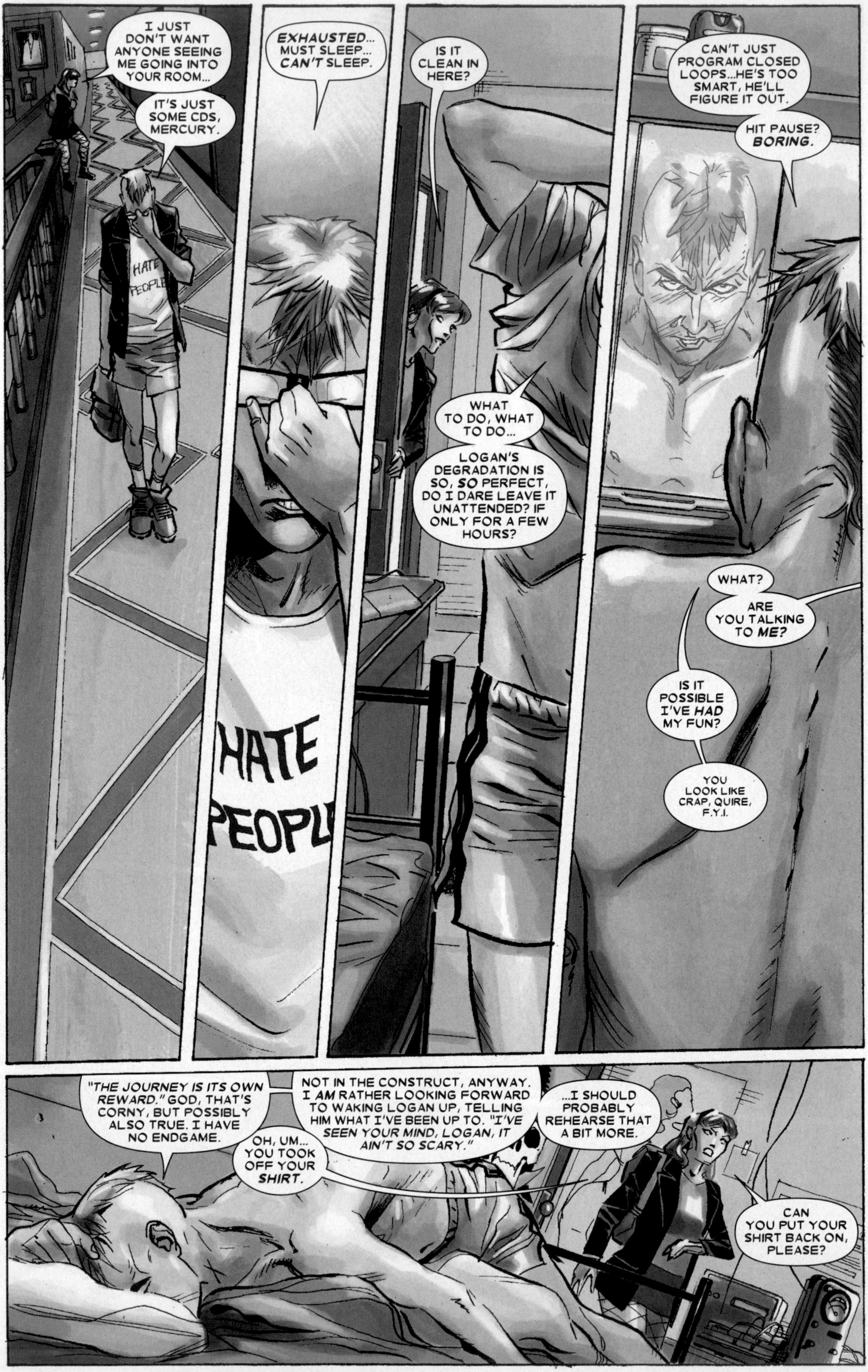
I JUST DON'T WANT ANYONE SEEING ME GOING INTO YOUR ROOM...
IT'S JUST SOME CDS, MERCURY.
HATE PEOPLE
EXHAUSTED... MUST SLEEP... CAN'T SLEEP.
HATE PEOPLE
IS IT CLEAN IN HERE?
WHAT TO DO, WHAT TO DO...
LOGAN'S DEGRADATION IS SO, SO PERFECT, DO I DARE LEAVE IT UNATTENDED? IF ONLY FOR A FEW HOURS?
CAN'T JUST PROGRAM CLOSED LOOPS...HE'S TOO SMART, HE'LL FIGURE IT OUT.
HIT PAUSE? BORING.
WHAT?
ARE YOU TALKING TO ME?
IS IT POSSIBLE I'VE HAD MY FUN?
YOU LOOK LIKE CRAP, QUIRE, F.Y.I.
"THE JOURNEY IS ITS OWN REWARD." GOD, THAT'S CORNY, BUT POSSIBLY ALSO TRUE. I HAVE NO ENDGAME.
NOT IN THE CONSTRUCT, ANYWAY. I AM RATHER LOOKING FORWARD TO WAKING LOGAN UP, TELLING HIM WHAT I'VE BEEN UP TO. "I'VE SEEN YOUR MIND, LOGAN, IT AIN'T SO SCARY."
OH, UM... YOU TOOK OFF YOUR SHIRT.
...I SHOULD PROBABLY REHEARSE THAT A BIT MORE.
CAN YOU PUT YOUR SHIRT BACK ON, PLEASE?

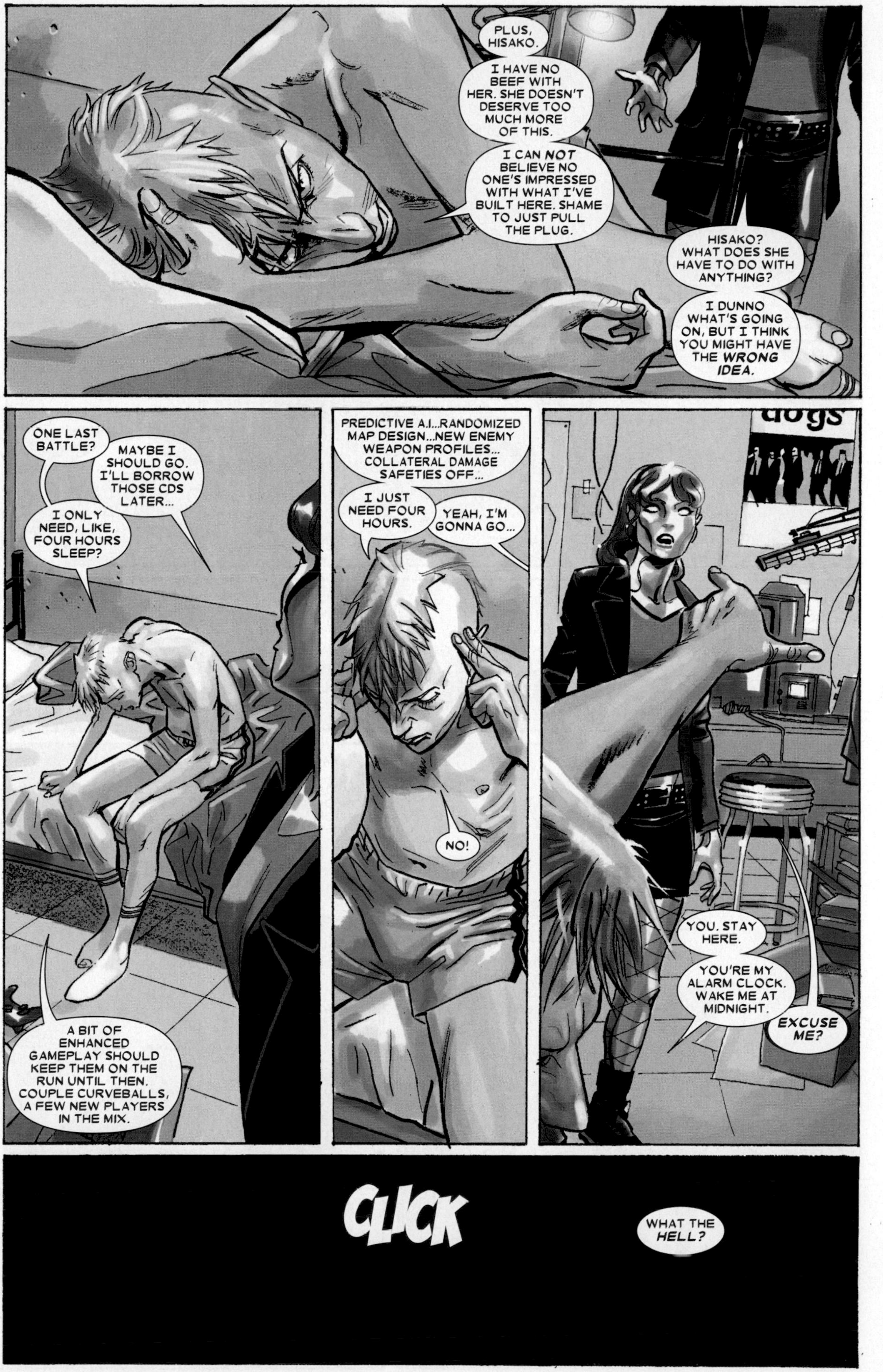
PLUS, HISAKO.
I HAVE NO BEEF WITH HER. SHE DOESN'T DESERVE TOO MUCH MORE OF THIS.
I CAN *NOT* BELIEVE NO ONE'S IMPRESSED WITH WHAT I'VE BUILT HERE. SHAME TO JUST PULL THE PLUG.
HISAKO? WHAT DOES SHE HAVE TO DO WITH ANYTHING?
I DUNNO WHAT'S GOING ON, BUT I THINK YOU MIGHT HAVE THE ***WRONG IDEA.***
ONE LAST BATTLE?
MAYBE I SHOULD GO. I'LL BORROW THOSE CDS LATER...
I ONLY NEED, LIKE, FOUR HOURS SLEEP?
A BIT OF ENHANCED GAMEPLAY SHOULD KEEP THEM ON THE RUN UNTIL THEN. COUPLE CURVEBALLS, A FEW NEW PLAYERS IN THE MIX.
PREDICTIVE A.I...RANDOMIZED MAP DESIGN...NEW ENEMY WEAPON PROFILES... COLLATERAL DAMAGE SAFETIES OFF...
I JUST NEED FOUR HOURS.
YEAH, I'M GONNA GO...
NO!
dogs
YOU. STAY HERE.
YOU'RE MY ALARM CLOCK. WAKE ME AT MIDNIGHT.
EXCUSE ME?
CLICK
WHAT THE *HELL?*

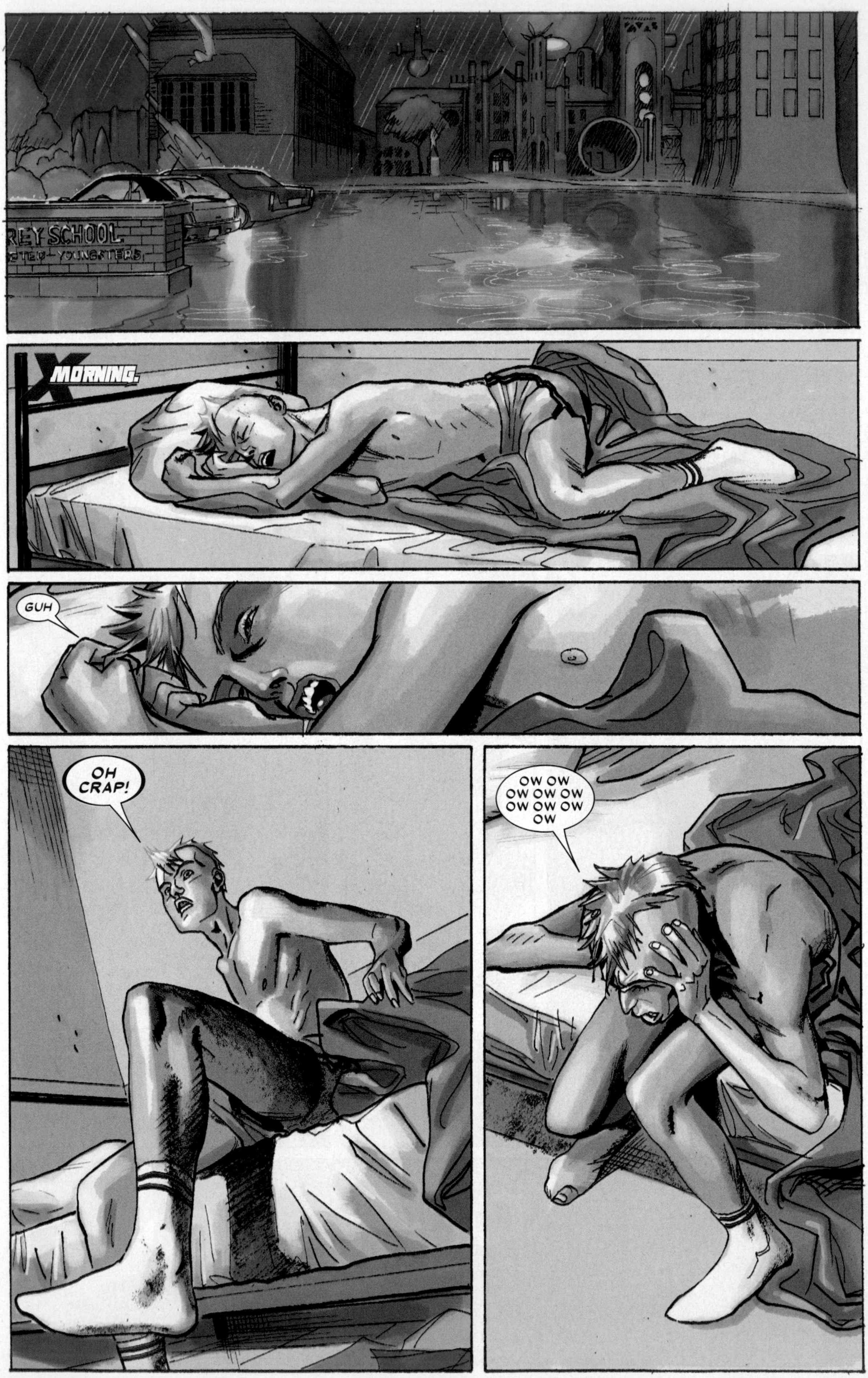
REY SCHOOL
YOUNGSTERS
MORNING.
GUH
OH CRAP!
OW OW OW OW OW OW OW OW OW

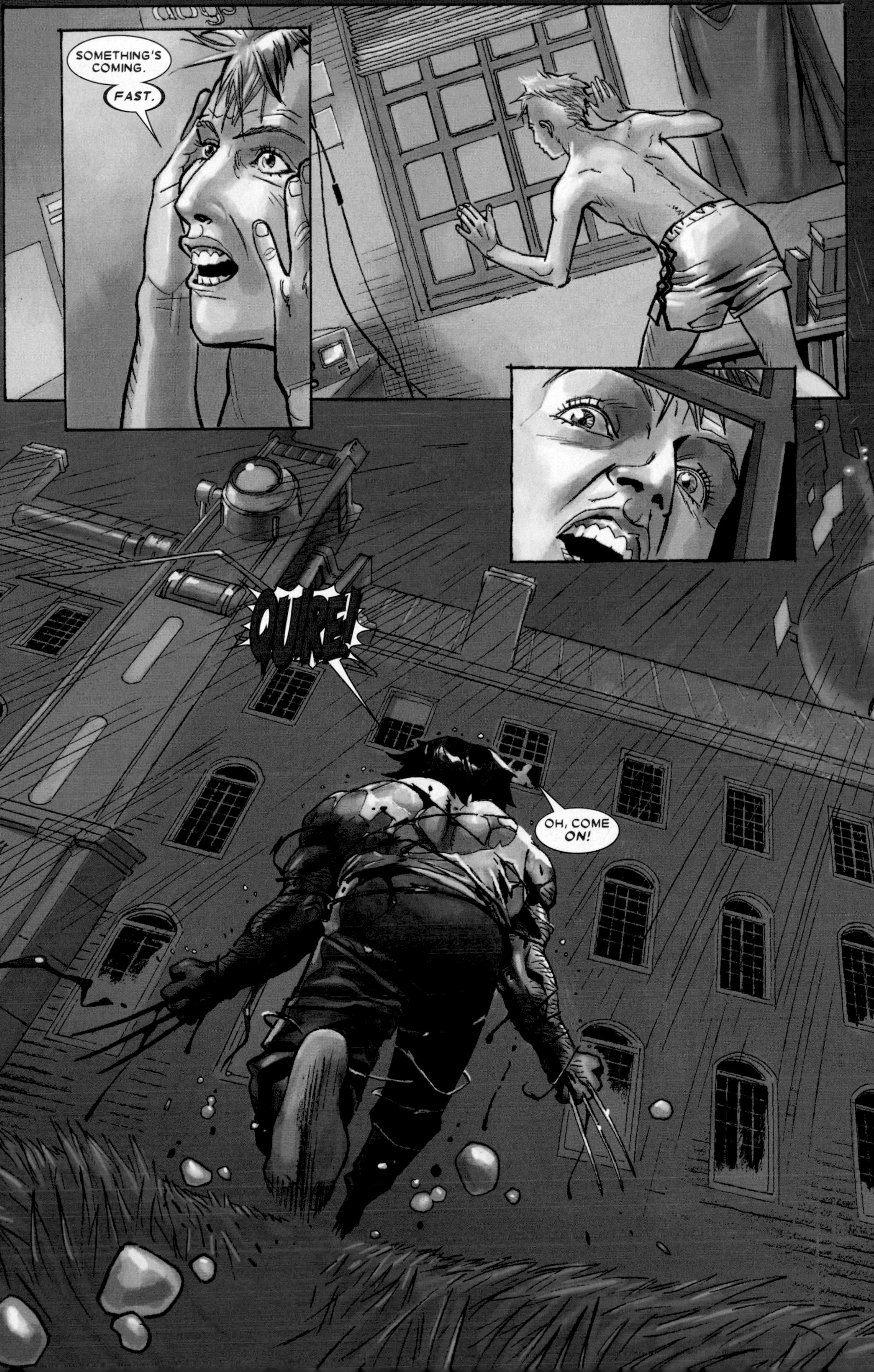
SOMETHING'S COMING.
FAST.
QUIRE!
OH, COME ON!

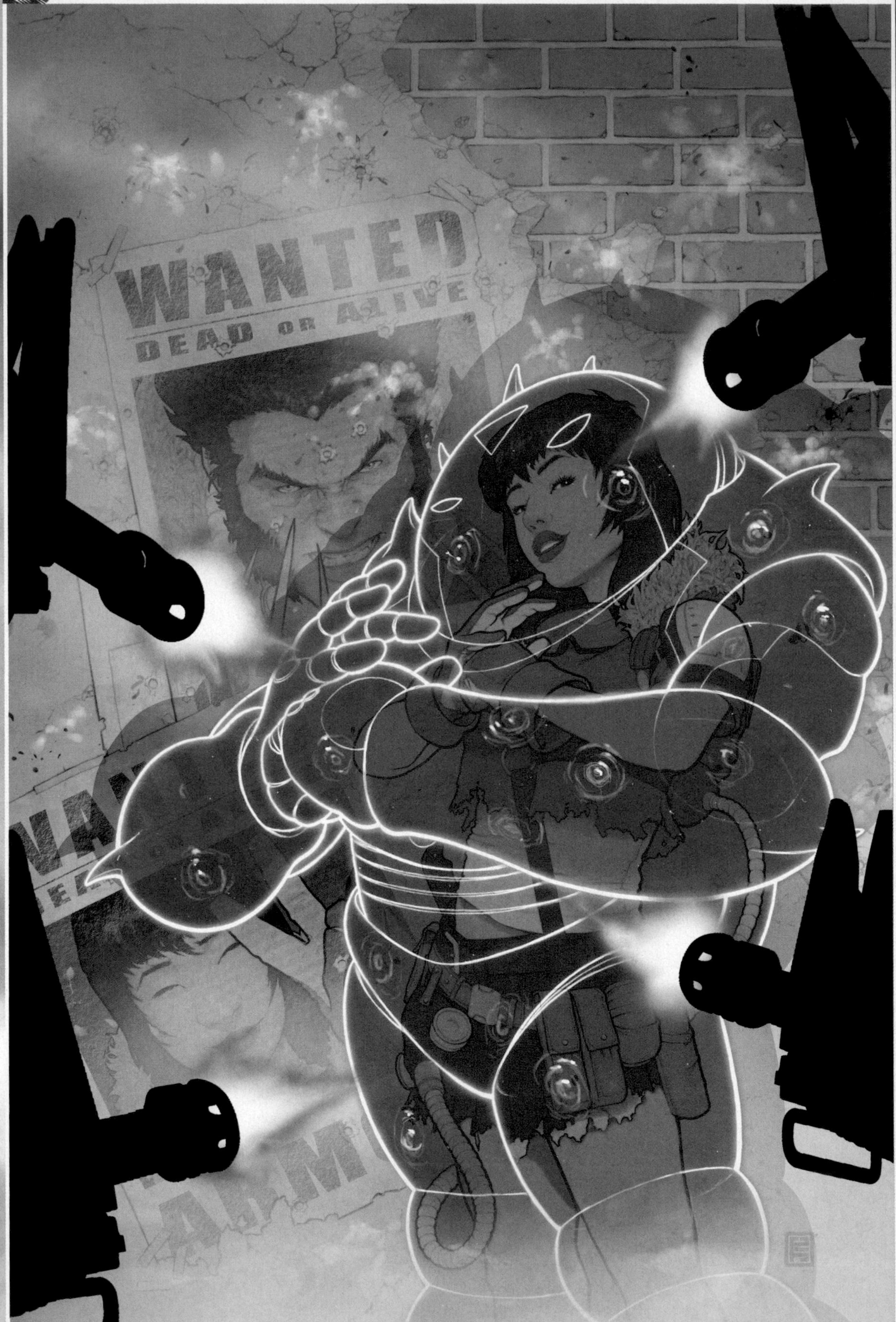
WANTED
DEAD OR ALIVE

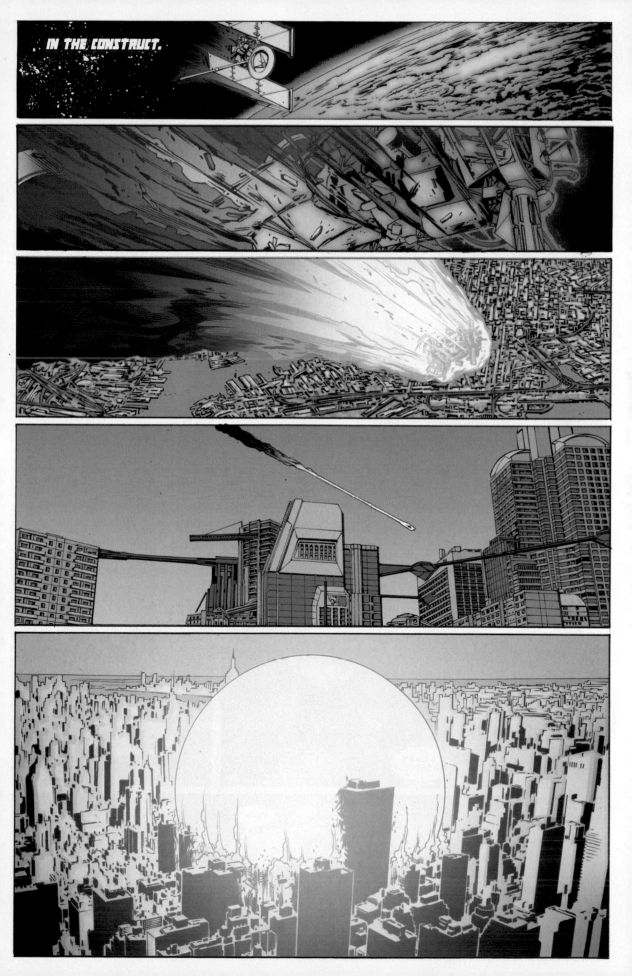

IN THE CONSTRUCT.

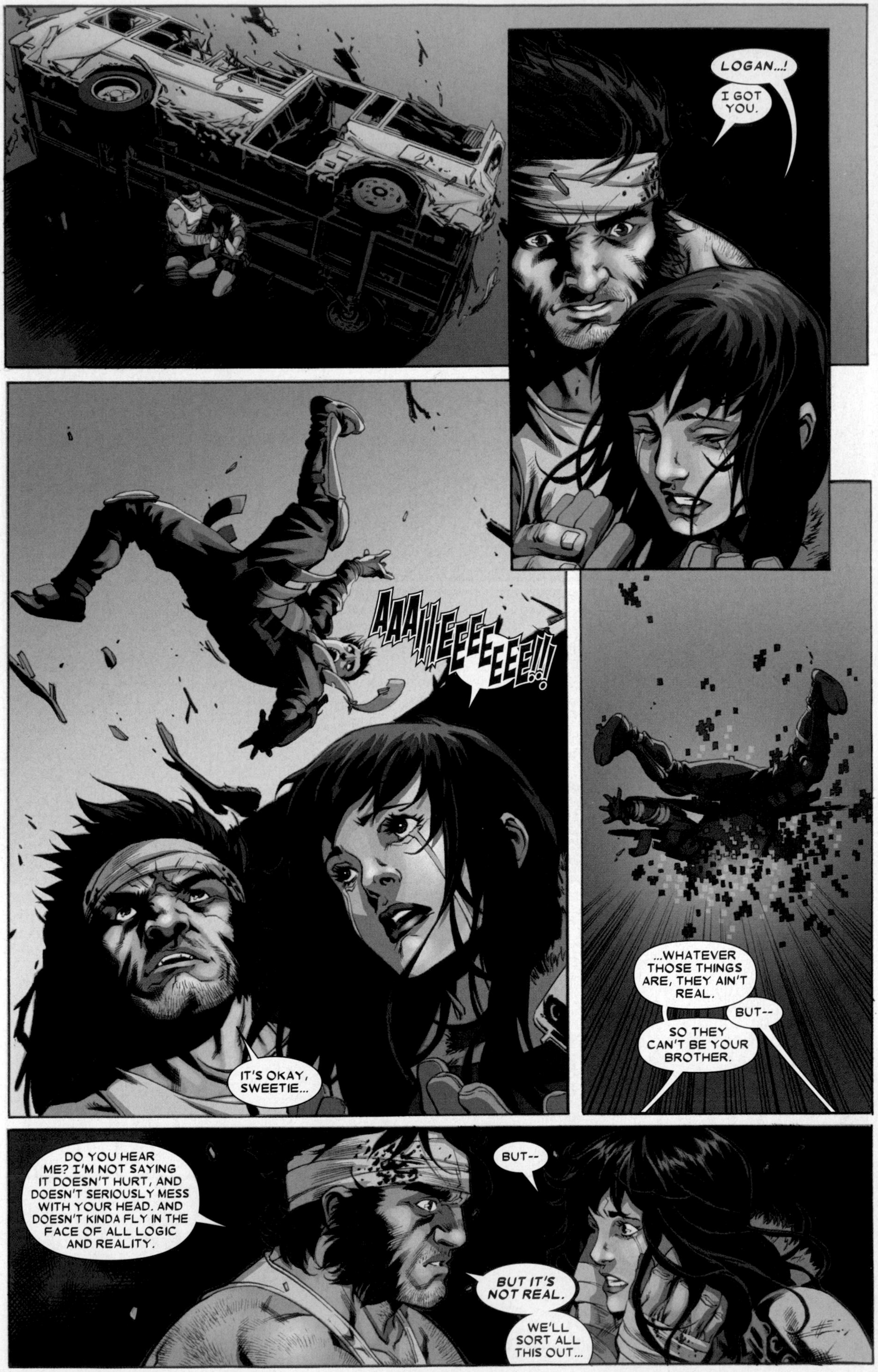
LOGAN...!
I GOT YOU.
AAAIIIEEEEEEEE!!!
IT'S OKAY, SWEETIE...
...WHATEVER THOSE THINGS ARE, THEY AIN'T REAL.
BUT--
SO THEY CAN'T BE YOUR BROTHER.
DO YOU HEAR ME? I'M NOT SAYING IT DOESN'T HURT, AND DOESN'T SERIOUSLY MESS WITH YOUR HEAD. AND DOESN'T KINDA FLY IN THE FACE OF ALL LOGIC AND REALITY.
BUT--
BUT IT'S NOT REAL.
WE'LL SORT ALL THIS OUT...

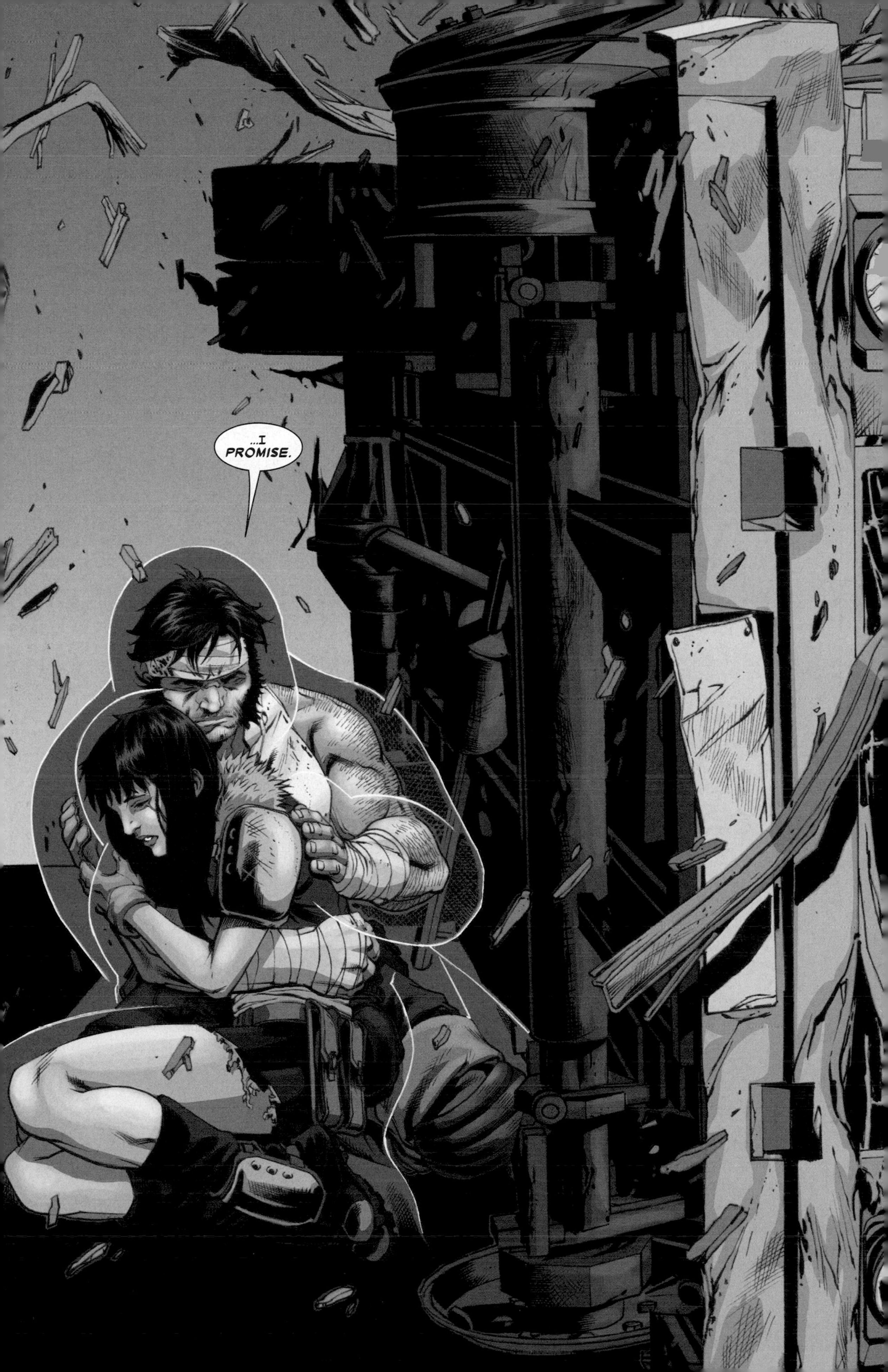
...I PROMISE.

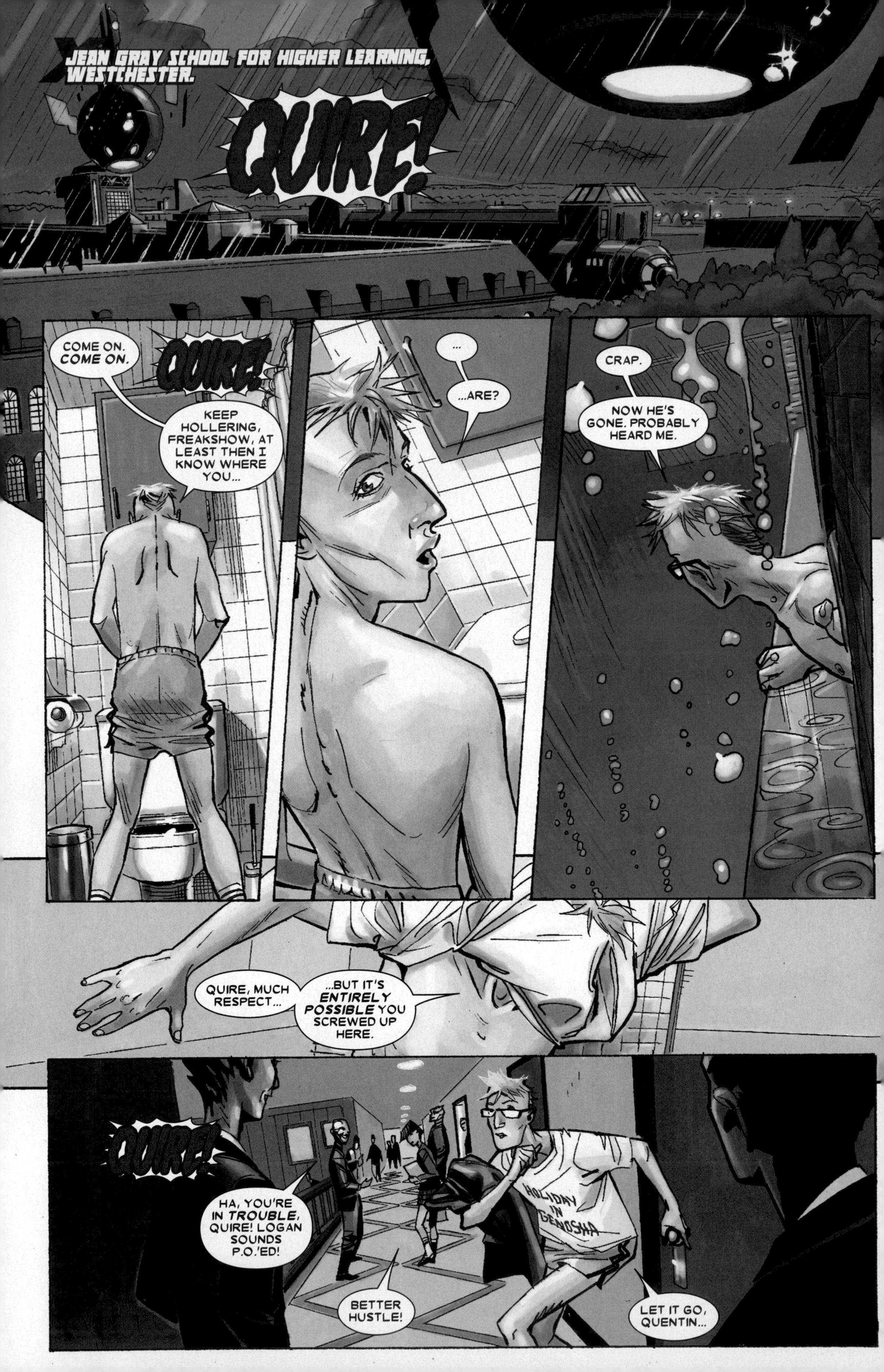

JEAN GRAY SCHOOL FOR HIGHER LEARNING, WESTCHESTER.
QUIRE!
COME ON. COME ON.
QUIRE!
KEEP HOLLERING, FREAKSHOW, AT LEAST THEN I KNOW WHERE YOU...
...
...ARE?
CRAP.
NOW HE'S GONE. PROBABLY HEARD ME.
QUIRE, MUCH RESPECT...
...BUT IT'S ENTIRELY POSSIBLE YOU SCREWED UP HERE.
QUIRE!
HA, YOU'RE IN TROUBLE, QUIRE! LOGAN SOUNDS P.O.'ED!
BETTER HUSTLE!
LET IT GO, QUENTIN...
HOLIDAY IN GENOSHA

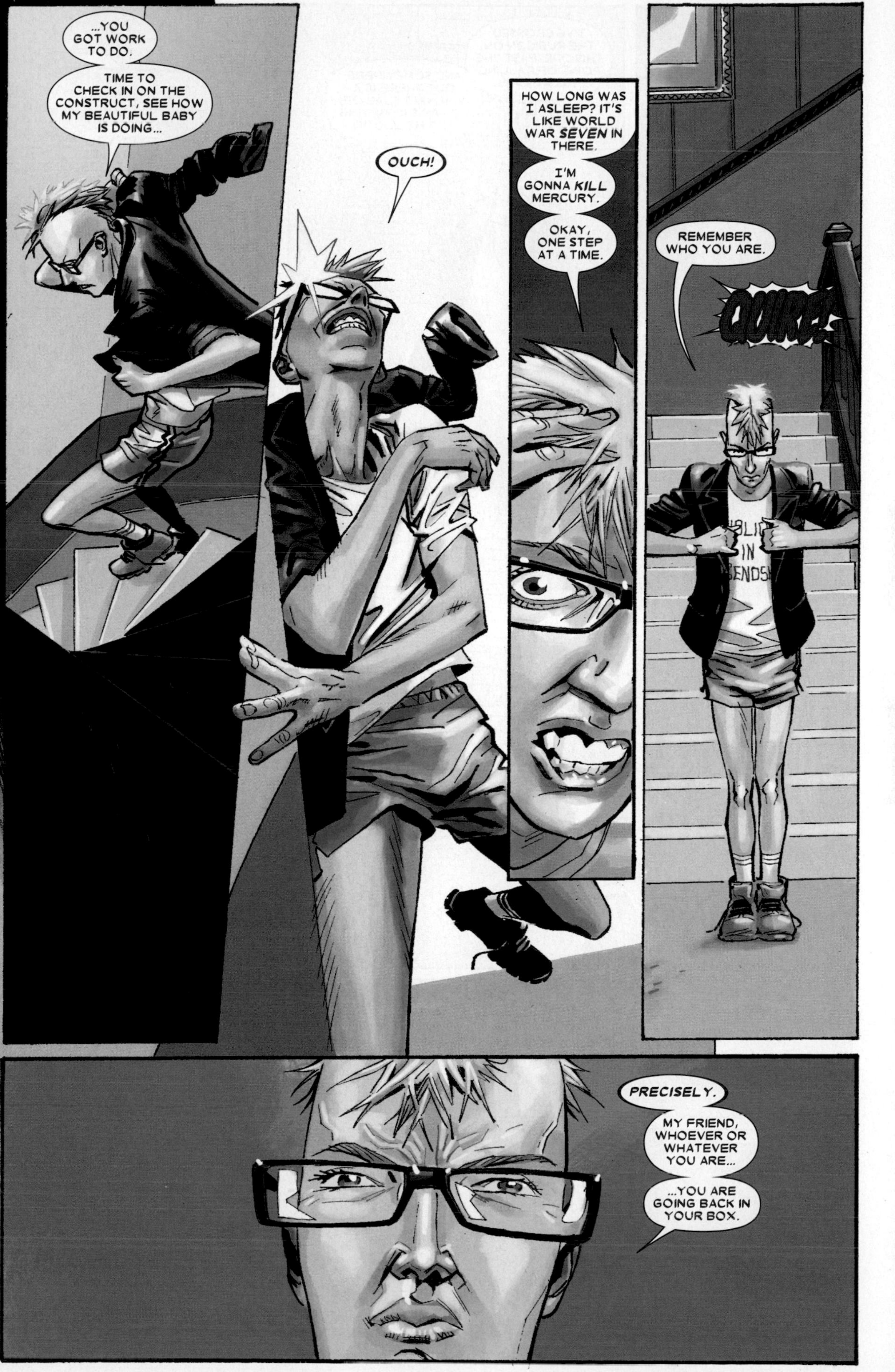
...YOU GOT WORK TO DO.
TIME TO CHECK IN ON THE CONSTRUCT, SEE HOW MY BEAUTIFUL BABY IS DOING...
OUCH!
HOW LONG WAS I ASLEEP? IT'S LIKE WORLD WAR SEVEN IN THERE.
I'M GONNA KILL MERCURY.
OKAY, ONE STEP AT A TIME.
REMEMBER WHO YOU ARE.
QUIRE!
PRECISELY.
MY FRIEND, WHOEVER OR WHATEVER YOU ARE...
...YOU ARE GOING BACK IN YOUR BOX.

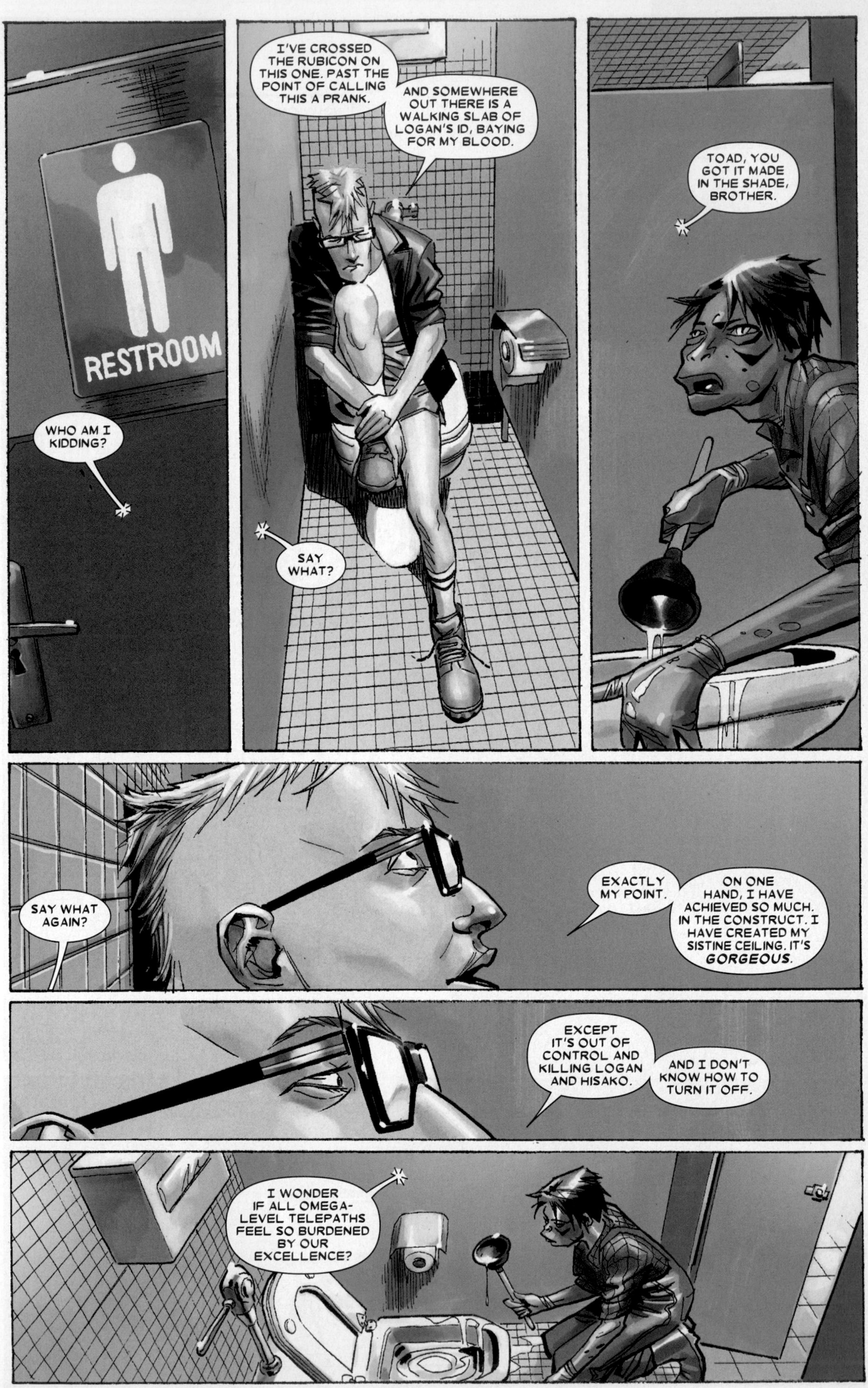
RESTROOM
WHO AM I KIDDING?
I'VE CROSSED THE RUBICON ON THIS ONE. PAST THE POINT OF CALLING THIS A PRANK.
AND SOMEWHERE OUT THERE IS A WALKING SLAB OF LOGAN'S ID, BAYING FOR MY BLOOD.
SAY WHAT?
TOAD, YOU GOT IT MADE IN THE SHADE, BROTHER.
SAY WHAT AGAIN?
EXACTLY MY POINT.
ON ONE HAND, I HAVE ACHIEVED SO MUCH. IN THE CONSTRUCT. I HAVE CREATED MY SISTINE CEILING. IT'S GORGEOUS.
EXCEPT IT'S OUT OF CONTROL AND KILLING LOGAN AND HISAKO.
AND I DON'T KNOW HOW TO TURN IT OFF.
I WONDER IF ALL OMEGA-LEVEL TELEPATHS FEEL SO BURDENED BY OUR EXCELLENCE?

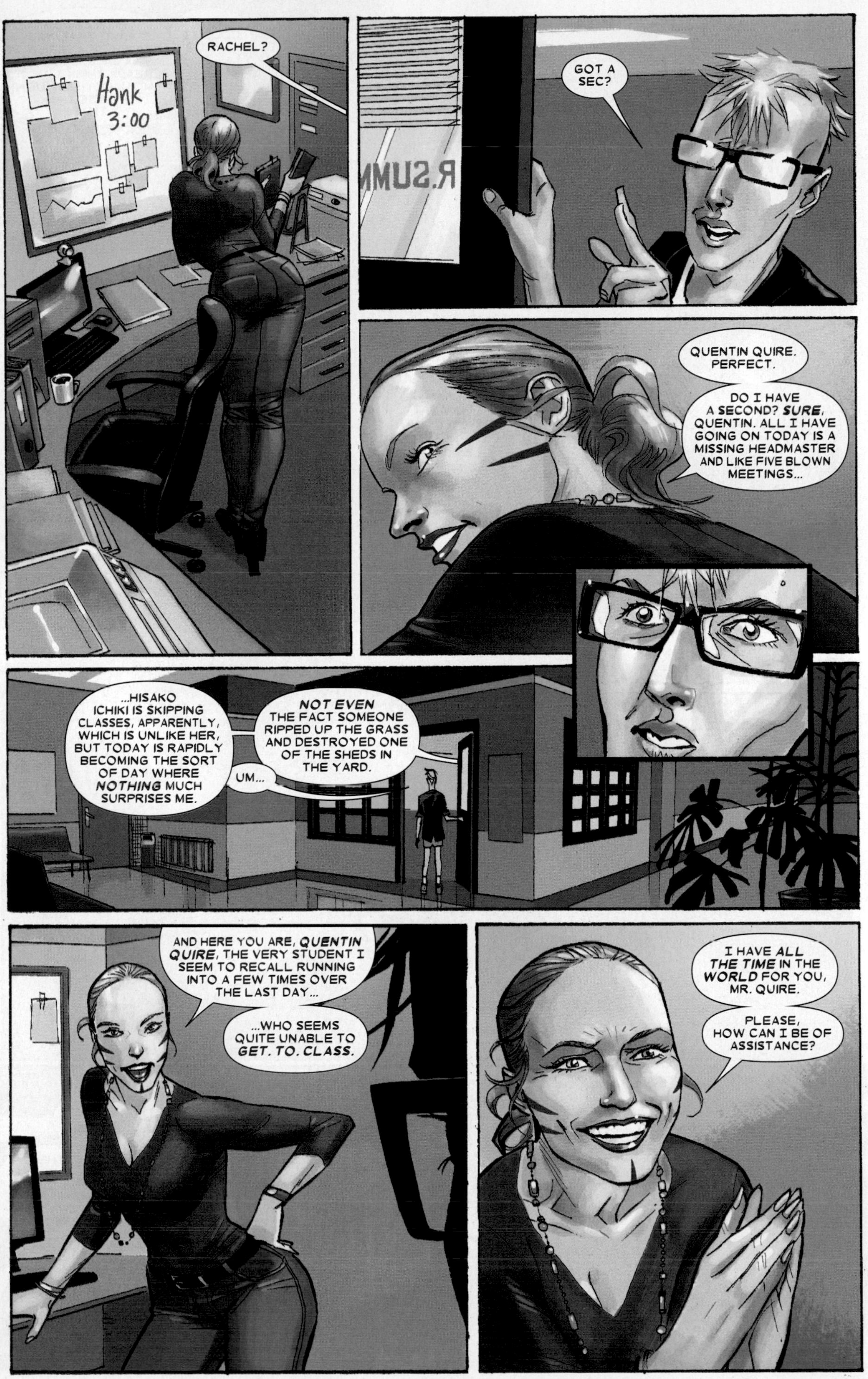
RACHEL?
GOT A SEC?
R.SUMM
Hank 3:00
QUENTIN QUIRE. PERFECT.
DO I HAVE A SECOND? SURE, QUENTIN. ALL I HAVE GOING ON TODAY IS A MISSING HEADMASTER AND LIKE FIVE BLOWN MEETINGS...
...HISAKO ICHIKI IS SKIPPING CLASSES, APPARENTLY, WHICH IS UNLIKE HER, BUT TODAY IS RAPIDLY BECOMING THE SORT OF DAY WHERE NOTHING MUCH SURPRISES ME.
NOT EVEN THE FACT SOMEONE RIPPED UP THE GRASS AND DESTROYED ONE OF THE SHEDS IN THE YARD.
UM...
AND HERE YOU ARE, QUENTIN QUIRE, THE VERY STUDENT I SEEM TO RECALL RUNNING INTO A FEW TIMES OVER THE LAST DAY...
...WHO SEEMS QUITE UNABLE TO GET. TO. CLASS.
I HAVE ALL THE TIME IN THE WORLD FOR YOU, MR. QUIRE.
PLEASE, HOW CAN I BE OF ASSISTANCE?

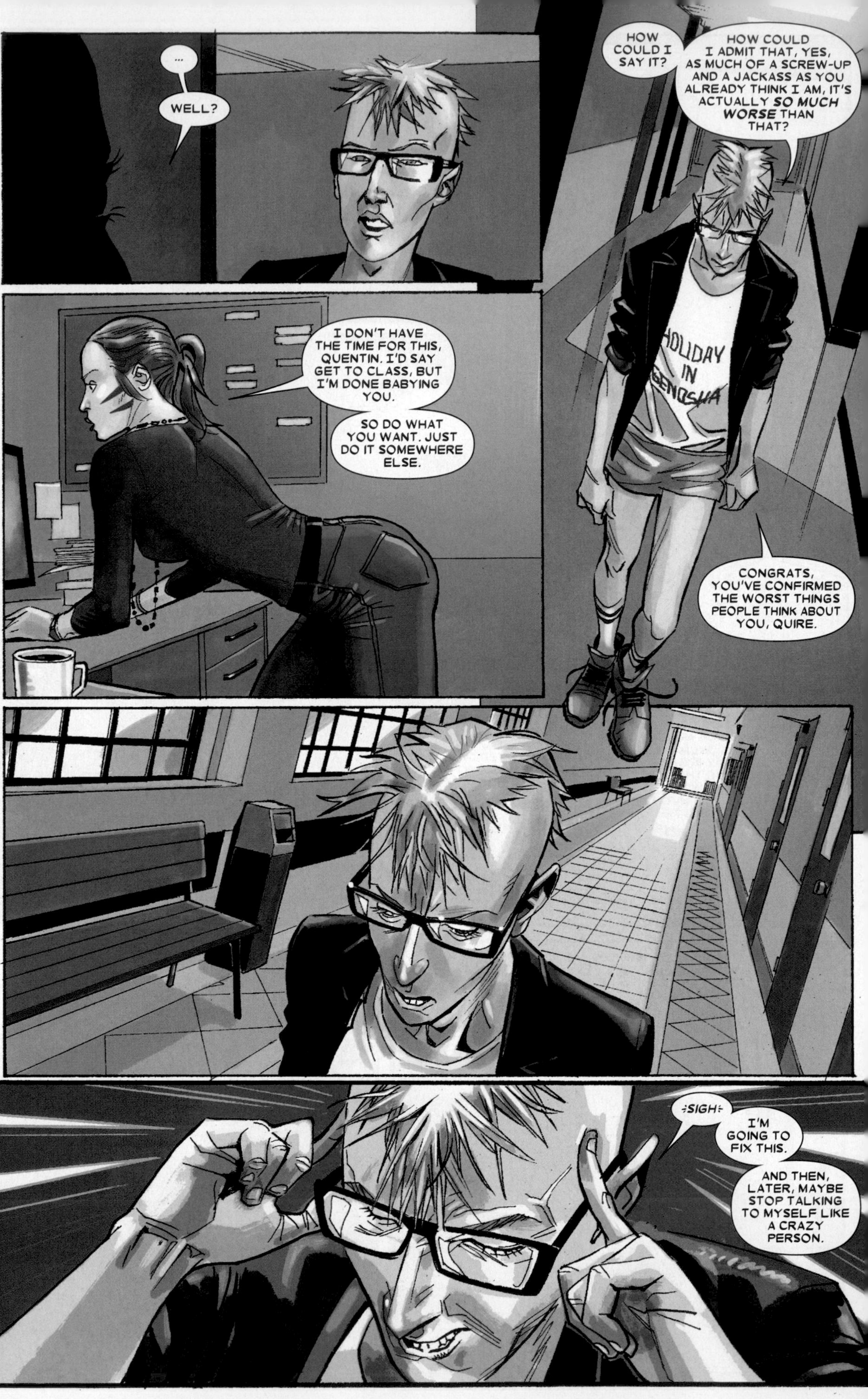
...
WELL?
HOW COULD I SAY IT?
HOW COULD I ADMIT THAT, YES, AS MUCH OF A SCREW-UP AND A JACKASS AS YOU ALREADY THINK I AM, IT'S ACTUALLY SO MUCH WORSE THAN THAT?
I DON'T HAVE THE TIME FOR THIS, QUENTIN. I'D SAY GET TO CLASS, BUT I'M DONE BABYING YOU.
SO DO WHAT YOU WANT. JUST DO IT SOMEWHERE ELSE.
HOLIDAY IN GENOSHA
CONGRATS, YOU'VE CONFIRMED THE WORST THINGS PEOPLE THINK ABOUT YOU, QUIRE.
SIGH
I'M GOING TO FIX THIS.
AND THEN, LATER, MAYBE STOP TALKING TO MYSELF LIKE A CRAZY PERSON.

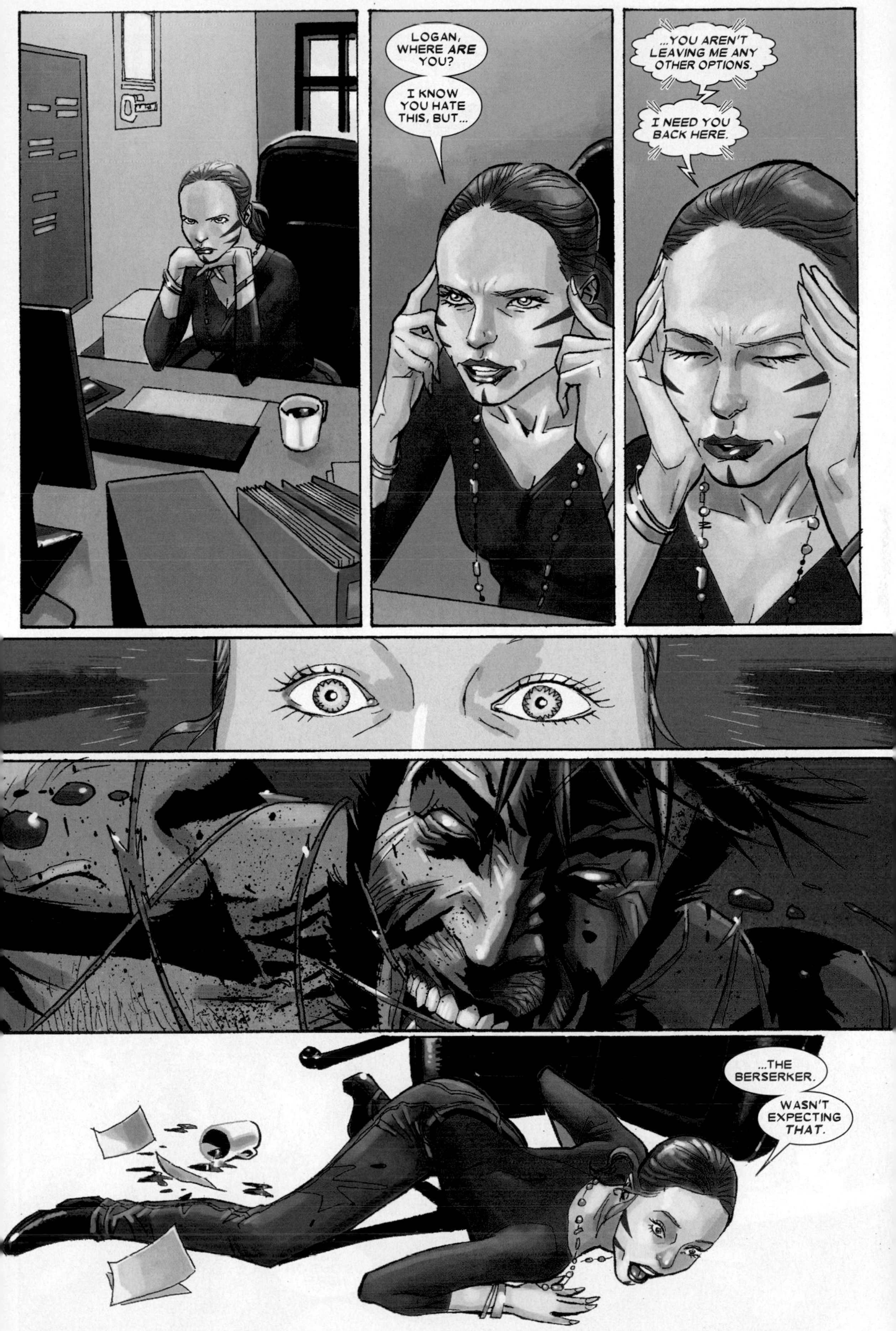
LOGAN, WHERE *ARE* YOU?
I KNOW YOU HATE THIS, BUT...
...YOU AREN'T LEAVING ME ANY OTHER OPTIONS.
I NEED YOU BACK HERE.
...THE BERSERKER.
WASN'T EXPECTING *THAT*.

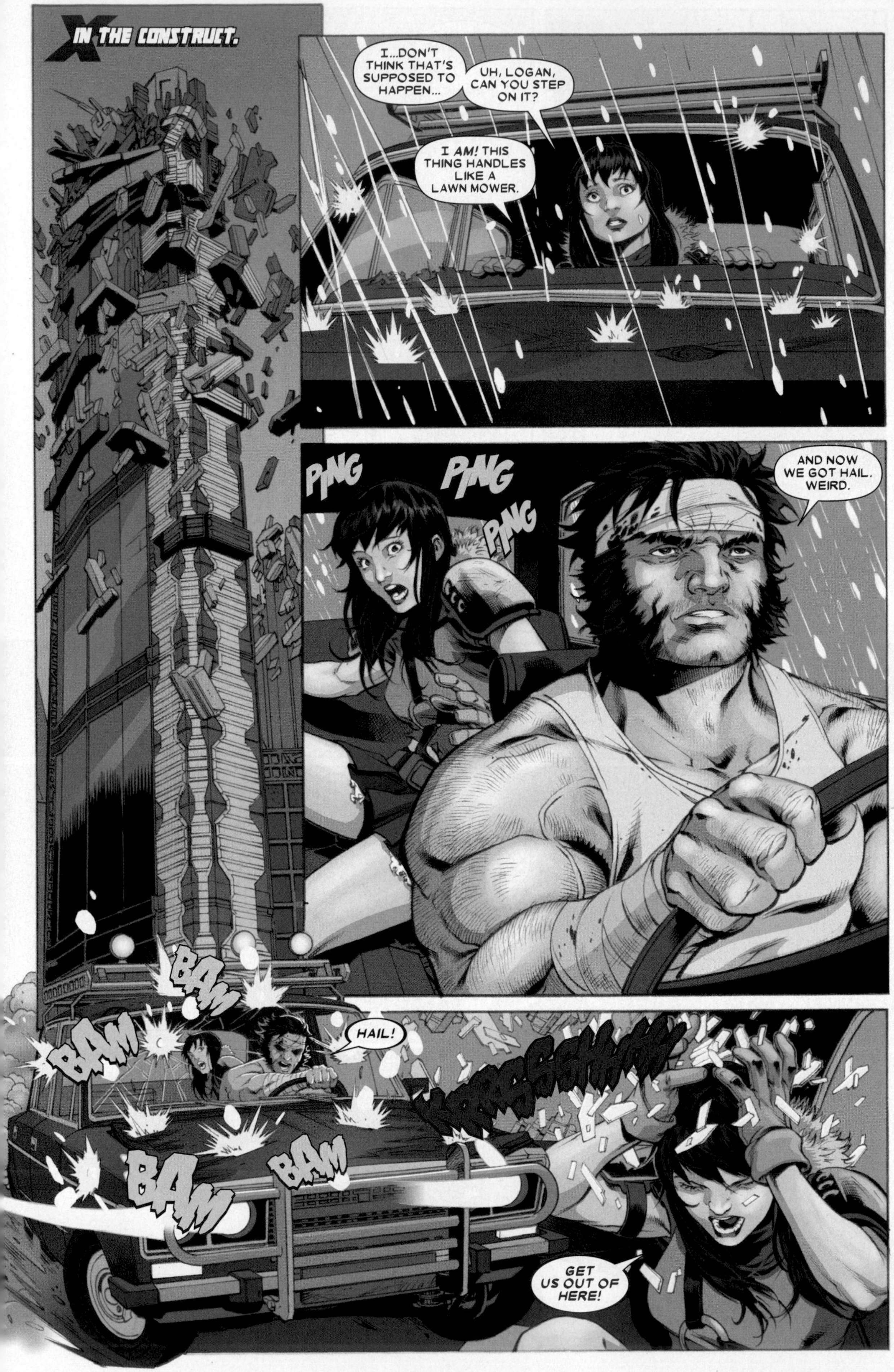
IN THE CONSTRUCT.
I...DON'T THINK THAT'S SUPPOSED TO HAPPEN...
UH, LOGAN, CAN YOU STEP ON IT?
I AM! THIS THING HANDLES LIKE A LAWN MOWER.
PING
PING
PING
AND NOW WE GOT HAIL. WEIRD.
BAM
BAM
HAIL!
BAM
BAM
GET US OUT OF HERE!

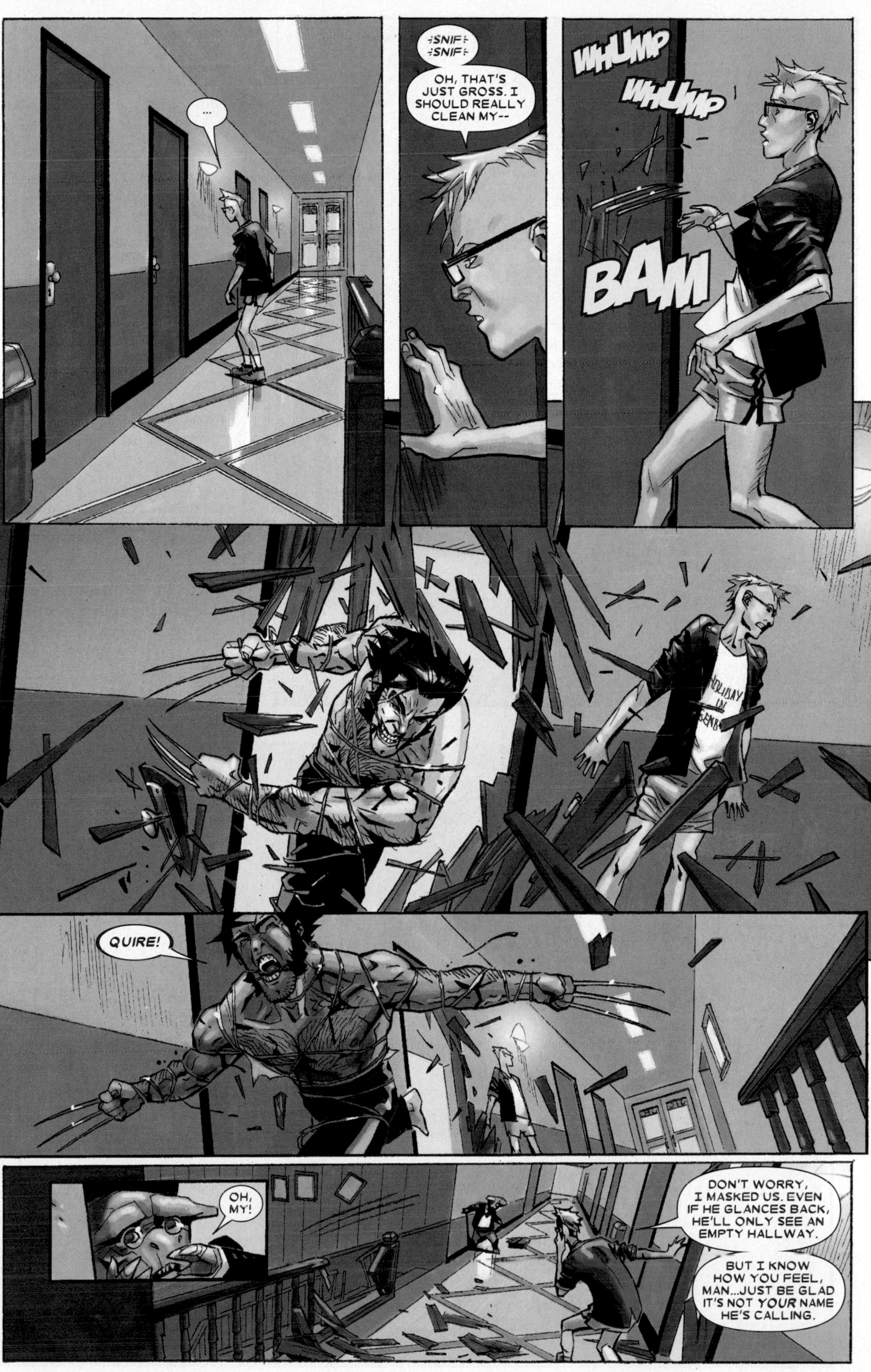
...
SNIF SNIF
OH, THAT'S JUST GROSS. I SHOULD REALLY CLEAN MY--
WHUMP
WHUMP
BAM
HOLIDAY IN
QUIRE!
OH, MY!
DON'T WORRY, I MASKED US. EVEN IF HE GLANCES BACK, HE'LL ONLY SEE AN EMPTY HALLWAY.
BUT I KNOW HOW YOU FEEL, MAN...JUST BE GLAD IT'S NOT YOUR NAME HE'S CALLING.

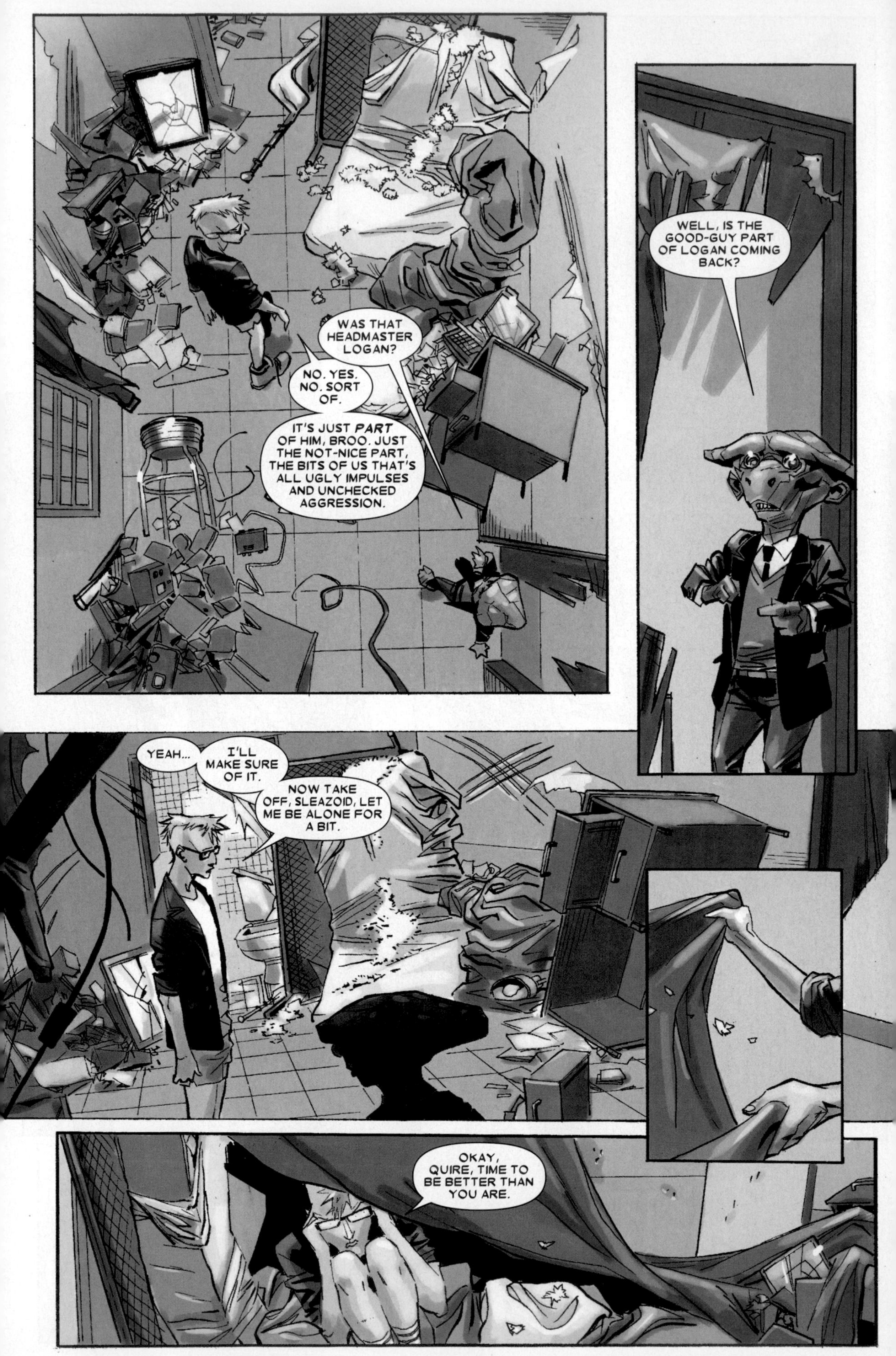
WAS THAT HEADMASTER LOGAN?
NO. YES. NO. SORT OF.
IT'S JUST *PART* OF HIM, BROO. JUST THE NOT-NICE PART, THE BITS OF US THAT'S ALL UGLY IMPULSES AND UNCHECKED AGGRESSION.
WELL, IS THE GOOD-GUY PART OF LOGAN COMING BACK?
YEAH...
I'LL MAKE SURE OF IT.
NOW TAKE OFF, SLEAZOID, LET ME BE ALONE FOR A BIT.
OKAY, QUIRE, TIME TO BE BETTER THAN YOU ARE.

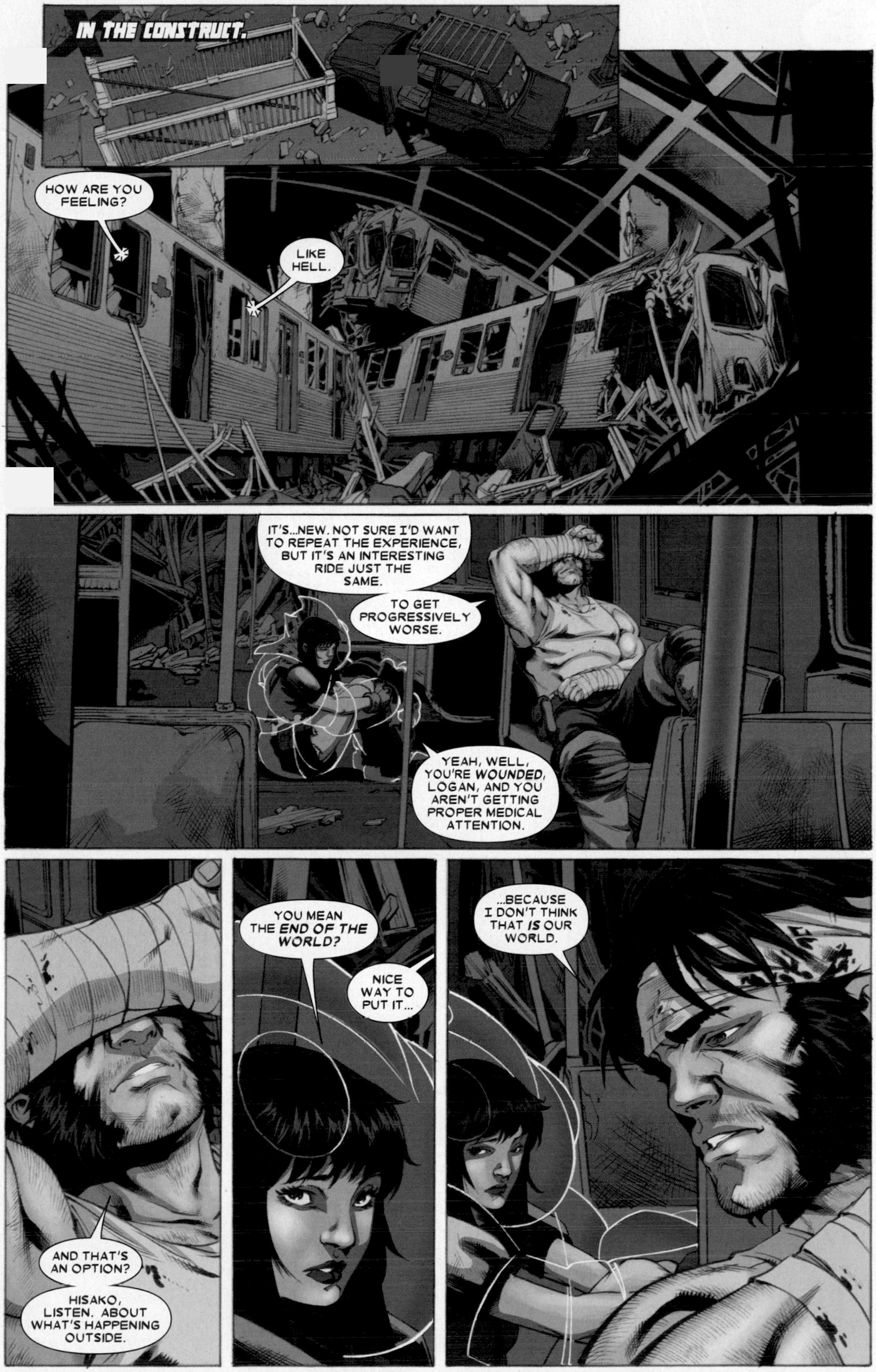
IN THE CONSTRUCT.
HOW ARE YOU FEELING?
LIKE HELL.
IT'S...NEW. NOT SURE I'D WANT TO REPEAT THE EXPERIENCE, BUT IT'S AN INTERESTING RIDE JUST THE SAME.
TO GET PROGRESSIVELY WORSE.
YEAH, WELL, YOU'RE WOUNDED, LOGAN, AND YOU AREN'T GETTING PROPER MEDICAL ATTENTION.
AND THAT'S AN OPTION?
HISAKO, LISTEN. ABOUT WHAT'S HAPPENING OUTSIDE.
YOU MEAN THE END OF THE WORLD?
NICE WAY TO PUT IT...
...BECAUSE I DON'T THINK THAT IS OUR WORLD.

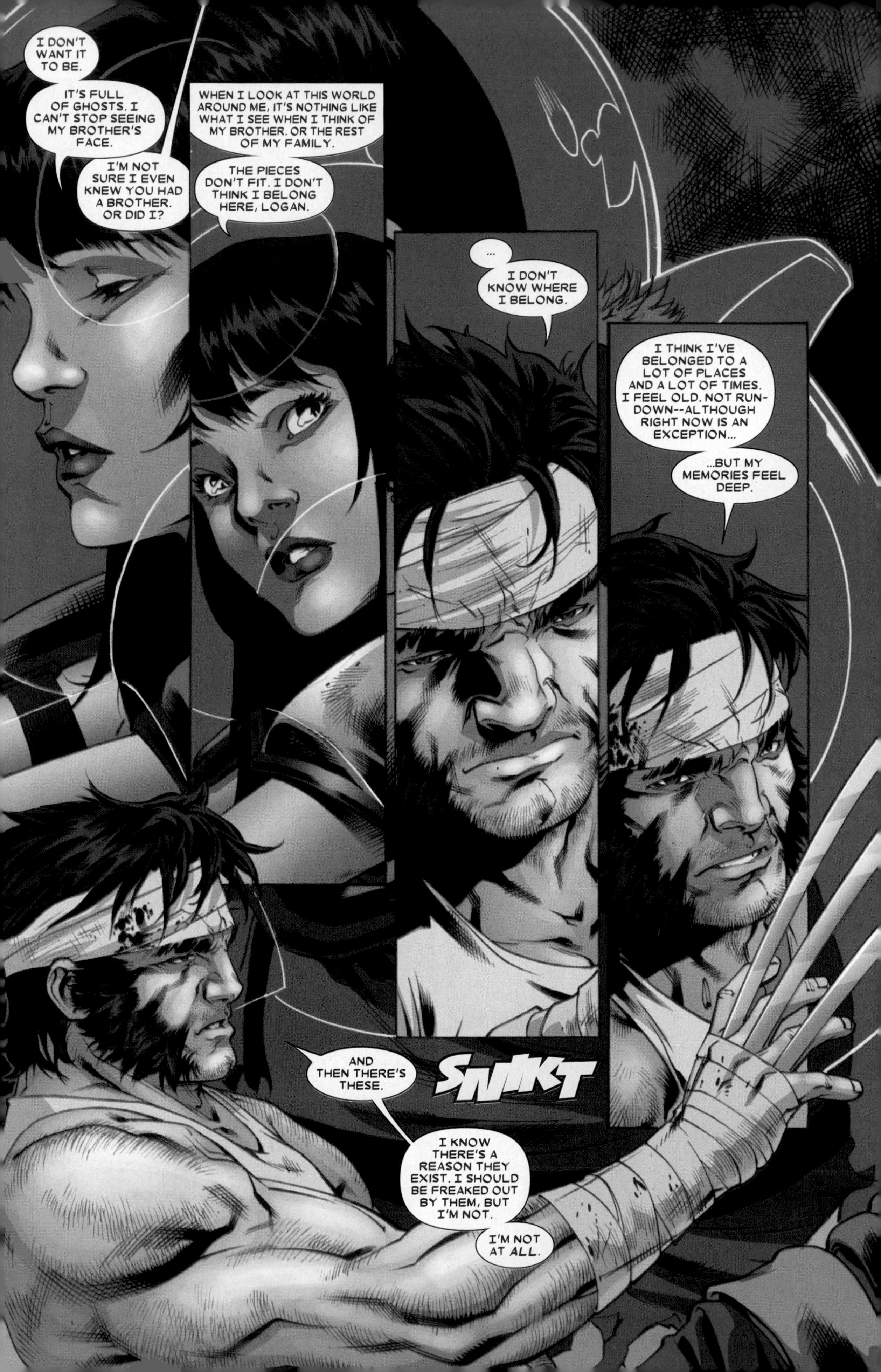
I DON'T WANT IT TO BE.
IT'S FULL OF GHOSTS. I CAN'T STOP SEEING MY BROTHER'S FACE.
I'M NOT SURE I EVEN KNEW YOU HAD A BROTHER. OR DID I?
WHEN I LOOK AT THIS WORLD AROUND ME, IT'S NOTHING LIKE WHAT I SEE WHEN I THINK OF MY BROTHER. OR THE REST OF MY FAMILY.
THE PIECES DON'T FIT. I DON'T THINK I BELONG HERE, LOGAN.
...
I DON'T KNOW WHERE I BELONG.
I THINK I'VE BELONGED TO A LOT OF PLACES AND A LOT OF TIMES. I FEEL OLD. NOT RUN-DOWN--ALTHOUGH RIGHT NOW IS AN EXCEPTION...
...BUT MY MEMORIES FEEL DEEP.
AND THEN THERE'S THESE.
SNIKT
I KNOW THERE'S A REASON THEY EXIST. I SHOULD BE FREAKED OUT BY THEM, BUT I'M NOT.
I'M NOT AT ALL.

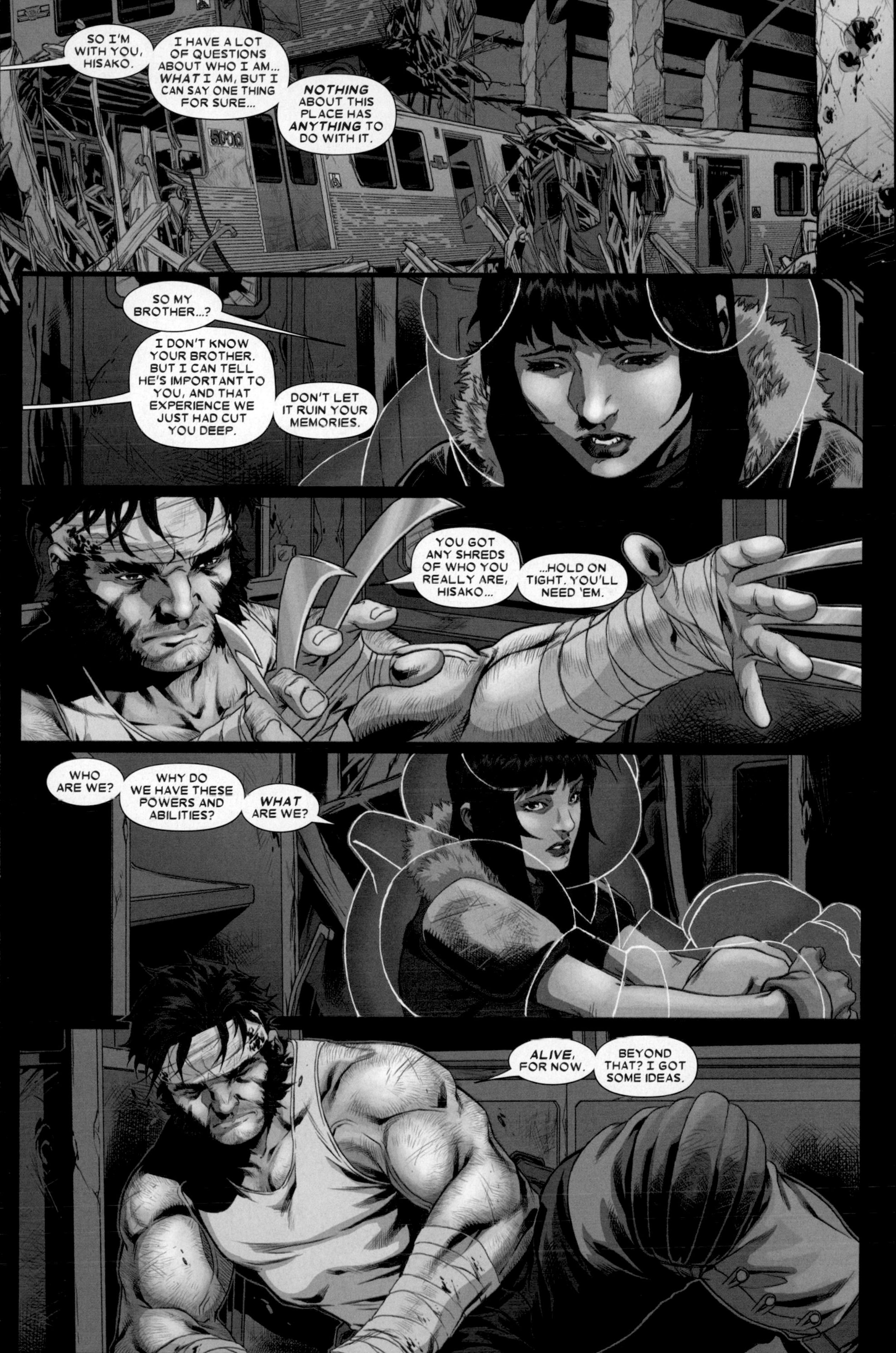
SO I'M WITH YOU, HISAKO.
I HAVE A LOT OF QUESTIONS ABOUT WHO I AM... WHAT I AM, BUT I CAN SAY ONE THING FOR SURE...
NOTHING ABOUT THIS PLACE HAS ANYTHING TO DO WITH IT.
5000
SO MY BROTHER...?
I DON'T KNOW YOUR BROTHER. BUT I CAN TELL HE'S IMPORTANT TO YOU, AND THAT EXPERIENCE WE JUST HAD CUT YOU DEEP.
DON'T LET IT RUIN YOUR MEMORIES.
YOU GOT ANY SHREDS OF WHO YOU REALLY ARE, HISAKO...
...HOLD ON TIGHT. YOU'LL NEED 'EM.
WHO ARE WE?
WHY DO WE HAVE THESE POWERS AND ABILITIES?
WHAT ARE WE?
ALIVE, FOR NOW.
BEYOND THAT? I GOT SOME IDEAS.

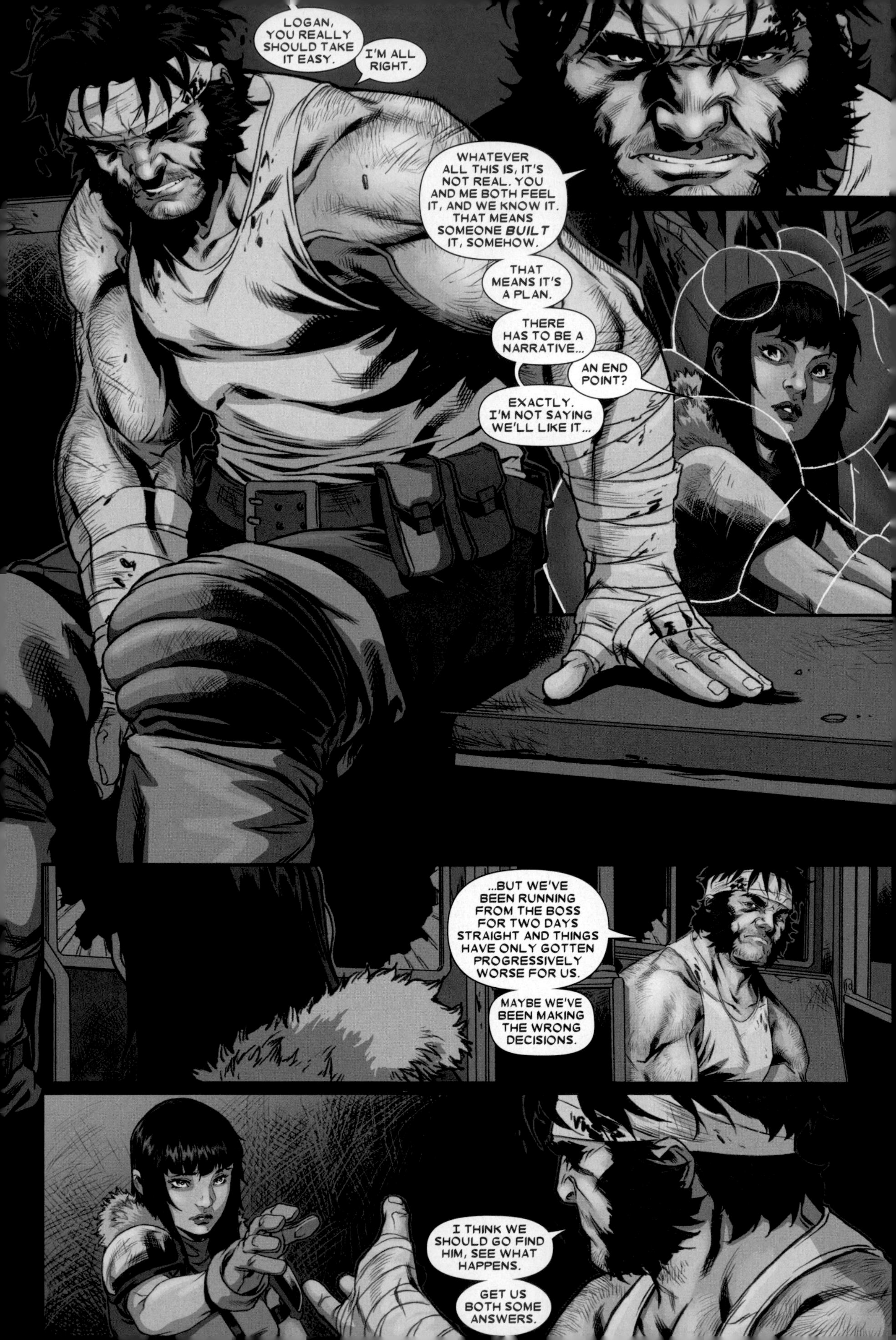
LOGAN, YOU REALLY SHOULD TAKE IT EASY.
I'M ALL RIGHT.
WHATEVER ALL THIS IS, IT'S NOT REAL. YOU AND ME BOTH FEEL IT, AND WE KNOW IT. THAT MEANS SOMEONE *BUILT* IT, SOMEHOW.
THAT MEANS IT'S A PLAN.
THERE HAS TO BE A NARRATIVE...
AN END POINT?
EXACTLY. I'M NOT SAYING WE'LL LIKE IT...
...BUT WE'VE BEEN RUNNING FROM THE BOSS FOR TWO DAYS STRAIGHT AND THINGS HAVE ONLY GOTTEN PROGRESSIVELY WORSE FOR US.
MAYBE WE'VE BEEN MAKING THE WRONG DECISIONS.
I THINK WE SHOULD GO FIND HIM, SEE WHAT HAPPENS.
GET US BOTH SOME ANSWERS.

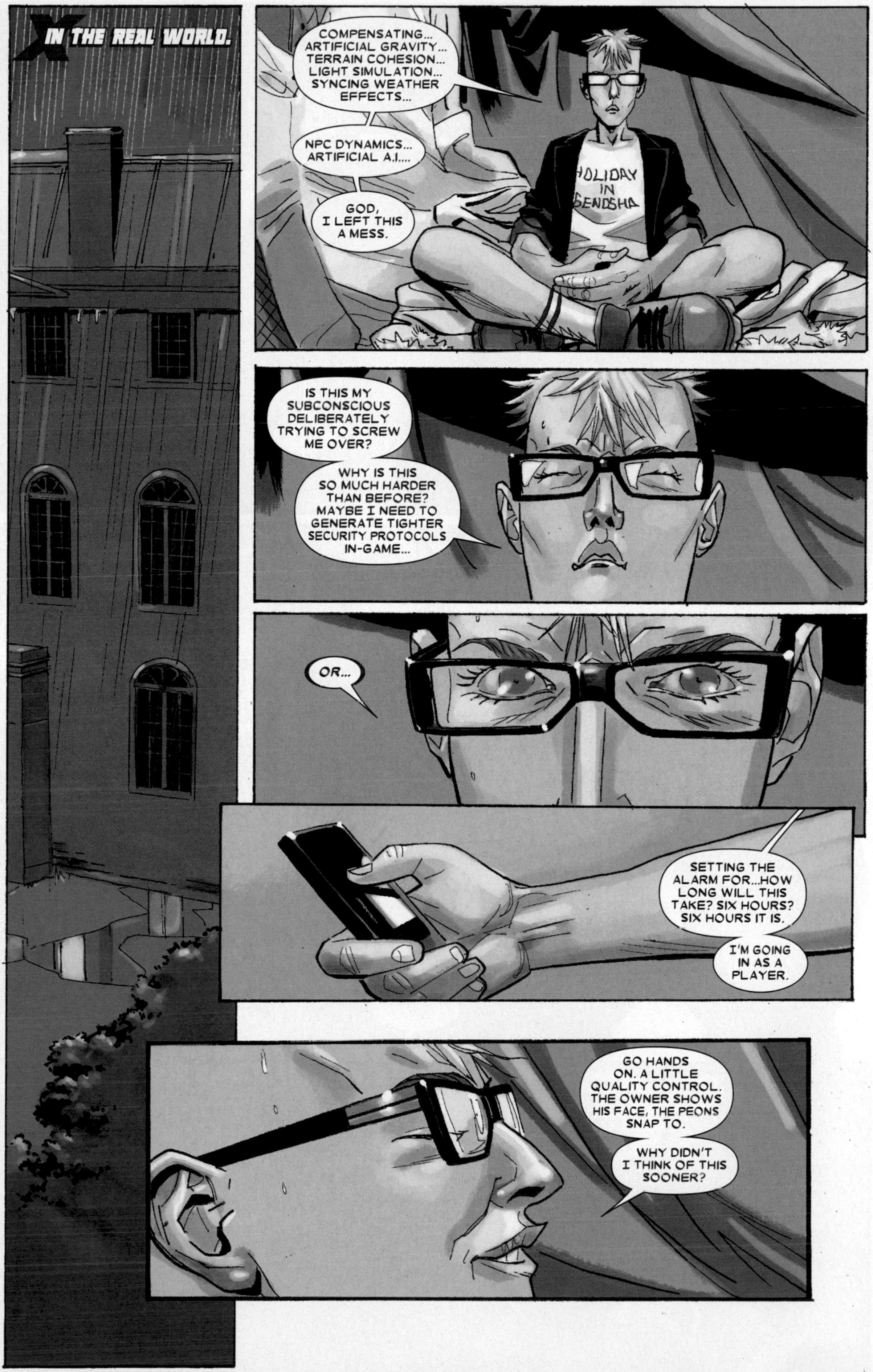
IN THE REAL WORLD.
COMPENSATING... ARTIFICIAL GRAVITY... TERRAIN COHESION... LIGHT SIMULATION... SYNCING WEATHER EFFECTS...
NPC DYNAMICS... ARTIFICIAL A.I....
GOD, I LEFT THIS A MESS.
HOLIDAY IN GENOSHA
IS THIS MY SUBCONSCIOUS DELIBERATELY TRYING TO SCREW ME OVER?
WHY IS THIS SO MUCH HARDER THAN BEFORE? MAYBE I NEED TO GENERATE TIGHTER SECURITY PROTOCOLS IN-GAME...
OR...
SETTING THE ALARM FOR...HOW LONG WILL THIS TAKE? SIX HOURS? SIX HOURS IT IS.
I'M GOING IN AS A PLAYER.
GO HANDS ON. A LITTLE QUALITY CONTROL. THE OWNER SHOWS HIS FACE, THE PEONS SNAP TO.
WHY DIDN'T I THINK OF THIS SOONER?

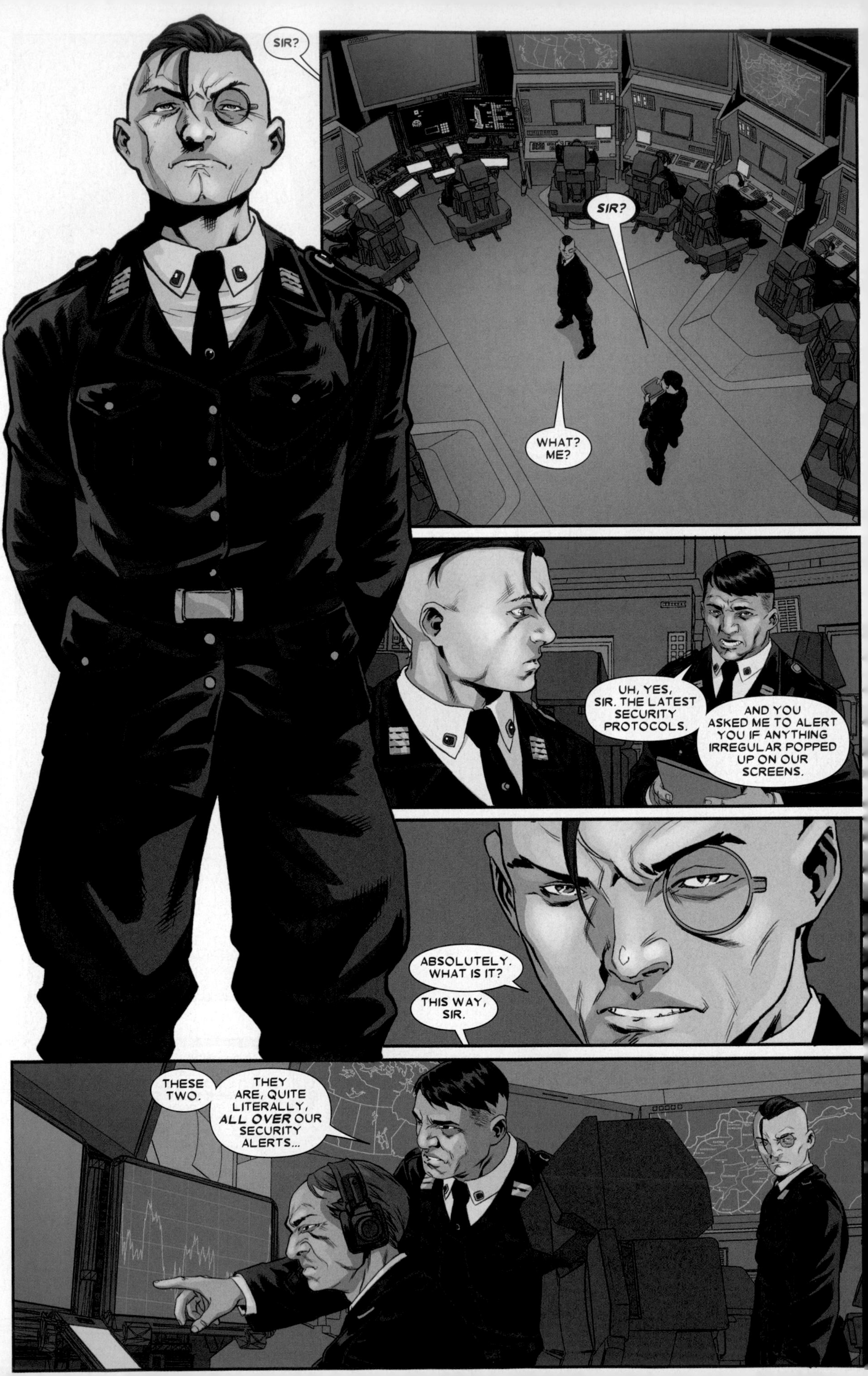
SIR?
SIR?
WHAT? ME?
UH, YES, SIR. THE LATEST SECURITY PROTOCOLS.
AND YOU ASKED ME TO ALERT YOU IF ANYTHING IRREGULAR POPPED UP ON OUR SCREENS.
ABSOLUTELY. WHAT IS IT?
THIS WAY, SIR.
THESE TWO.
THEY ARE, QUITE LITERALLY, ALL OVER OUR SECURITY ALERTS...

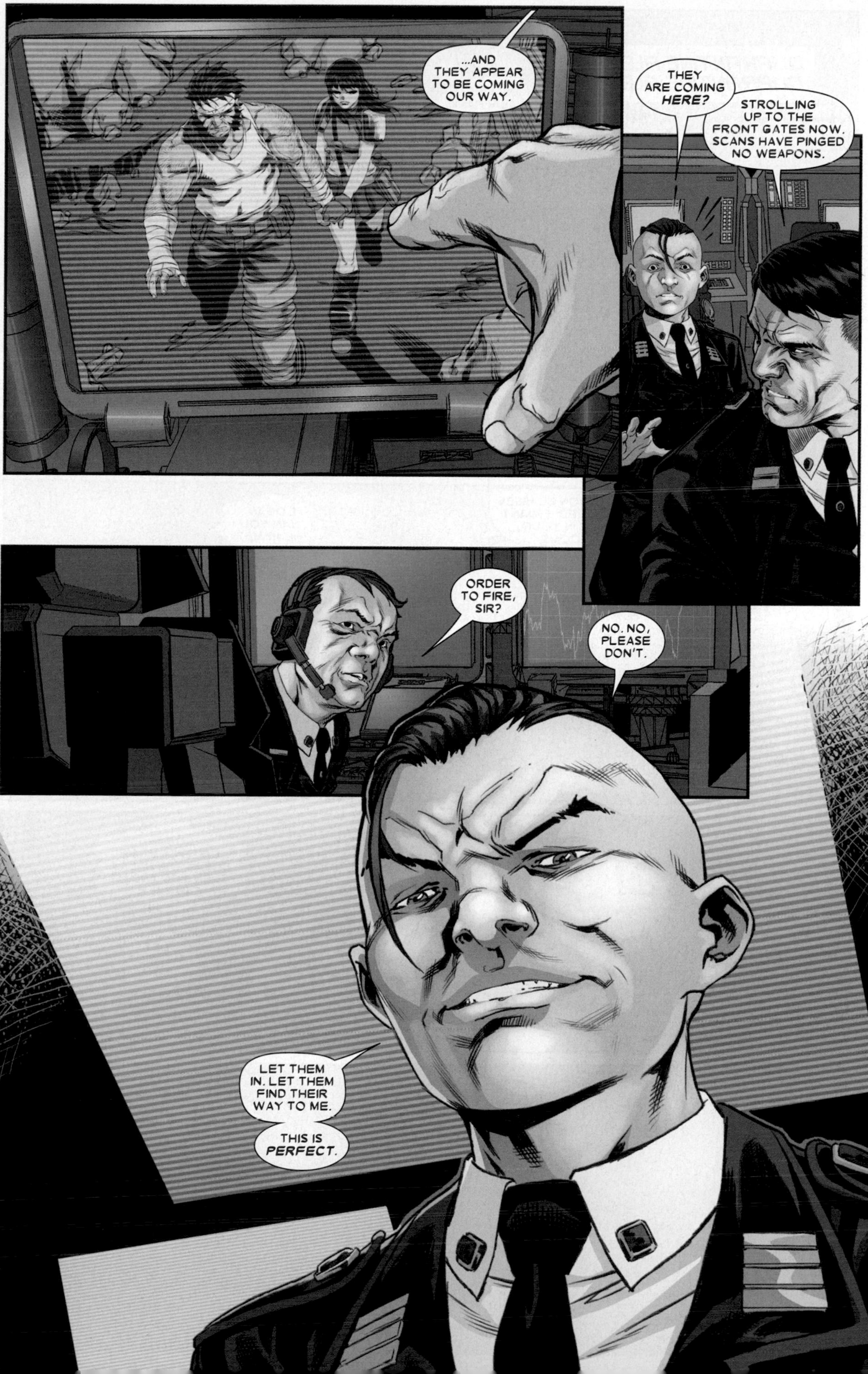
...AND THEY APPEAR TO BE COMING OUR WAY.
THEY ARE COMING *HERE?*
STROLLING UP TO THE FRONT GATES NOW. SCANS HAVE PINGED NO WEAPONS.
ORDER TO FIRE, SIR?
NO. NO, PLEASE DON'T.
LET THEM IN. LET THEM FIND THEIR WAY TO ME.
THIS IS *PERFECT*.

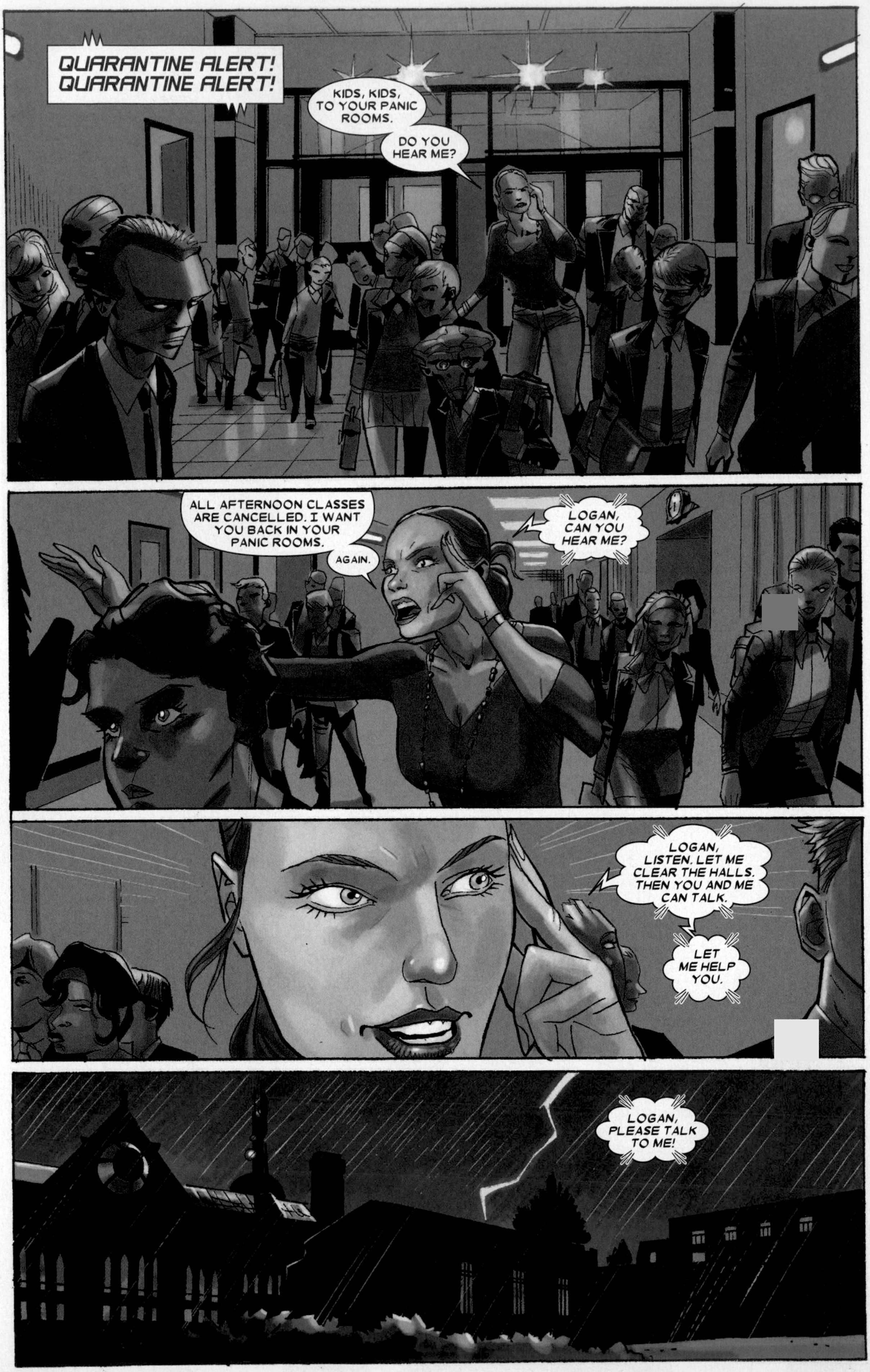
QUARANTINE ALERT! QUARANTINE ALERT!
KIDS, KIDS, TO YOUR PANIC ROOMS.
DO YOU HEAR ME?
ALL AFTERNOON CLASSES ARE CANCELLED. I WANT YOU BACK IN YOUR PANIC ROOMS.
AGAIN.
LOGAN, CAN YOU HEAR ME?
LOGAN, LISTEN. LET ME CLEAR THE HALLS. THEN YOU AND ME CAN TALK.
LET ME HELP YOU.
LOGAN, PLEASE TALK TO ME!

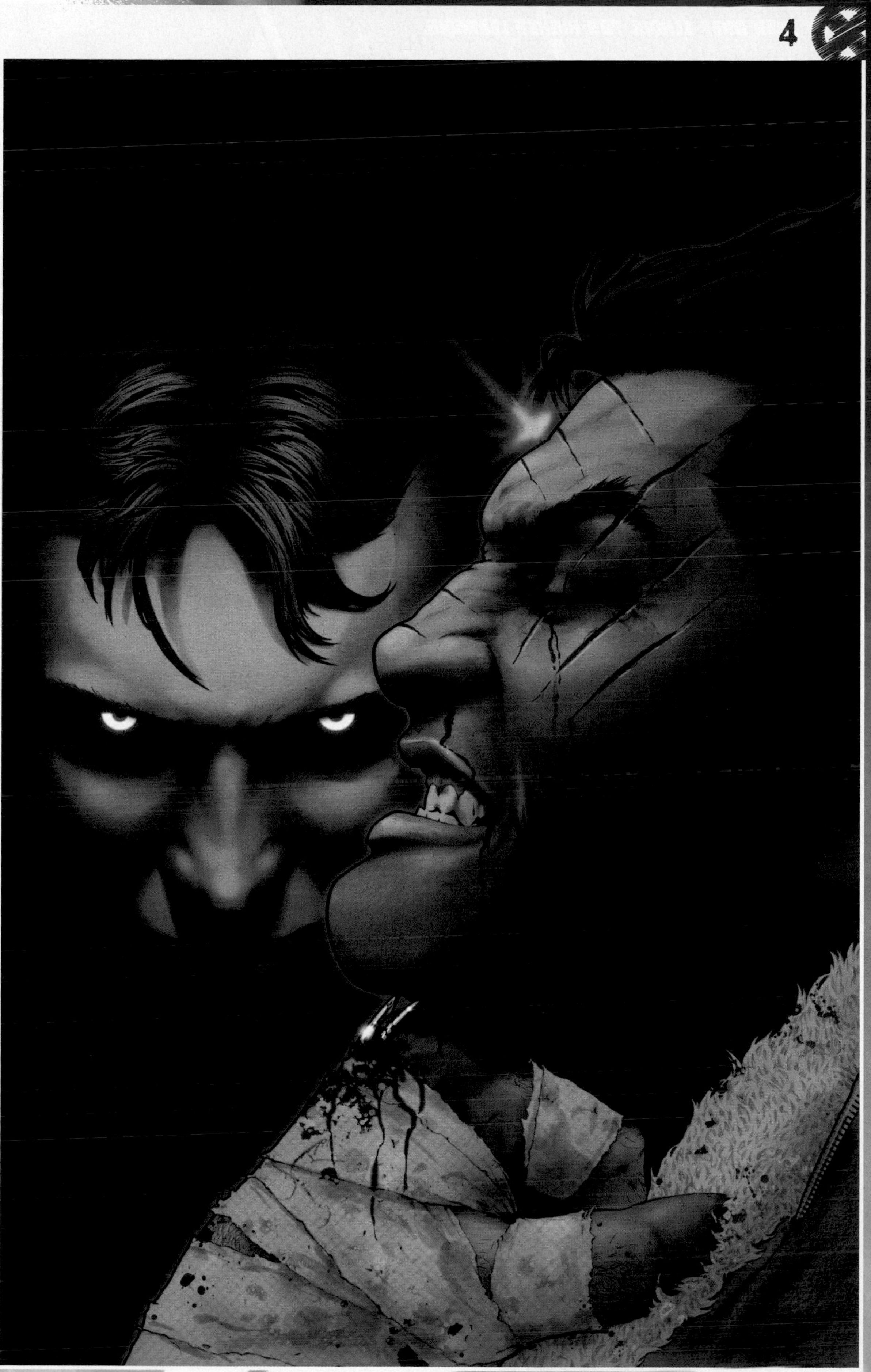
4

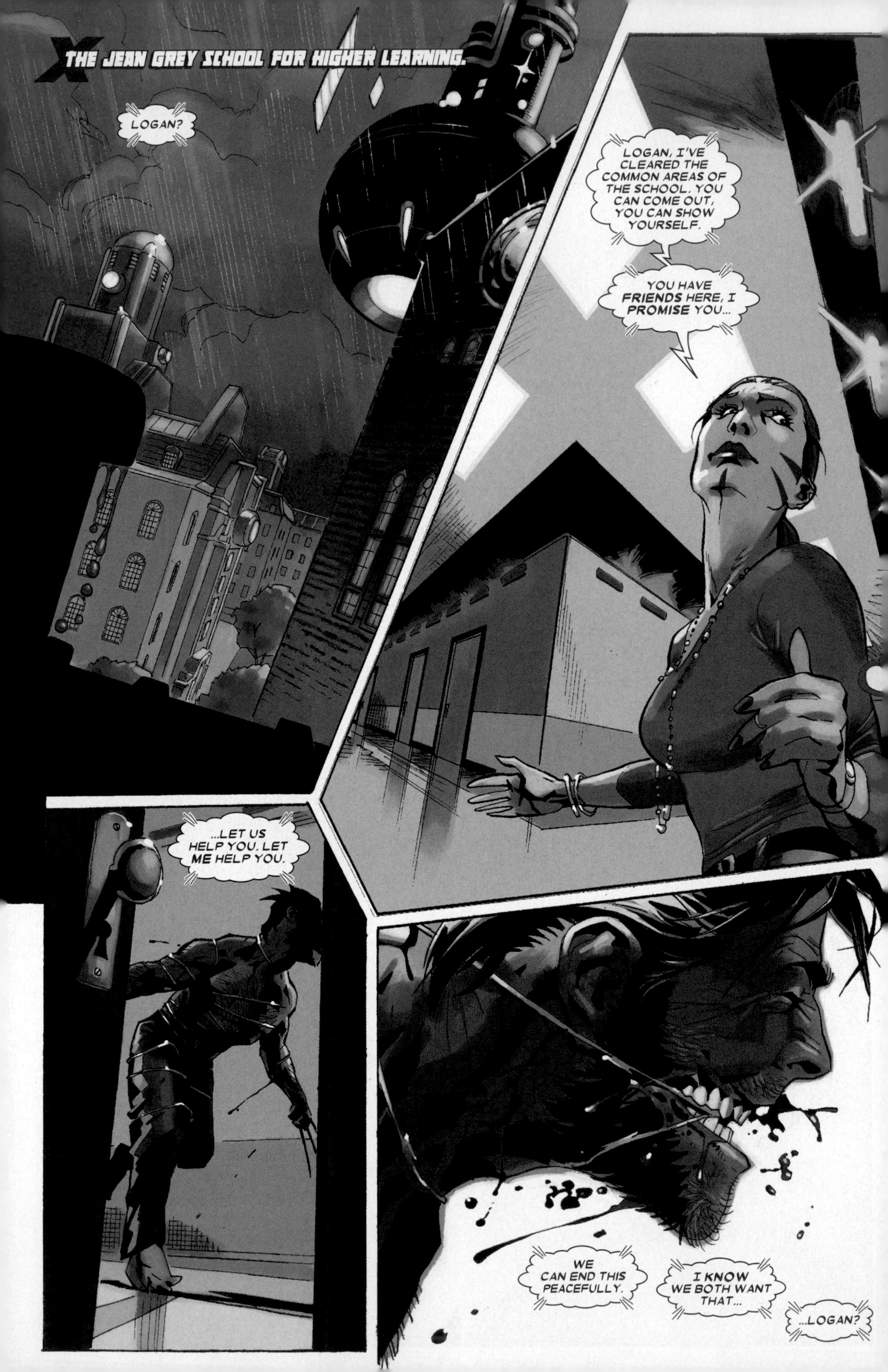
THE JEAN GREY SCHOOL FOR HIGHER LEARNING.
LOGAN?
LOGAN, I'VE CLEARED THE COMMON AREAS OF THE SCHOOL. YOU CAN COME OUT, YOU CAN SHOW YOURSELF.
YOU HAVE FRIENDS HERE, I PROMISE YOU...
...LET US HELP YOU. LET ME HELP YOU.
WE CAN END THIS PEACEFULLY.
I KNOW WE BOTH WANT THAT...
...LOGAN?

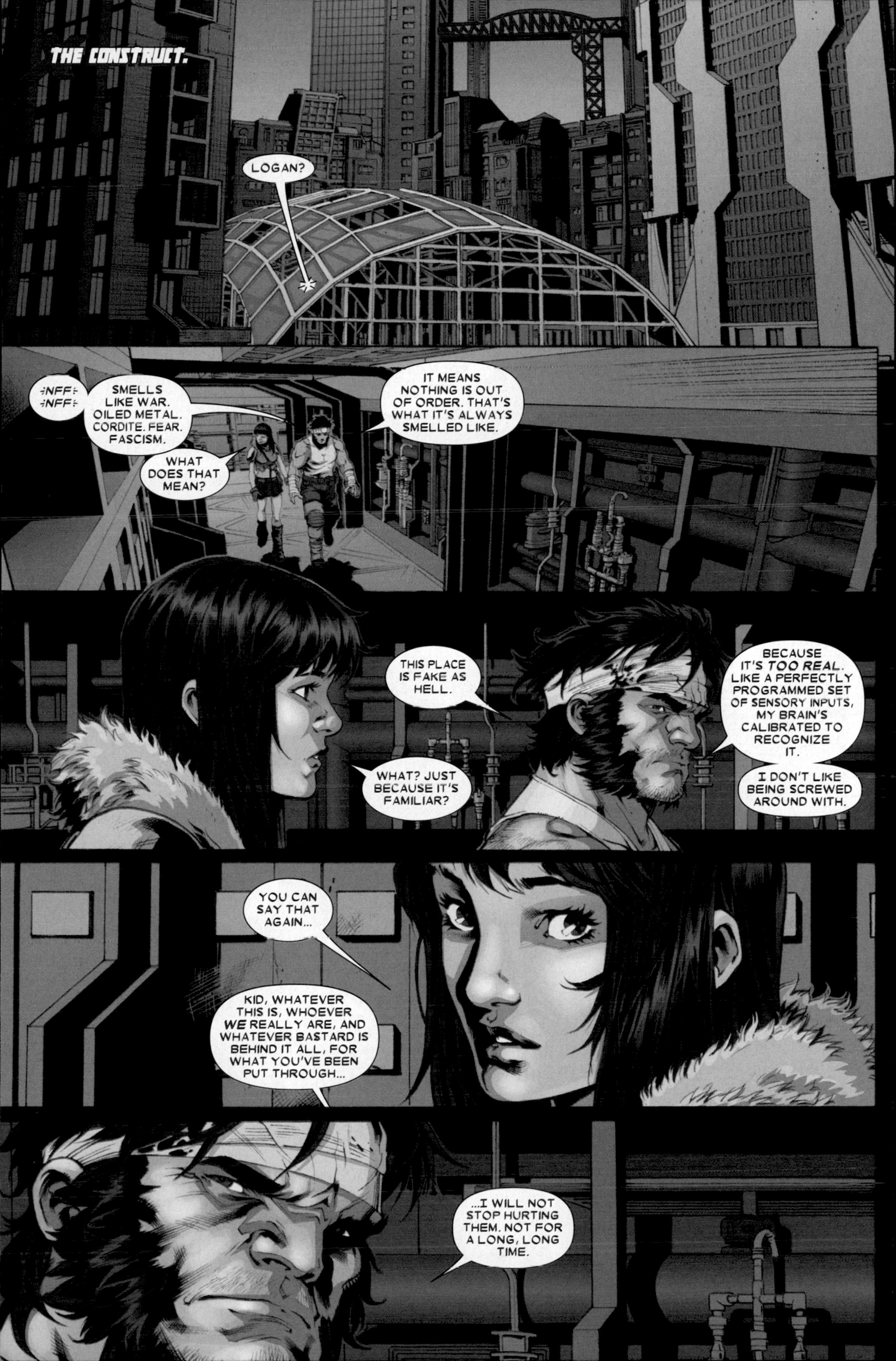
THE CONSTRUCT.
LOGAN?
≠NFF≠ ≠NFF≠
SMELLS LIKE WAR. OILED METAL. CORDITE. FEAR. FASCISM.
WHAT DOES THAT MEAN?
IT MEANS NOTHING IS OUT OF ORDER. THAT'S WHAT IT'S ALWAYS SMELLED LIKE.
THIS PLACE IS FAKE AS HELL.
WHAT? JUST BECAUSE IT'S FAMILIAR?
BECAUSE IT'S *TOO REAL*. LIKE A PERFECTLY PROGRAMMED SET OF SENSORY INPUTS, MY BRAIN'S CALIBRATED TO RECOGNIZE IT.
I DON'T LIKE BEING SCREWED AROUND WITH.
YOU CAN SAY THAT AGAIN...
KID, WHATEVER THIS IS, WHOEVER *WE* REALLY ARE, AND WHATEVER BASTARD IS BEHIND IT ALL, FOR WHAT YOU'VE BEEN PUT THROUGH...
...I WILL NOT STOP HURTING THEM. NOT FOR A LONG, LONG TIME.

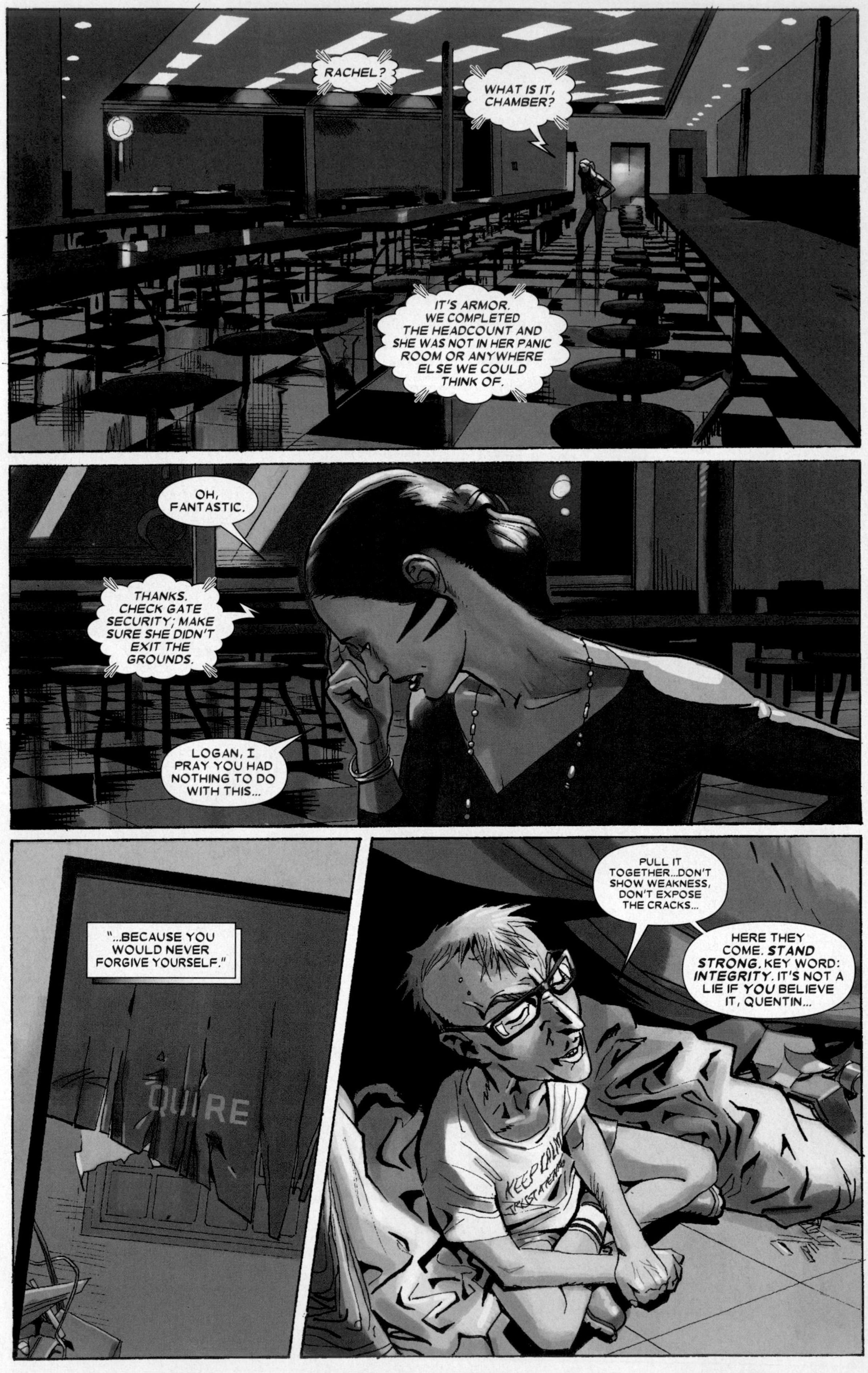
RACHEL?
WHAT IS IT, CHAMBER?
IT'S ARMOR. WE COMPLETED THE HEADCOUNT AND SHE WAS NOT IN HER PANIC ROOM OR ANYWHERE ELSE WE COULD THINK OF.
OH, FANTASTIC.
THANKS. CHECK GATE SECURITY; MAKE SURE SHE DIDN'T EXIT THE GROUNDS.
LOGAN, I PRAY YOU HAD NOTHING TO DO WITH THIS...
"...BECAUSE YOU WOULD NEVER FORGIVE YOURSELF."
QUIRE
PULL IT TOGETHER...DON'T SHOW WEAKNESS, DON'T EXPOSE THE CRACKS...
HERE THEY COME. STAND STRONG. KEY WORD: INTEGRITY. IT'S NOT A LIE IF YOU BELIEVE IT, QUENTIN...

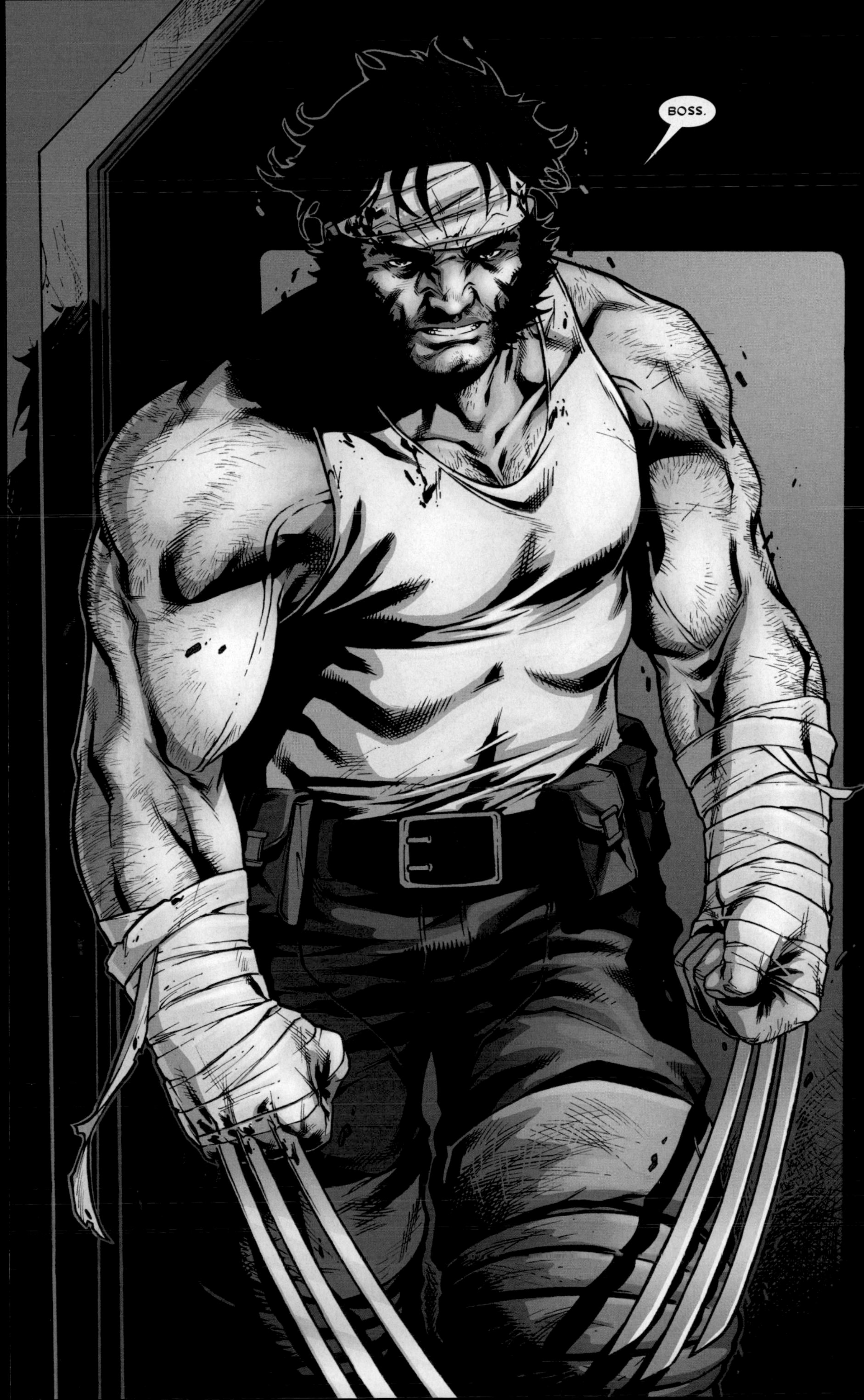
BOSS.

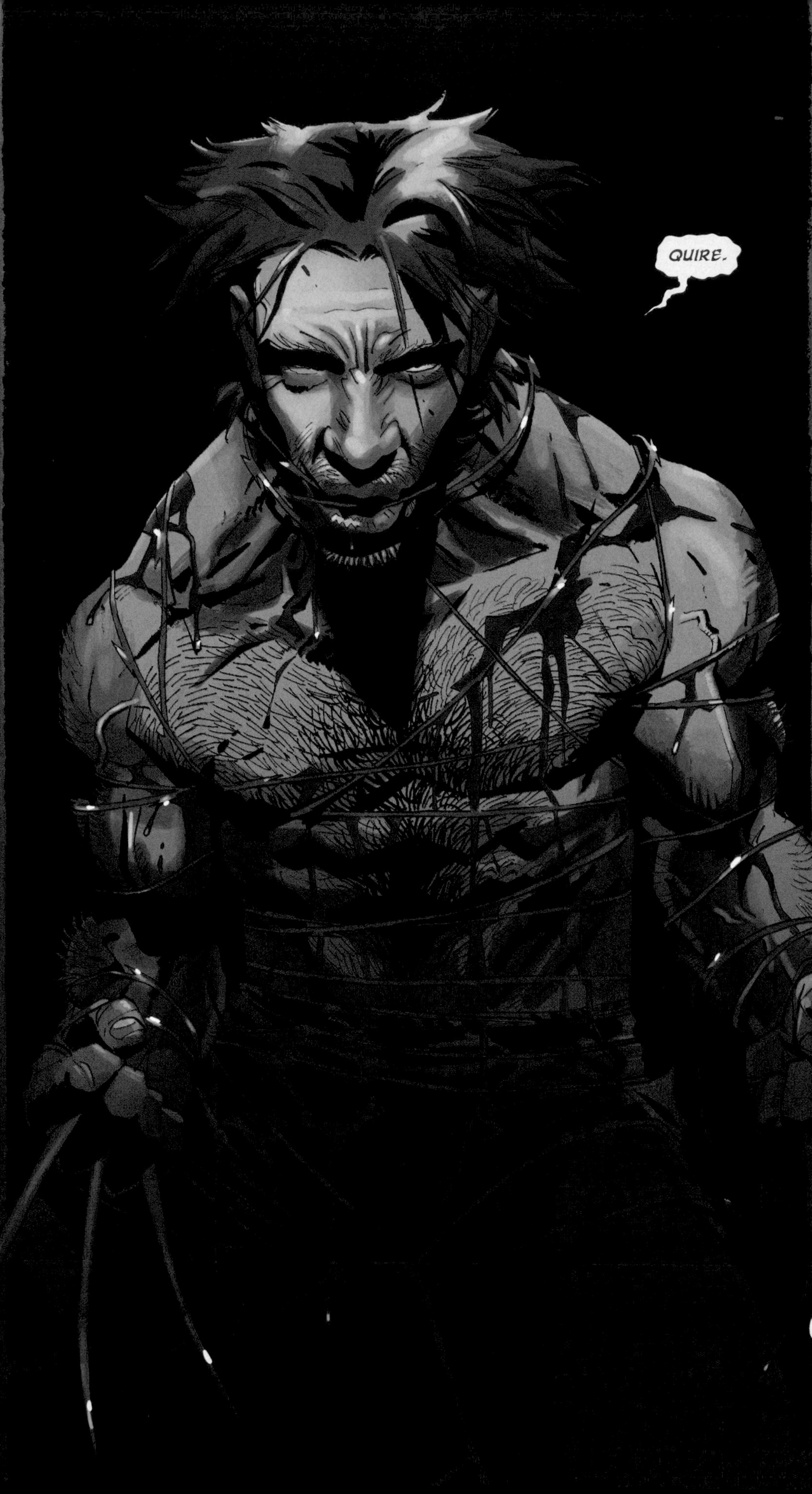
QUIRE.

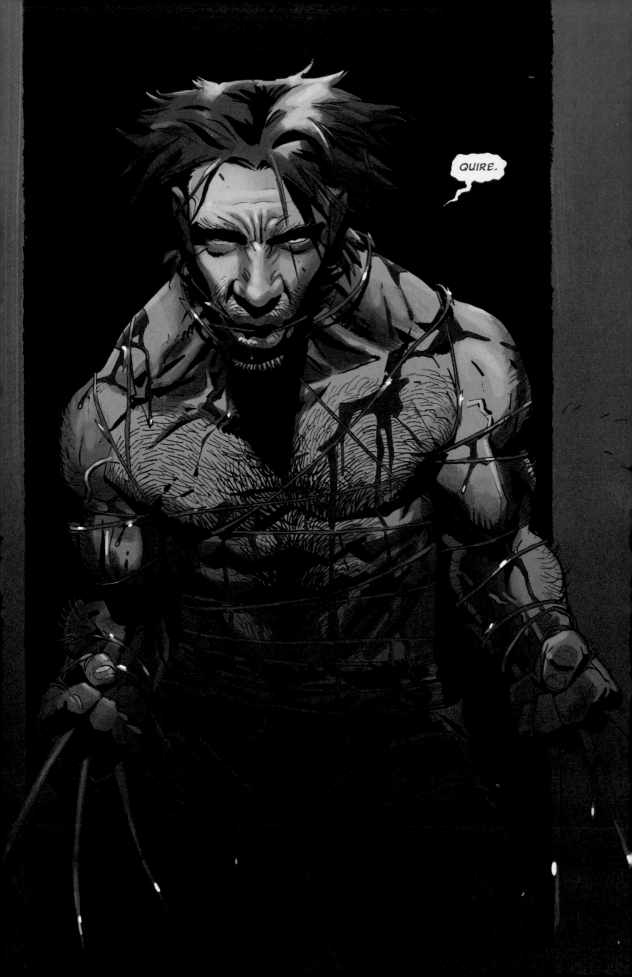

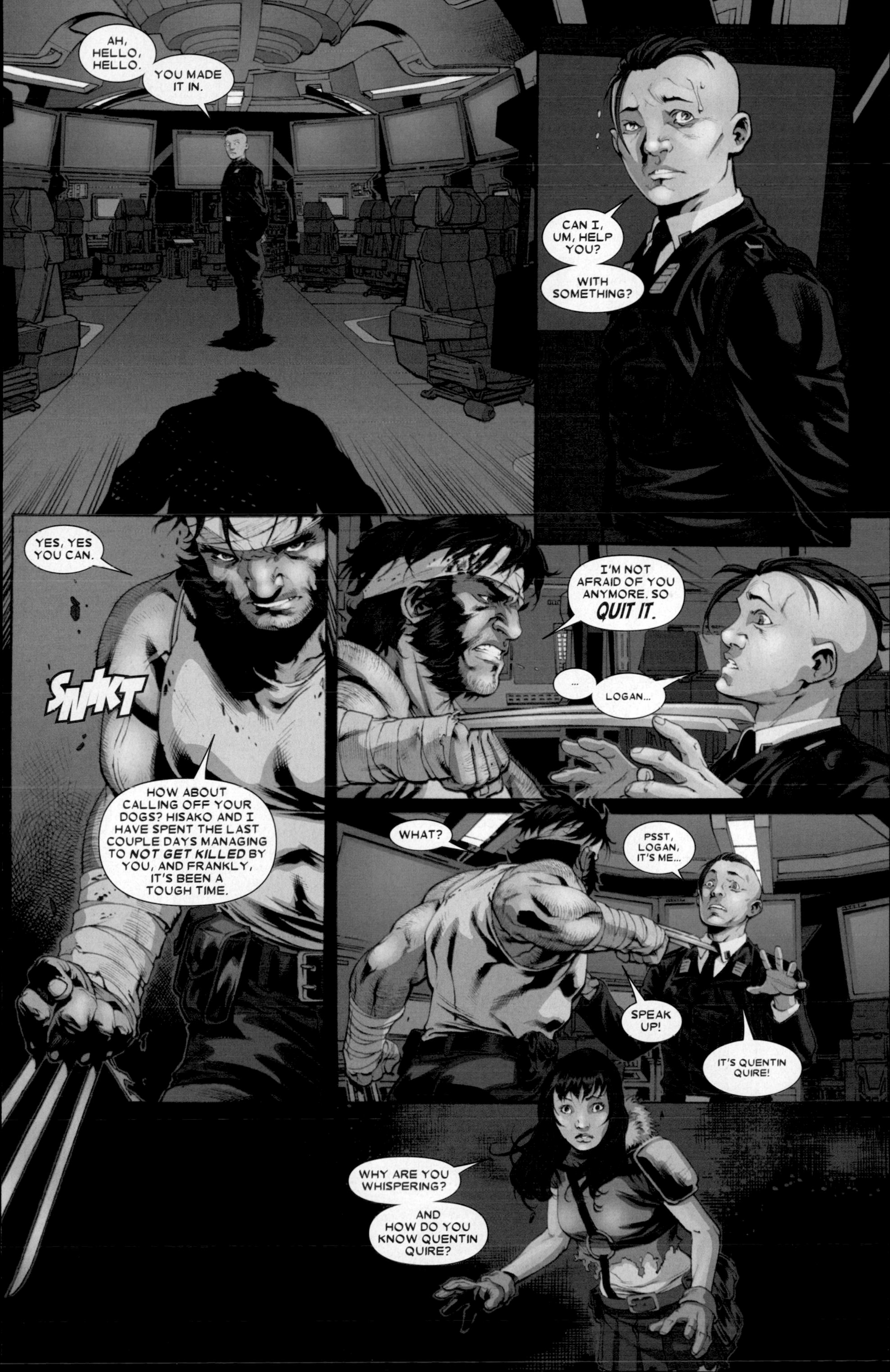
AH, HELLO, HELLO.
YOU MADE IT IN.
CAN I, UM, HELP YOU?
WITH SOMETHING?
YES, YES YOU CAN.
SNIKT
HOW ABOUT CALLING OFF YOUR DOGS? HISAKO AND I HAVE SPENT THE LAST COUPLE DAYS MANAGING TO NOT GET KILLED BY YOU, AND FRANKLY, IT'S BEEN A TOUGH TIME.
I'M NOT AFRAID OF YOU ANYMORE. SO QUIT IT.
...
LOGAN...
WHAT?
PSST, LOGAN, IT'S ME...
SPEAK UP!
IT'S QUENTIN QUIRE!
WHY ARE YOU WHISPERING?
AND HOW DO YOU KNOW QUENTIN QUIRE?

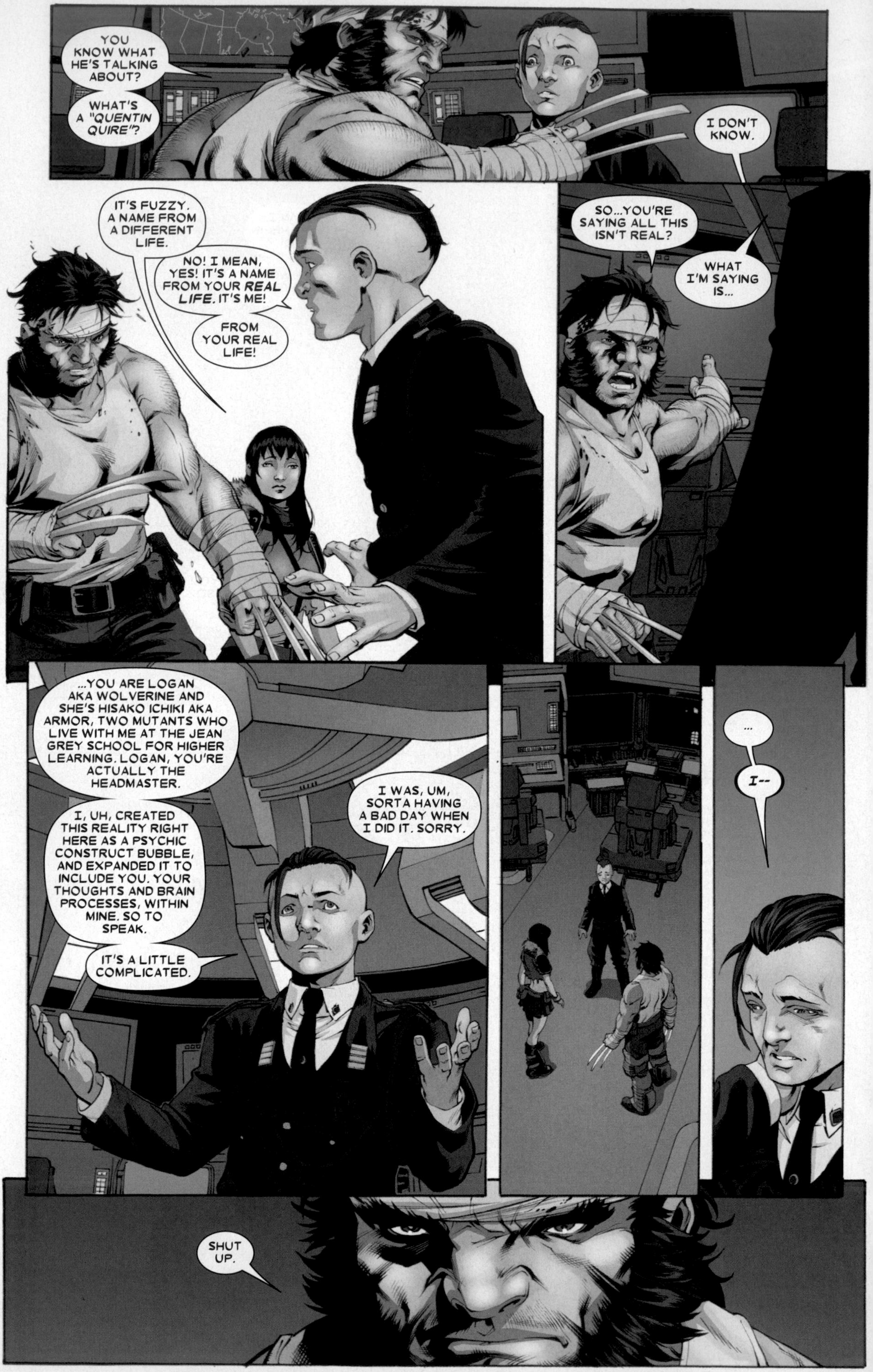
YOU KNOW WHAT HE'S TALKING ABOUT?
WHAT'S A "QUENTIN QUIRE"?
I DON'T KNOW.
IT'S FUZZY. A NAME FROM A DIFFERENT LIFE.
NO! I MEAN, YES! IT'S A NAME FROM YOUR REAL LIFE. IT'S ME!
FROM YOUR REAL LIFE!
SO...YOU'RE SAYING ALL THIS ISN'T REAL?
WHAT I'M SAYING IS...
...YOU ARE LOGAN AKA WOLVERINE AND SHE'S HISAKO ICHIKI AKA ARMOR, TWO MUTANTS WHO LIVE WITH ME AT THE JEAN GREY SCHOOL FOR HIGHER LEARNING. LOGAN, YOU'RE ACTUALLY THE HEADMASTER.
I, UH, CREATED THIS REALITY RIGHT HERE AS A PSYCHIC CONSTRUCT BUBBLE, AND EXPANDED IT TO INCLUDE YOU. YOUR THOUGHTS AND BRAIN PROCESSES, WITHIN MINE. SO TO SPEAK.
IT'S A LITTLE COMPLICATED.
I WAS, UM, SORTA HAVING A BAD DAY WHEN I DID IT. SORRY.
...
I--
SHUT UP.

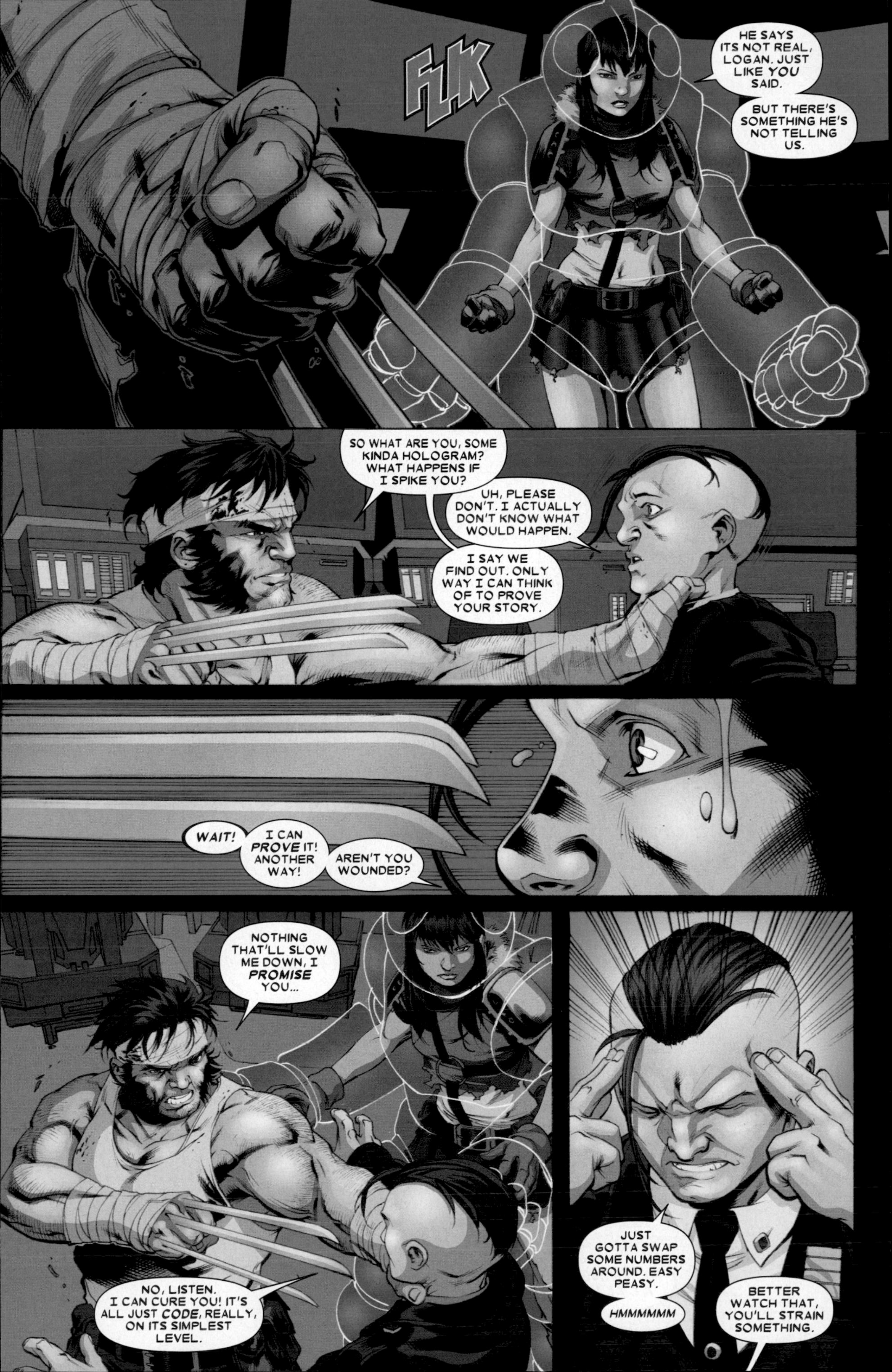
FLIK
HE SAYS ITS NOT REAL, LOGAN. JUST LIKE YOU SAID.
BUT THERE'S SOMETHING HE'S NOT TELLING US.
SO WHAT ARE YOU, SOME KINDA HOLOGRAM? WHAT HAPPENS IF I SPIKE YOU?
UH, PLEASE DON'T. I ACTUALLY DON'T KNOW WHAT WOULD HAPPEN.
I SAY WE FIND OUT. ONLY WAY I CAN THINK OF TO PROVE YOUR STORY.
WAIT!
I CAN PROVE IT! ANOTHER WAY!
AREN'T YOU WOUNDED?
NOTHING THAT'LL SLOW ME DOWN, I PROMISE YOU...
NO, LISTEN. I CAN CURE YOU! IT'S ALL JUST CODE, REALLY, ON ITS SIMPLEST LEVEL.
JUST GOTTA SWAP SOME NUMBERS AROUND. EASY PEASY.
HMMMMMM
BETTER WATCH THAT, YOU'LL STRAIN SOMETHING.

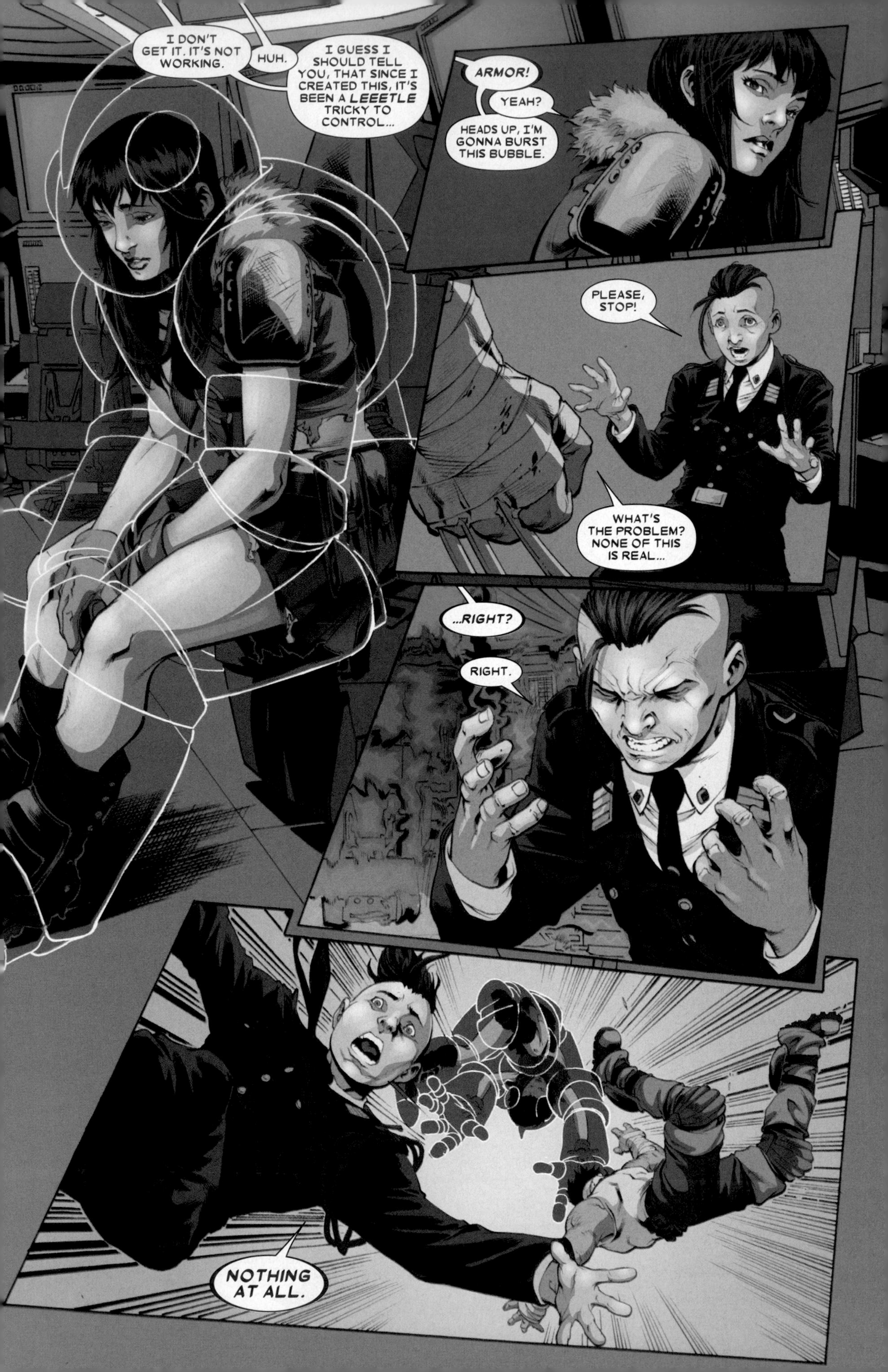

I DON'T GET IT. IT'S NOT WORKING.
HUH.
I GUESS I SHOULD TELL YOU, THAT SINCE I CREATED THIS, IT'S BEEN A *LEEETLE* TRICKY TO CONTROL...
ARMOR!
YEAH?
HEADS UP, I'M GONNA BURST THIS BUBBLE.
PLEASE, STOP!
WHAT'S THE PROBLEM? NONE OF THIS IS REAL...
...RIGHT?
RIGHT.
NOTHING AT ALL.

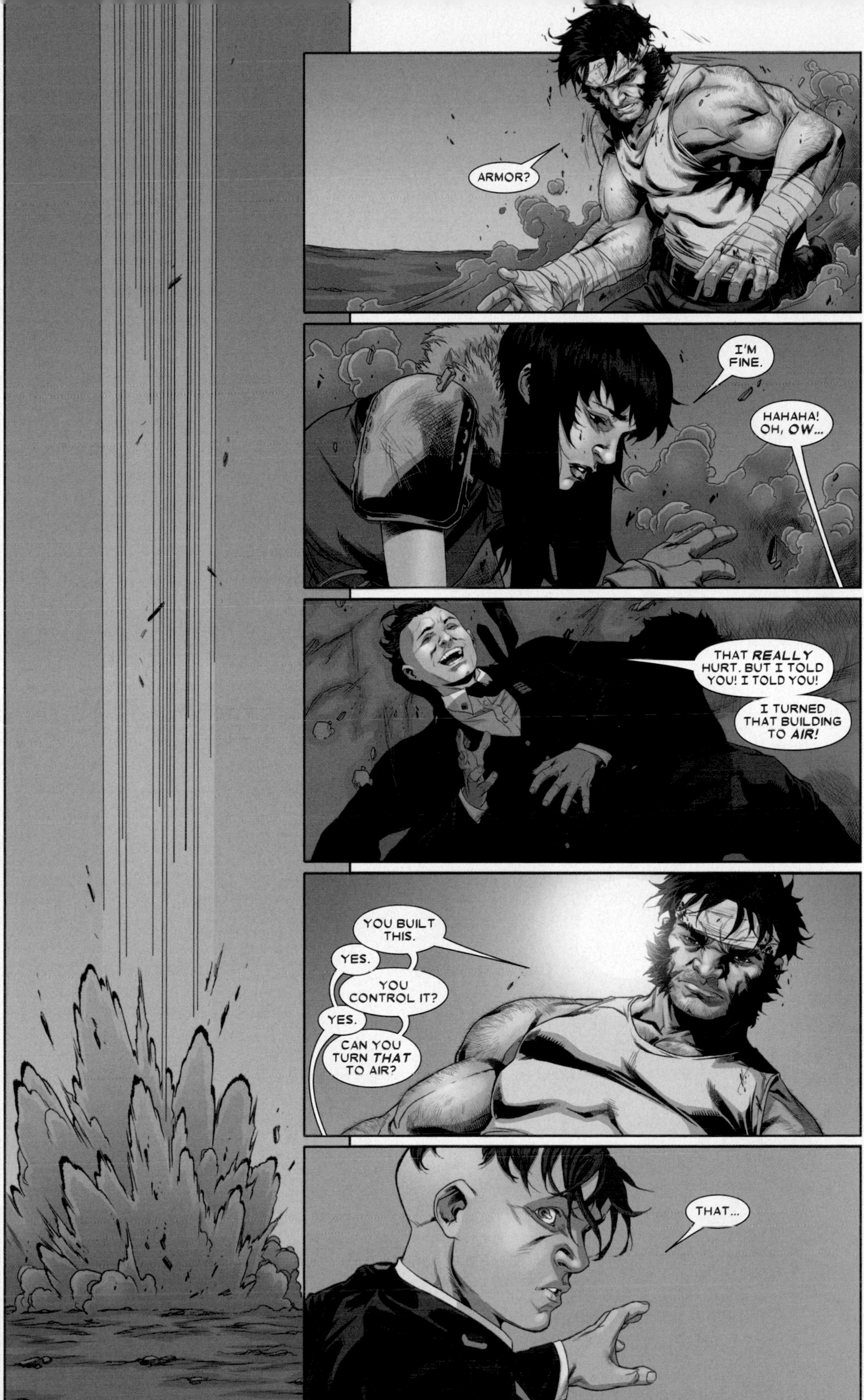
ARMOR?
I'M FINE.
HAHAHA! OH, *OW*...
THAT *REALLY* HURT. BUT I TOLD YOU! I TOLD YOU!
I TURNED THAT BUILDING TO *AIR!*
YOU BUILT THIS.
YES.
YOU CONTROL IT?
YES.
CAN YOU TURN *THAT* TO AIR?
THAT...

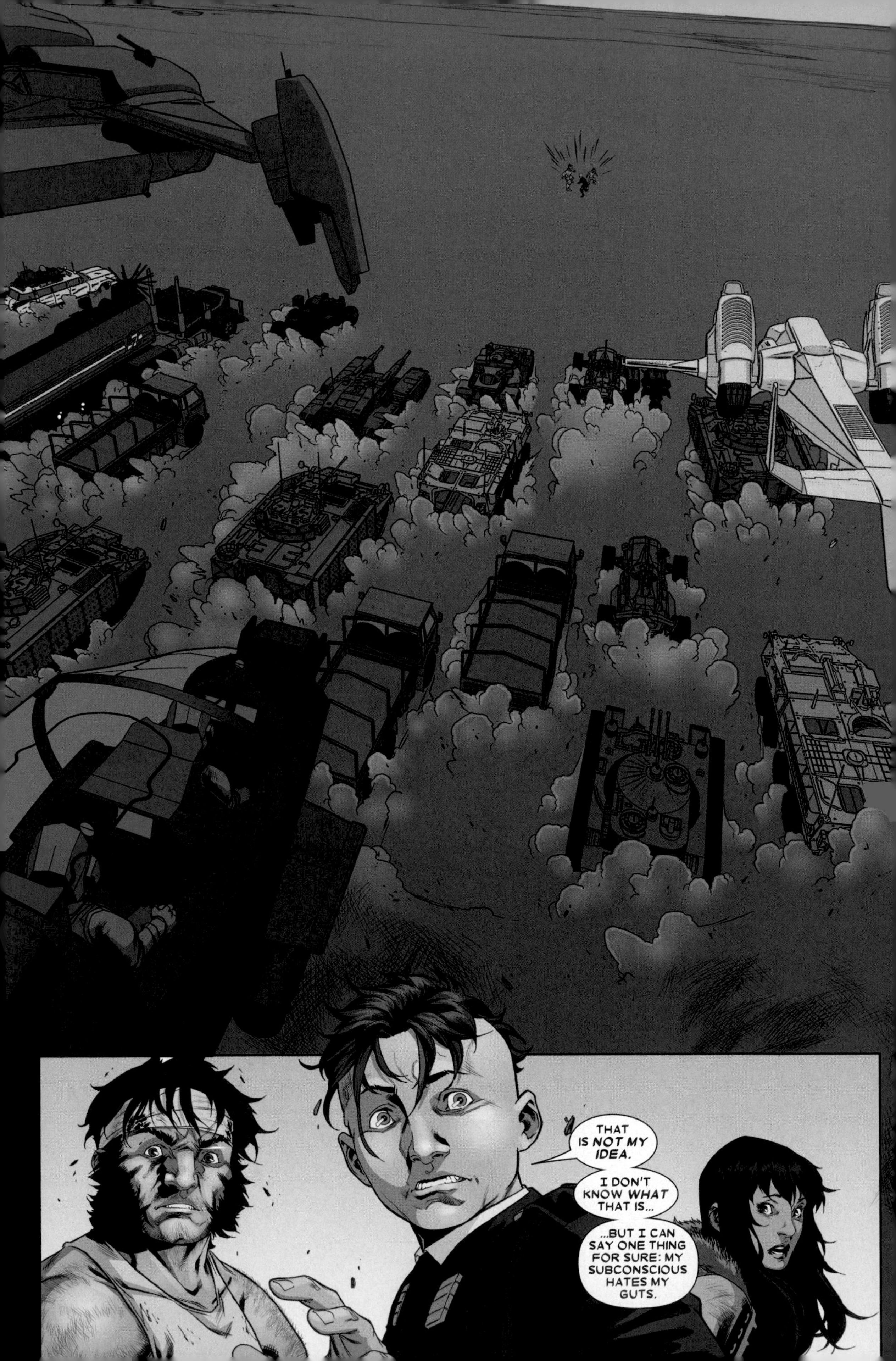
THAT IS NOT MY IDEA.
I DON'T KNOW WHAT THAT IS...
...BUT I CAN SAY ONE THING FOR SURE: MY SUBCONSCIOUS HATES MY GUTS.

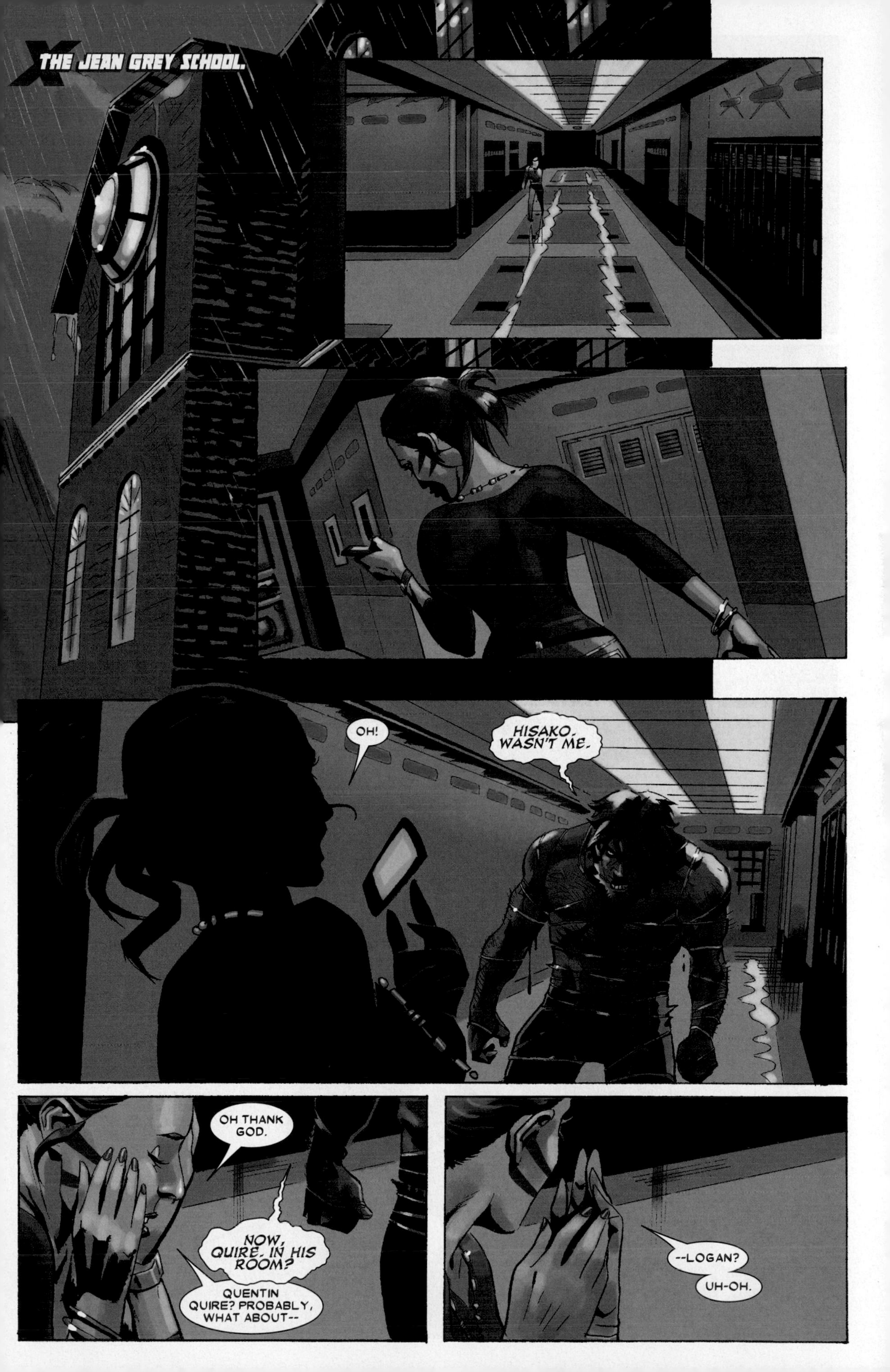
THE JEAN GREY SCHOOL.
OH!
HISAKO. WASN'T ME.
OH THANK GOD.
NOW, QUIRE. IN HIS ROOM?
QUENTIN QUIRE? PROBABLY, WHAT ABOUT--
--LOGAN?
UH-OH.

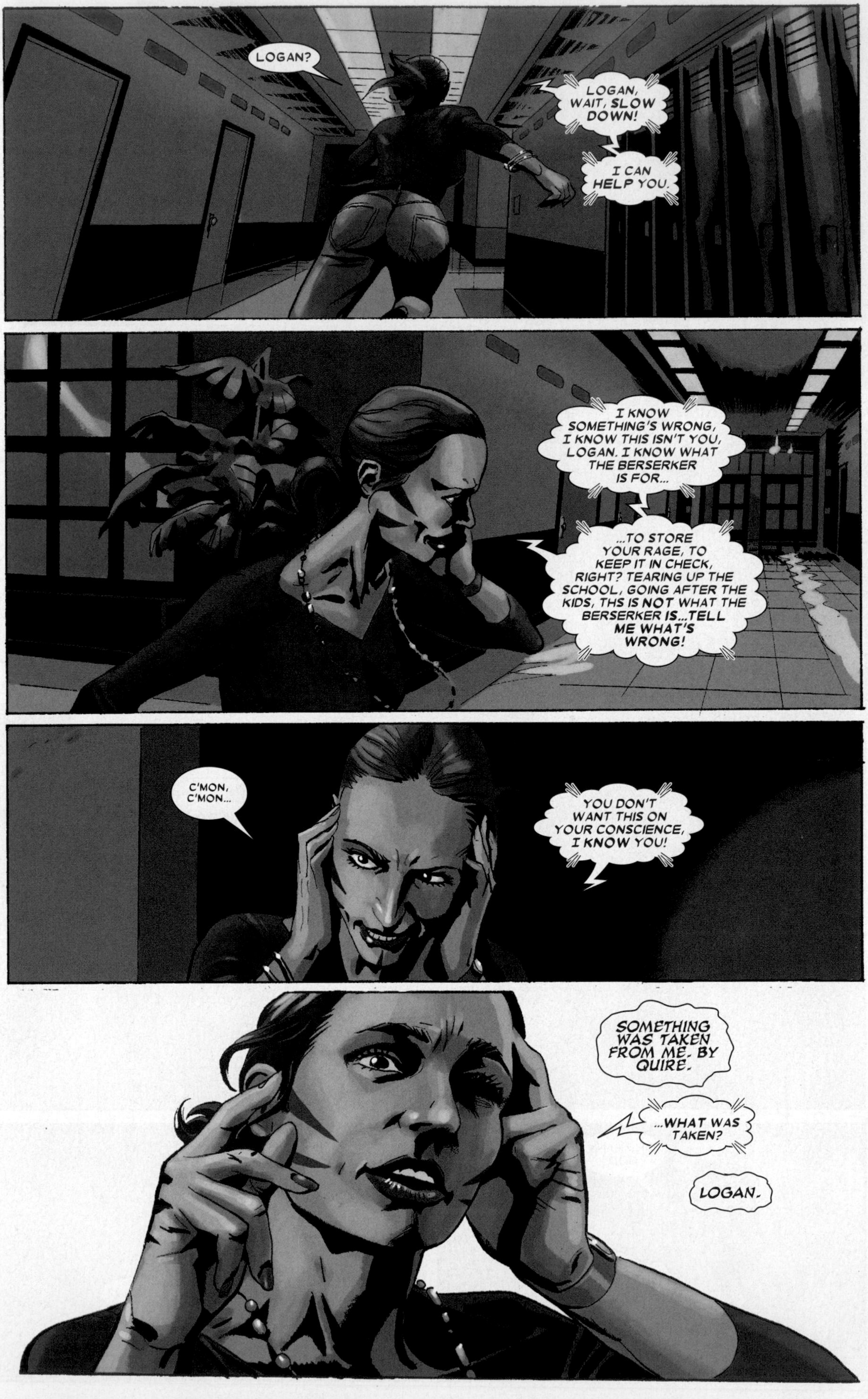
LOGAN?
LOGAN, WAIT, SLOW DOWN!
I CAN HELP YOU.
I KNOW SOMETHING'S WRONG, I KNOW THIS ISN'T YOU, LOGAN. I KNOW WHAT THE BERSERKER IS FOR...
...TO STORE YOUR RAGE, TO KEEP IT IN CHECK, RIGHT? TEARING UP THE SCHOOL, GOING AFTER THE KIDS, THS IS NOT WHAT THE BERSERKER IS...TELL ME WHAT'S WRONG!
C'MON, C'MON...
YOU DON'T WANT THIS ON YOUR CONSCIENCE, I KNOW YOU!
SOMETHING WAS TAKEN FROM ME. BY QUIRE.
...WHAT WAS TAKEN?
LOGAN.

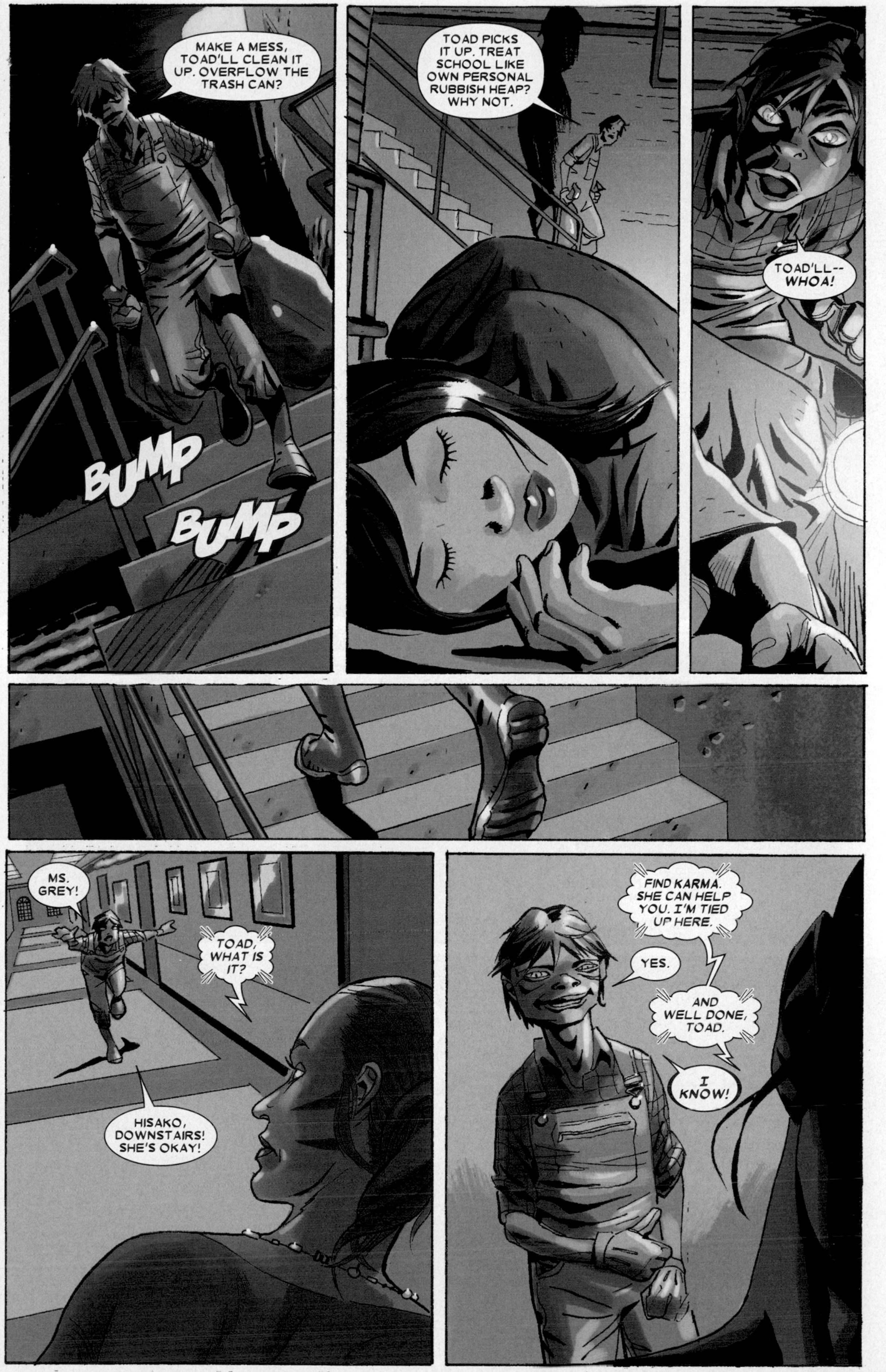
MAKE A MESS, TOAD'LL CLEAN IT UP. OVERFLOW THE TRASH CAN?
BUMP
BUMP
TOAD PICKS IT UP. TREAT SCHOOL LIKE OWN PERSONAL RUBBISH HEAP? WHY NOT.
TOAD'LL-- WHOA!
MS. GREY!
TOAD, WHAT IS IT?
HISAKO, DOWNSTAIRS! SHE'S OKAY!
FIND KARMA. SHE CAN HELP YOU. I'M TIED UP HERE.
YES.
AND WELL DONE, TOAD.
I KNOW!

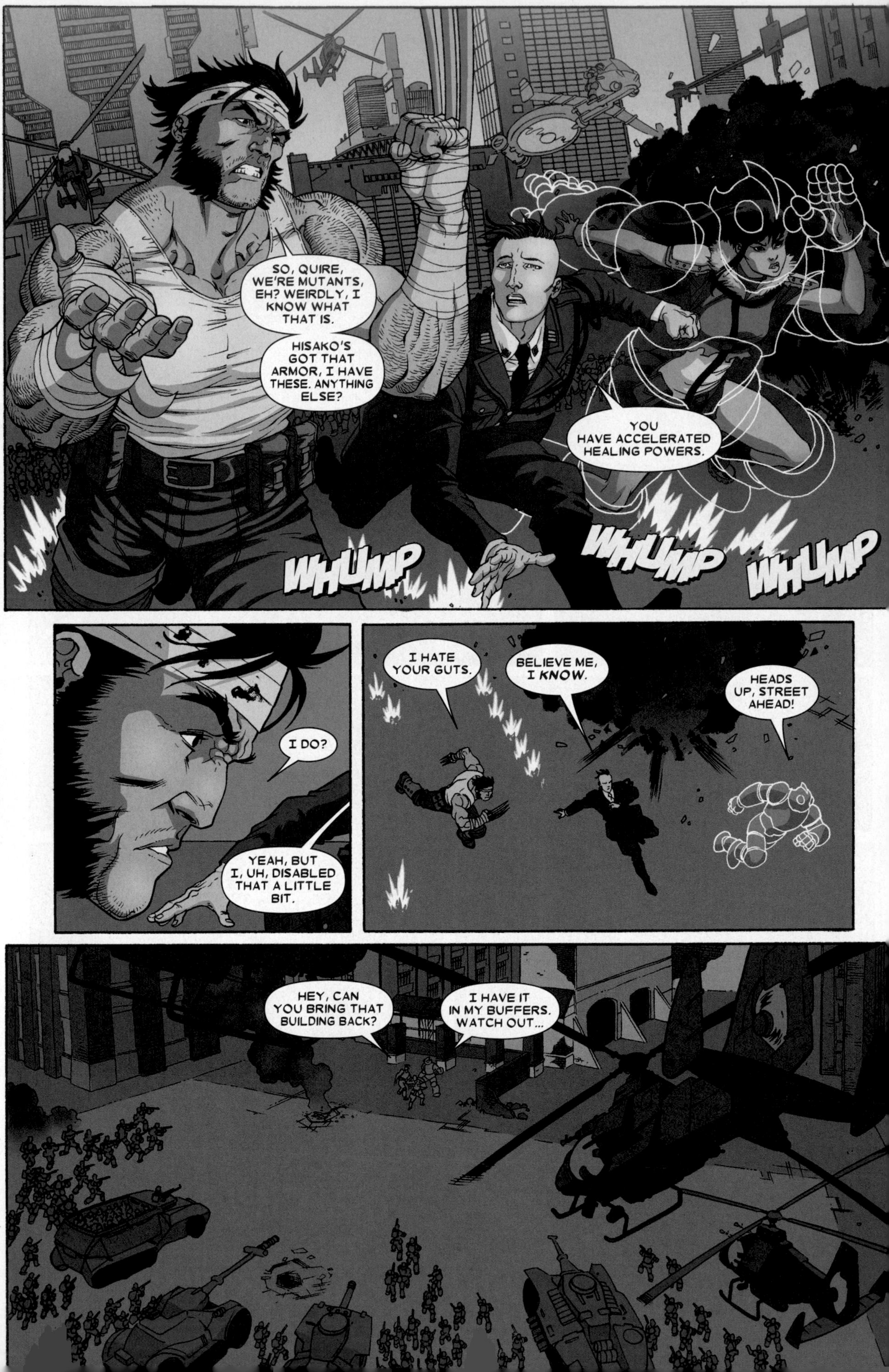
SO, QUIRE, WE'RE MUTANTS, EH? WEIRDLY, I KNOW WHAT THAT IS.
HISAKO'S GOT THAT ARMOR, I HAVE THESE. ANYTHING ELSE?
YOU HAVE ACCELERATED HEALING POWERS.
WHUMP
WHUMP
WHUMP
I DO?
YEAH, BUT I, UH, DISABLED THAT A LITTLE BIT.
I HATE YOUR GUTS.
BELIEVE ME, I *KNOW*.
HEADS UP, STREET AHEAD!
HEY, CAN YOU BRING THAT BUILDING BACK?
I HAVE IT IN MY BUFFERS. WATCH OUT...

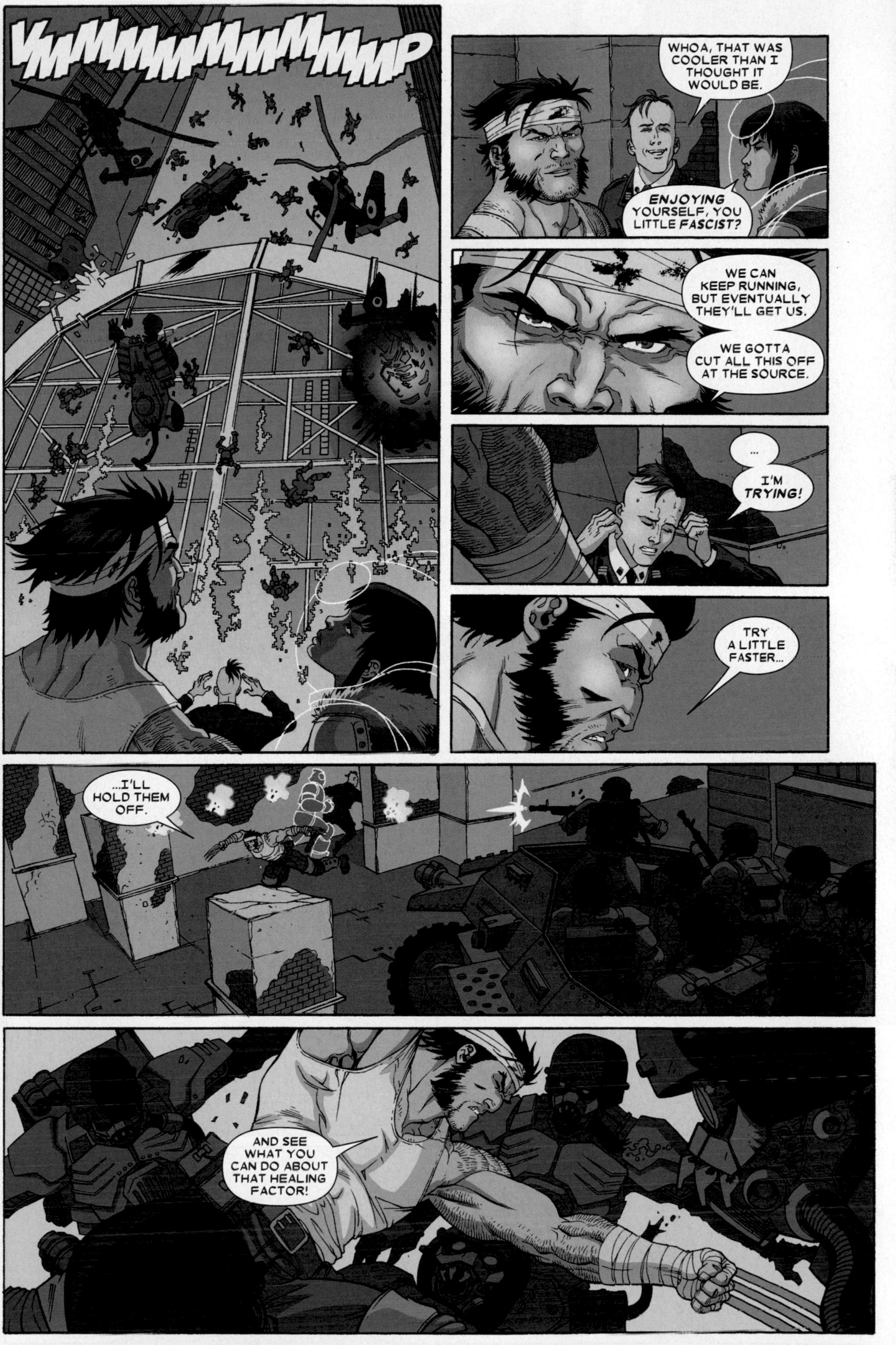
VMMMMMMMMMMMMP
WHOA, THAT WAS COOLER THAN I THOUGHT IT WOULD BE.
ENJOYING YOURSELF, YOU LITTLE FASCIST?
WE CAN KEEP RUNNING, BUT EVENTUALLY THEY'LL GET US.
WE GOTTA CUT ALL THIS OFF AT THE SOURCE.
...
I'M TRYING!
TRY A LITTLE FASTER...
...I'LL HOLD THEM OFF.
AND SEE WHAT YOU CAN DO ABOUT THAT HEALING FACTOR!

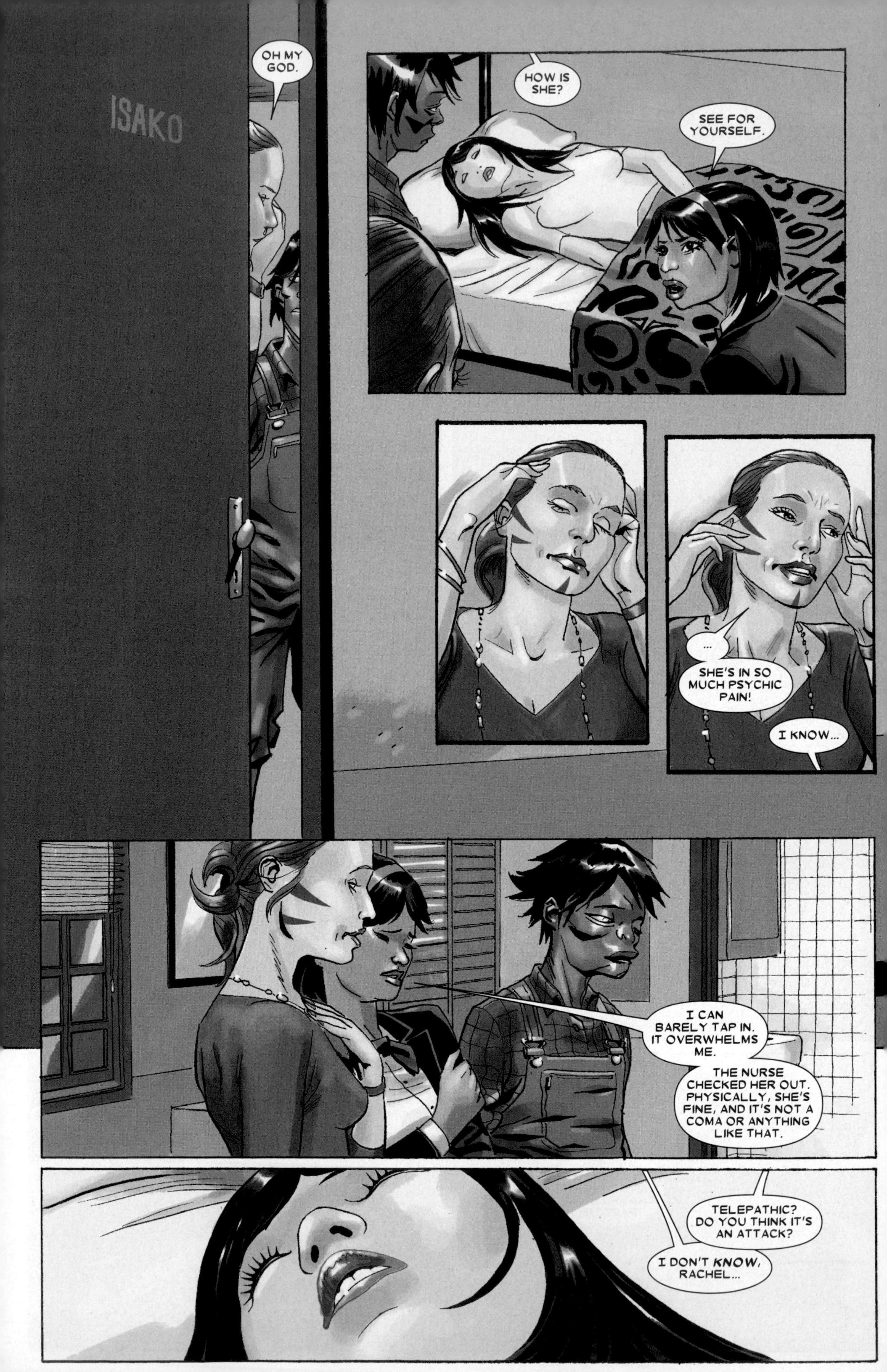
ISAKO
OH MY GOD.
HOW IS SHE?
SEE FOR YOURSELF.
...
SHE'S IN SO MUCH PSYCHIC PAIN!
I KNOW...
I CAN BARELY TAP IN. IT OVERWHELMS ME.
THE NURSE CHECKED HER OUT. PHYSICALLY, SHE'S FINE, AND IT'S NOT A COMA OR ANYTHING LIKE THAT.
TELEPATHIC? DO YOU THINK IT'S AN ATTACK?
I DON'T *KNOW*, RACHEL...

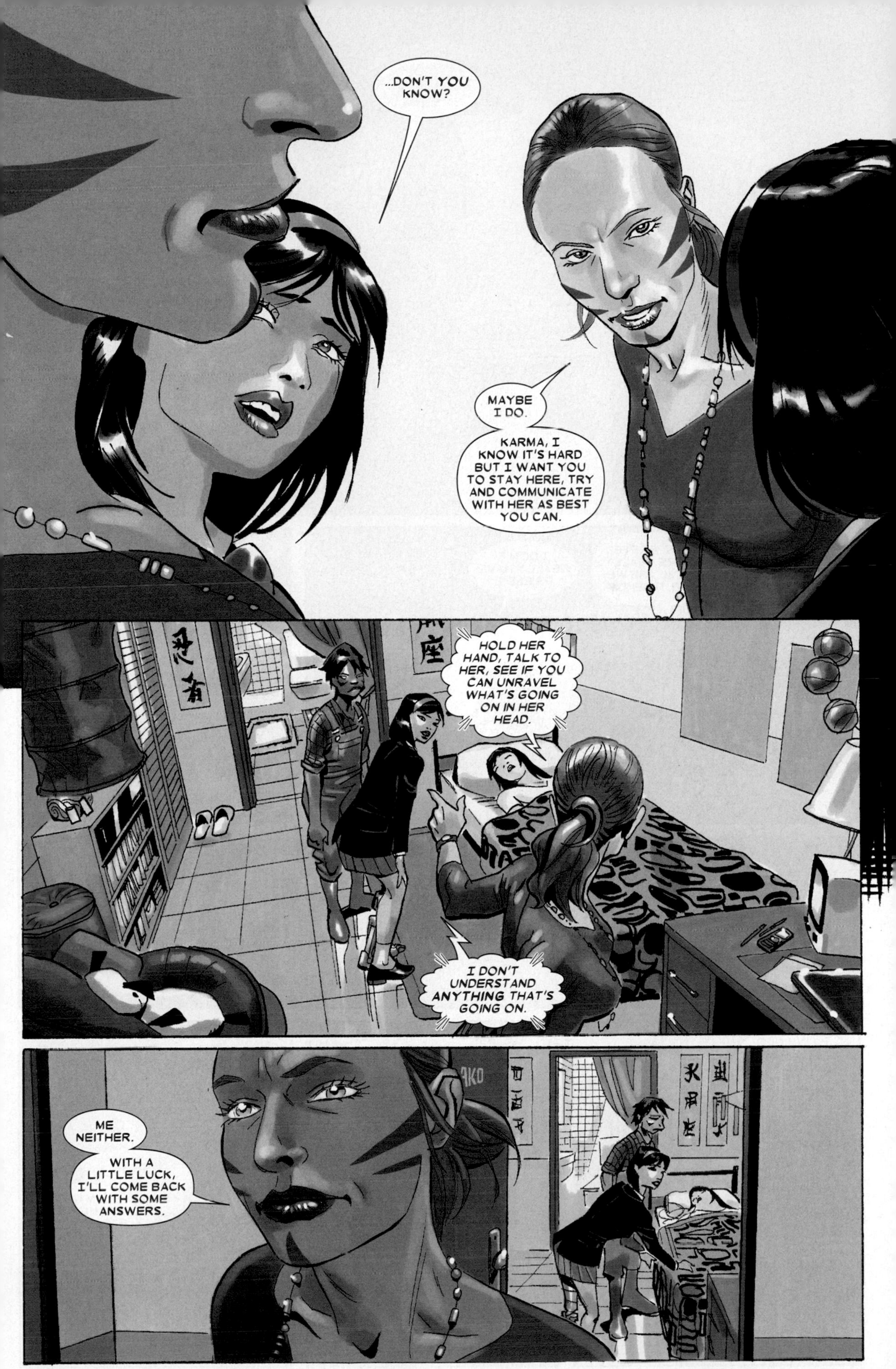

...DON'T YOU KNOW?
MAYBE I DO.
KARMA, I KNOW IT'S HARD BUT I WANT YOU TO STAY HERE, TRY AND COMMUNICATE WITH HER AS BEST YOU CAN.
HOLD HER HAND, TALK TO HER, SEE IF YOU CAN UNRAVEL WHAT'S GOING ON IN HER HEAD.
I DON'T UNDERSTAND ANYTHING THAT'S GOING ON.
ME NEITHER.
WITH A LITTLE LUCK, I'LL COME BACK WITH SOME ANSWERS.

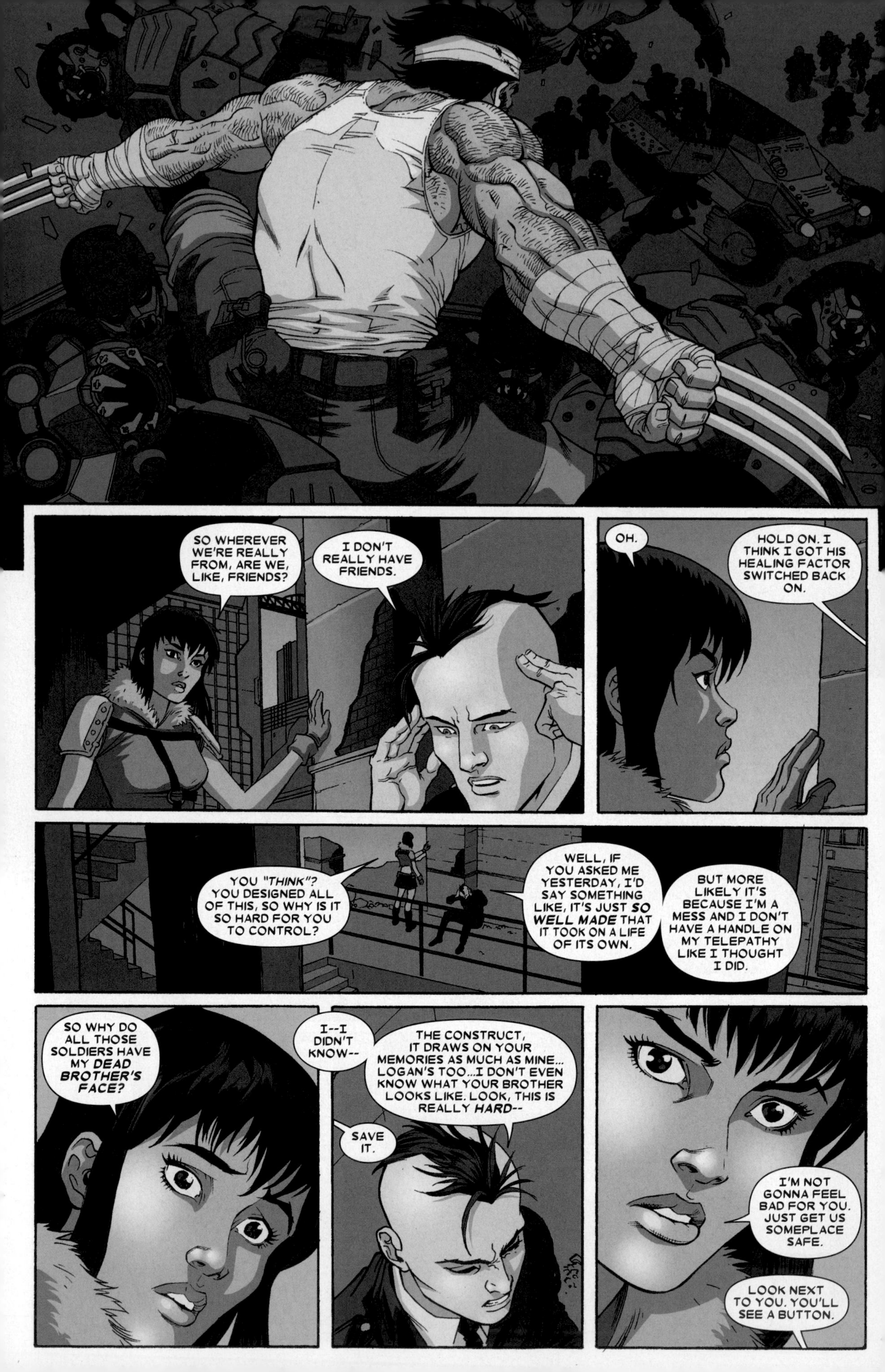
SO WHEREVER WE'RE REALLY FROM, ARE WE, LIKE, FRIENDS?
I DON'T REALLY HAVE FRIENDS.
OH.
HOLD ON. I THINK I GOT HIS HEALING FACTOR SWITCHED BACK ON.
YOU "THINK"? YOU DESIGNED ALL OF THIS, SO WHY IS IT SO HARD FOR YOU TO CONTROL?
WELL, IF YOU ASKED ME YESTERDAY, I'D SAY SOMETHING LIKE, IT'S JUST SO WELL MADE THAT IT TOOK ON A LIFE OF ITS OWN.
BUT MORE LIKELY IT'S BECAUSE I'M A MESS AND I DON'T HAVE A HANDLE ON MY TELEPATHY LIKE I THOUGHT I DID.
SO WHY DO ALL THOSE SOLDIERS HAVE MY DEAD BROTHER'S FACE?
I--I DIDN'T KNOW--
THE CONSTRUCT, IT DRAWS ON YOUR MEMORIES AS MUCH AS MINE... LOGAN'S TOO...I DON'T EVEN KNOW WHAT YOUR BROTHER LOOKS LIKE. LOOK, THIS IS REALLY HARD--
SAVE IT.
I'M NOT GONNA FEEL BAD FOR YOU. JUST GET US SOMEPLACE SAFE.
LOOK NEXT TO YOU. YOU'LL SEE A BUTTON.

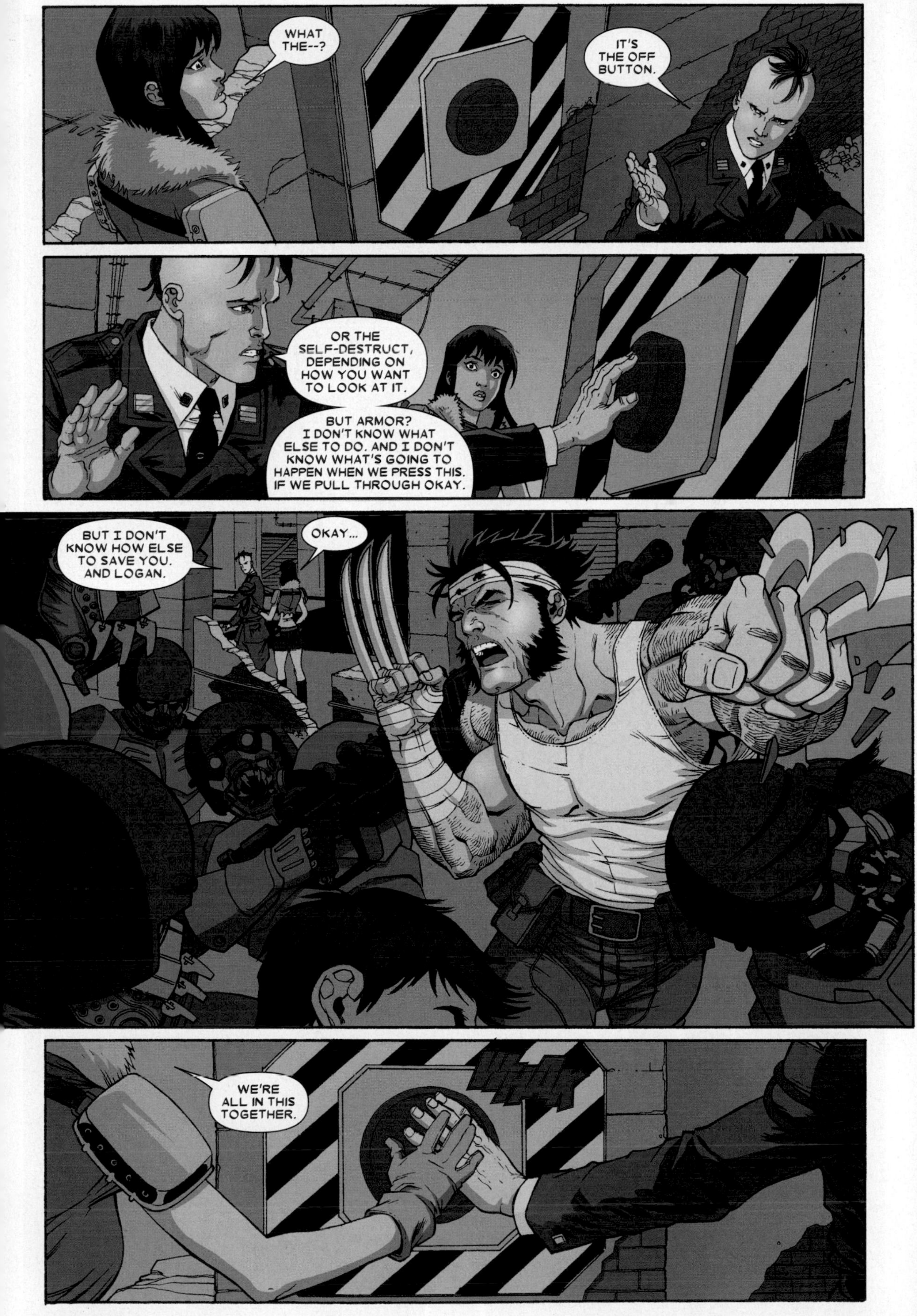
WHAT THE--?
IT'S THE OFF BUTTON.
OR THE SELF-DESTRUCT, DEPENDING ON HOW YOU WANT TO LOOK AT IT.
BUT ARMOR? I DON'T KNOW WHAT ELSE TO DO. AND I DON'T KNOW WHAT'S GOING TO HAPPEN WHEN WE PRESS THIS. IF WE PULL THROUGH OKAY.
BUT I DON'T KNOW HOW ELSE TO SAVE YOU. AND LOGAN.
OKAY...
WE'RE ALL IN THIS TOGETHER.

5

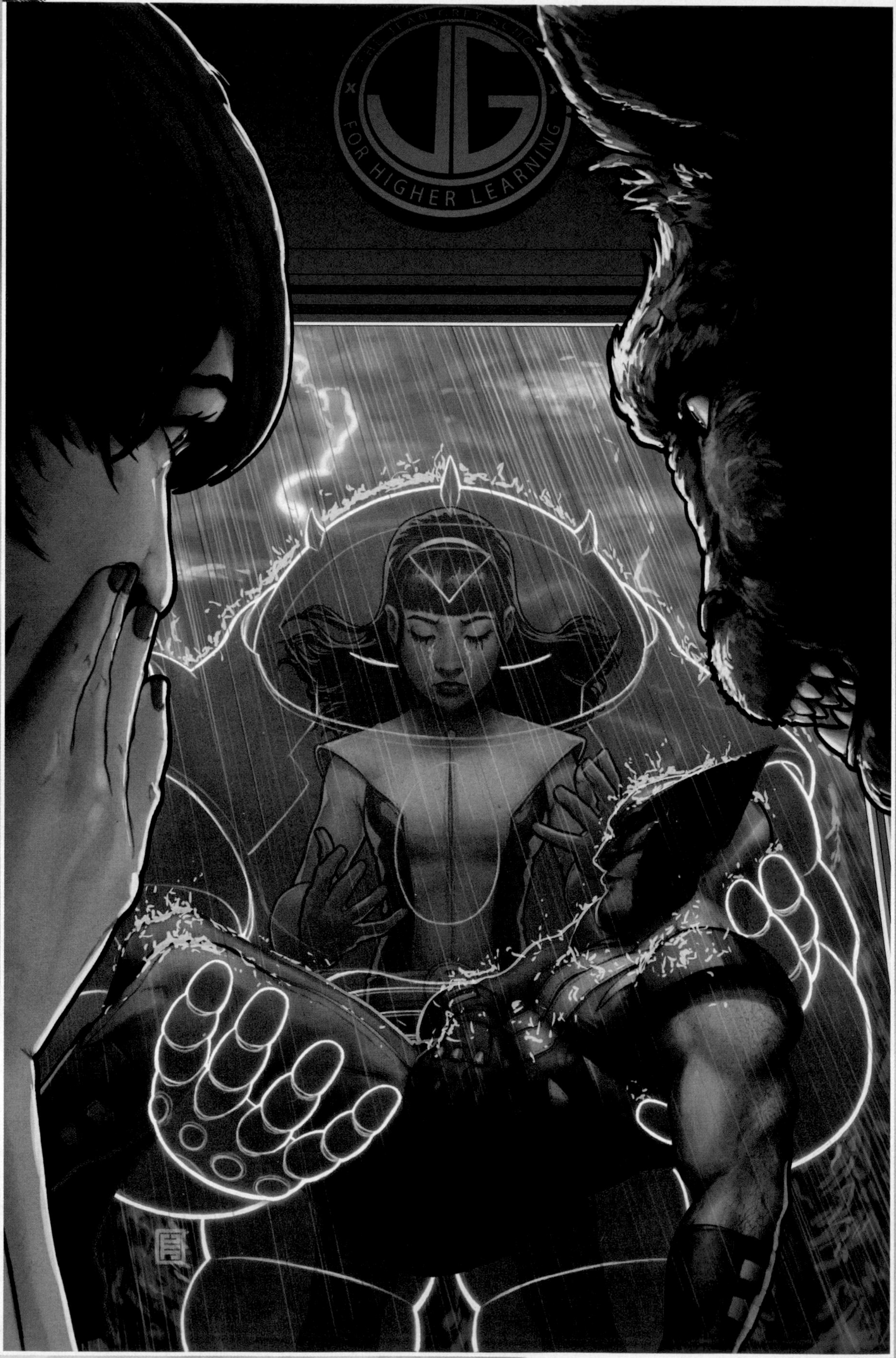
JG
FOR HIGHER LEARNING

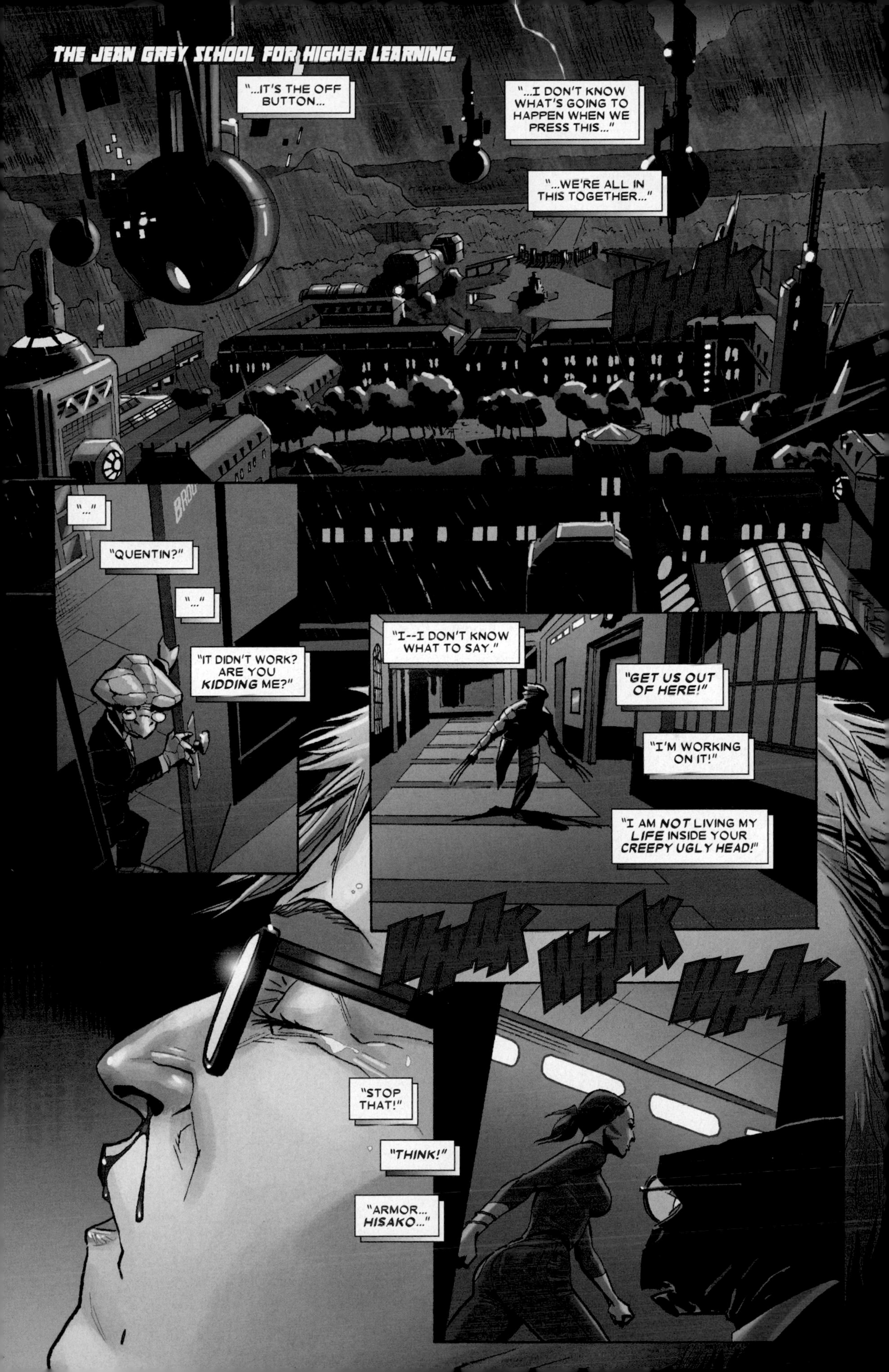
THE JEAN GREY SCHOOL FOR HIGHER LEARNING.
"...IT'S THE OFF BUTTON...
"...I DON'T KNOW WHAT'S GOING TO HAPPEN WHEN WE PRESS THIS..."
"...WE'RE ALL IN THIS TOGETHER..."
"..."
"QUENTIN?"
"..."
"IT DIDN'T WORK? ARE YOU KIDDING ME?"
"I--I DON'T KNOW WHAT TO SAY."
"GET US OUT OF HERE!"
"I'M WORKING ON IT!"
"I AM NOT LIVING MY LIFE INSIDE YOUR CREEPY UGLY HEAD!"
WHAK WHAK WHAK
"STOP THAT!"
"THINK!"
"ARMOR... HISAKO..."

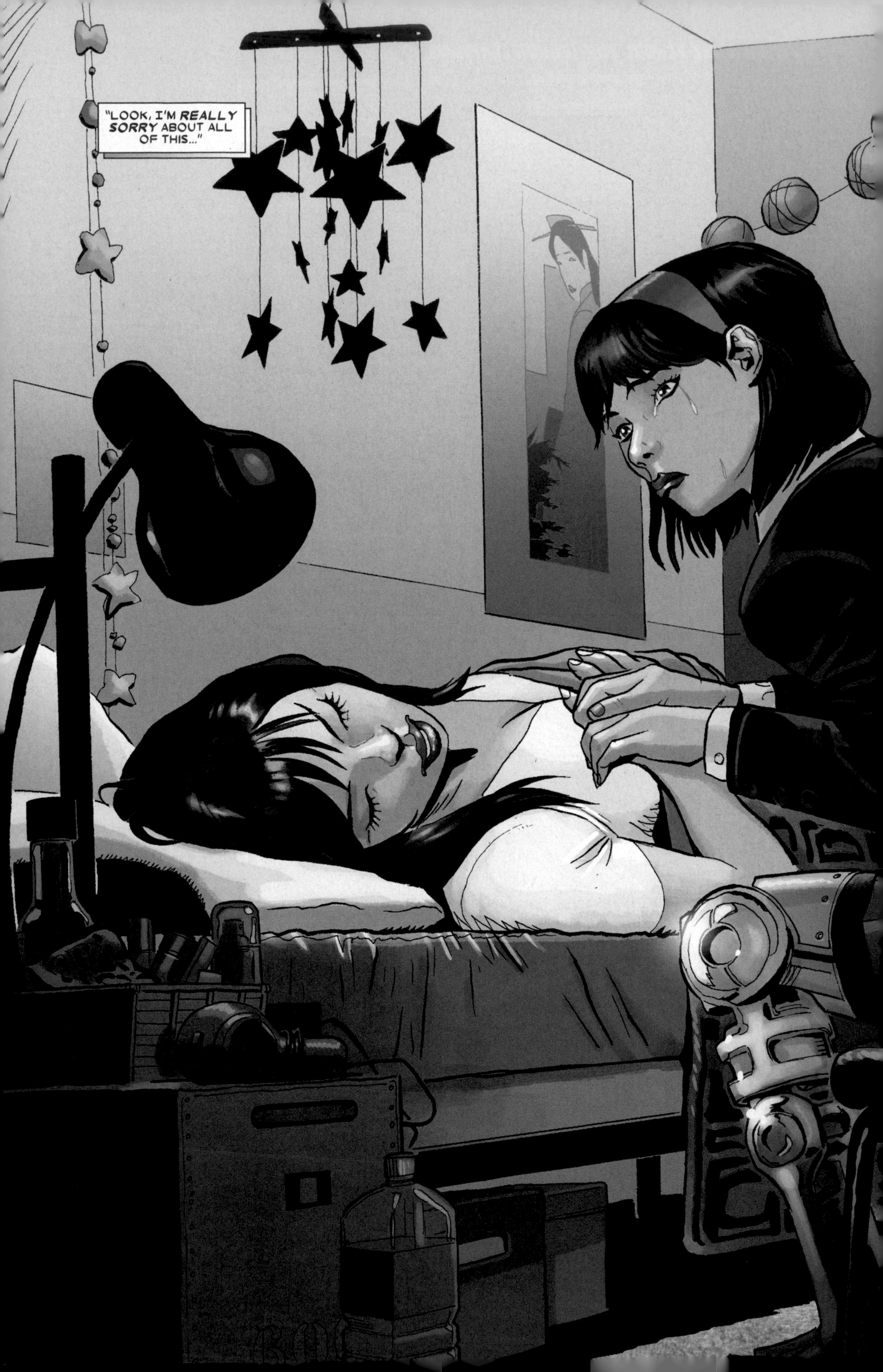
"LOOK, I'M REALLY SORRY ABOUT ALL OF THIS..."

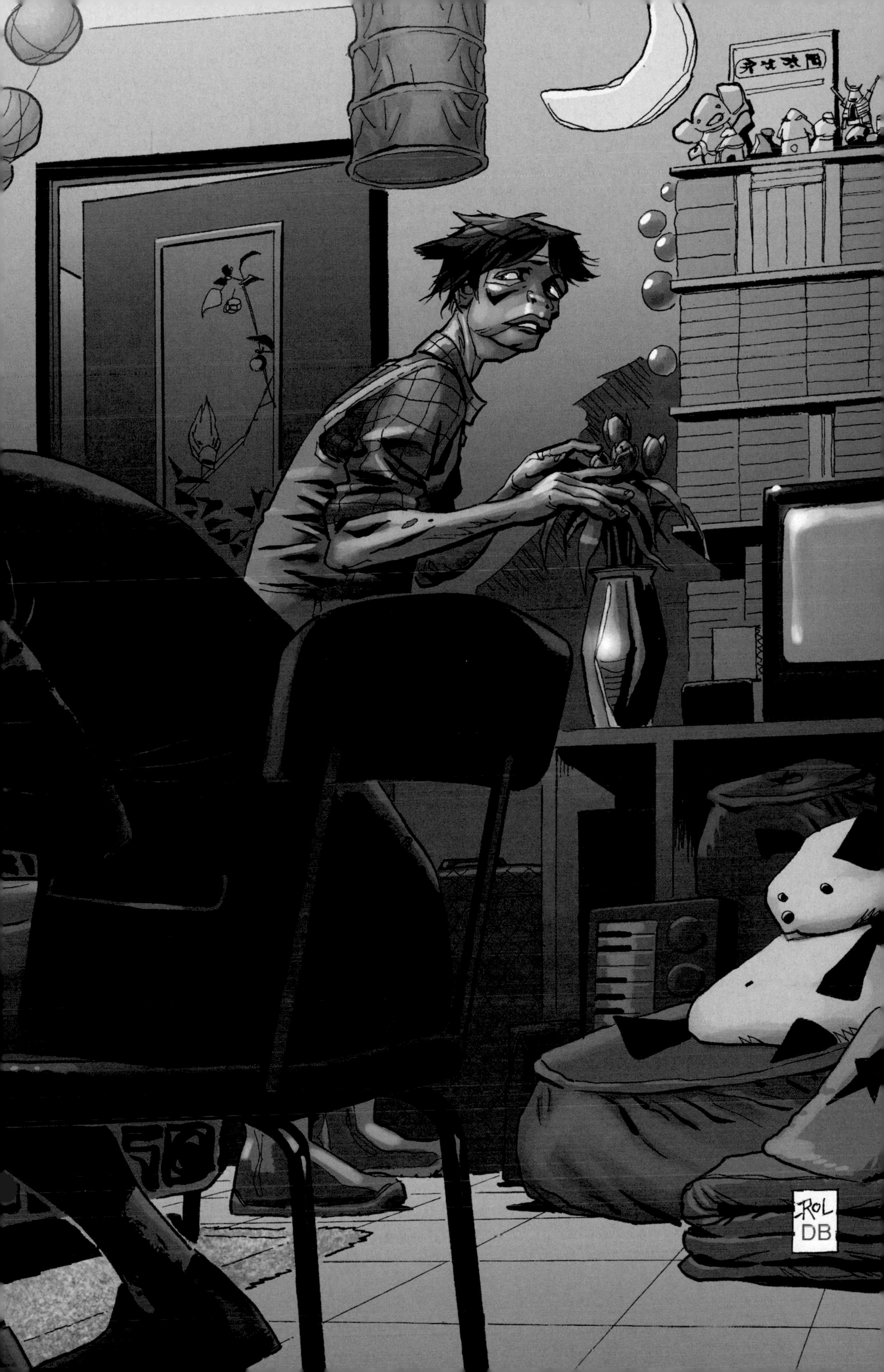

ROL
DB

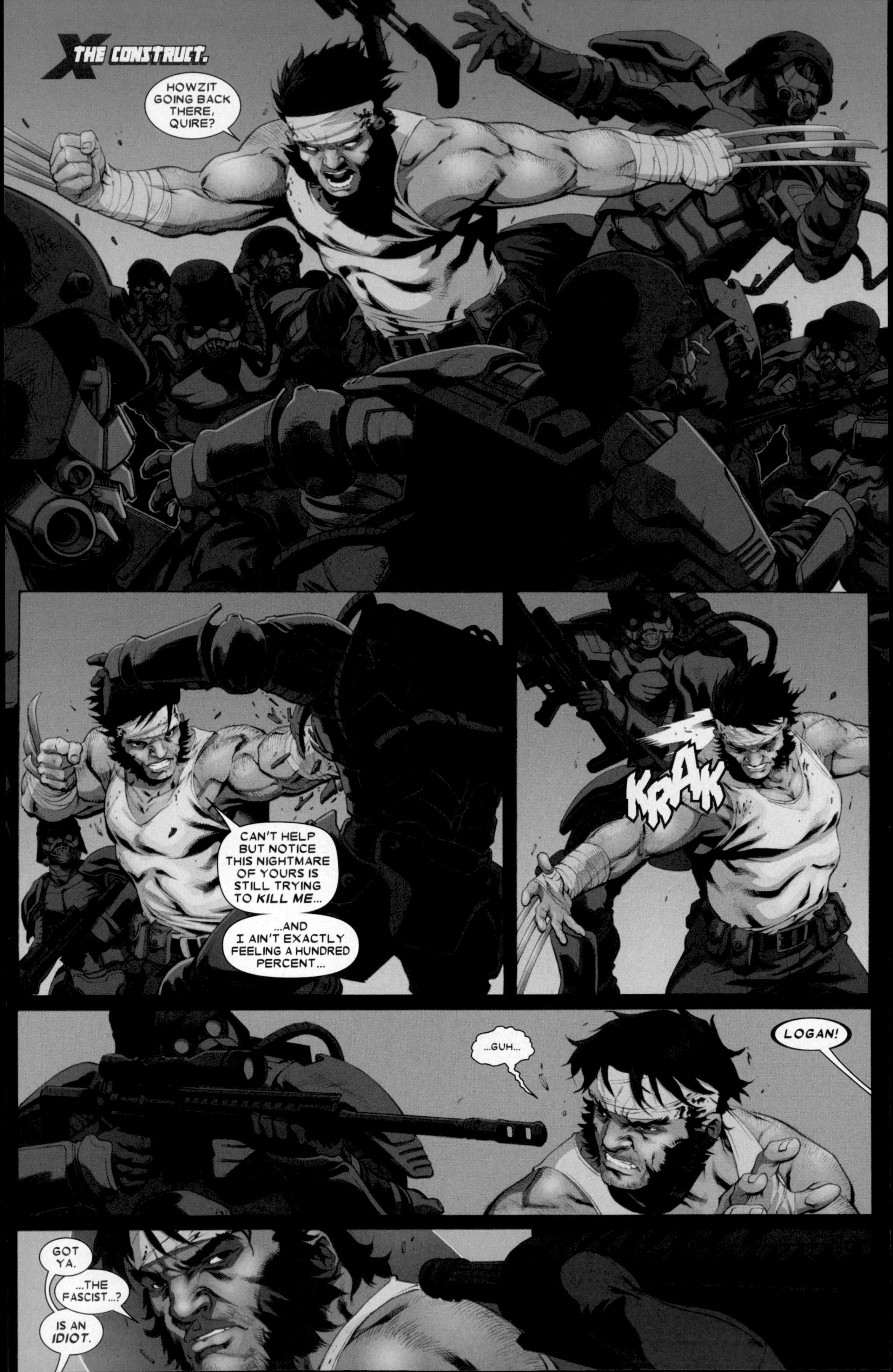
THE CONSTRUCT.
HOWZIT GOING BACK THERE, QUIRE?
CAN'T HELP BUT NOTICE THIS NIGHTMARE OF YOURS IS STILL TRYING TO KILL ME...
...AND I AIN'T EXACTLY FEELING A HUNDRED PERCENT...
KRAK
...GUH...
LOGAN!
GOT YA.
...THE FASCIST...?
IS AN IDIOT.

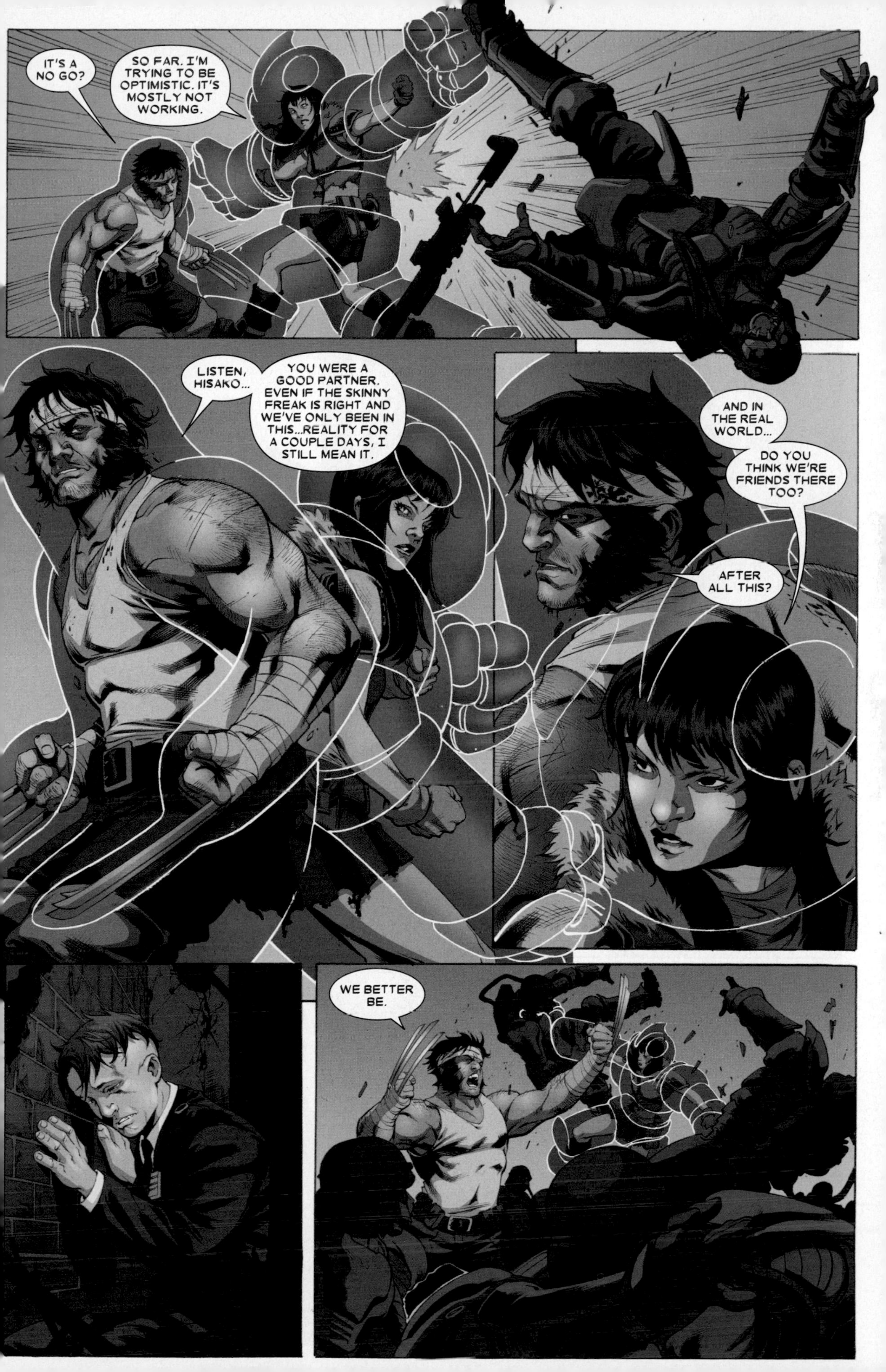
IT'S A NO GO?
SO FAR. I'M TRYING TO BE OPTIMISTIC. IT'S MOSTLY NOT WORKING.
LISTEN, HISAKO...
YOU WERE A GOOD PARTNER. EVEN IF THE SKINNY FREAK IS RIGHT AND WE'VE ONLY BEEN IN THIS...REALITY FOR A COUPLE DAYS, I STILL MEAN IT.
AND IN THE REAL WORLD...
DO YOU THINK WE'RE FRIENDS THERE TOO?
AFTER ALL THIS?
WE BETTER BE.

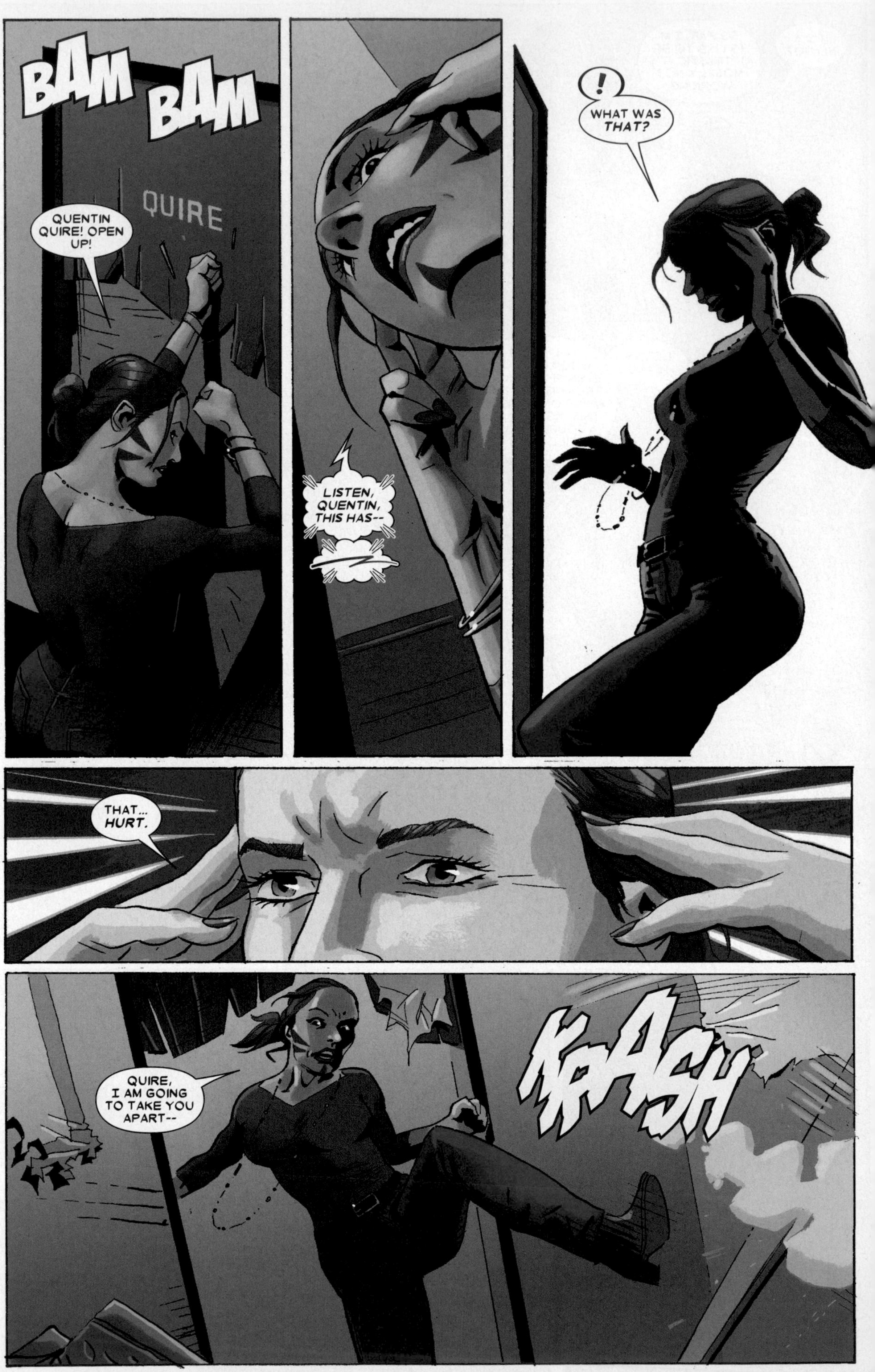
BAM BAM
QUIRE
QUENTIN QUIRE! OPEN UP!
LISTEN, QUENTIN, THIS HAS--
!
WHAT WAS THAT?
THAT... HURT.
KRASH
QUIRE, I AM GOING TO TAKE YOU APART--

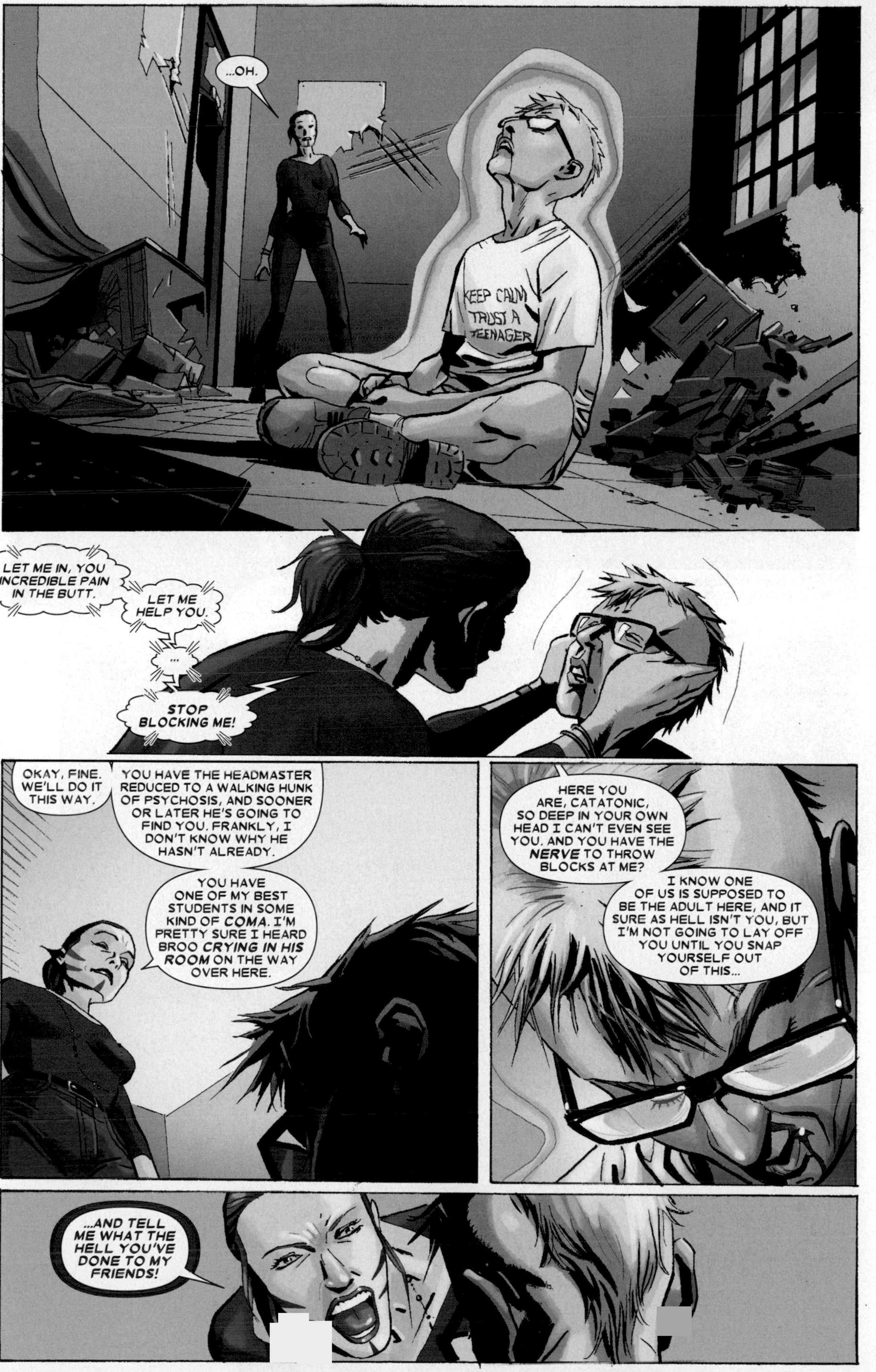
...OH.
KEEP CALM TRUST A TEENAGER
LET ME IN, YOU INCREDIBLE PAIN IN THE BUTT.
LET ME HELP YOU.
...
STOP BLOCKING ME!
OKAY, FINE. WE'LL DO IT THIS WAY.
YOU HAVE THE HEADMASTER REDUCED TO A WALKING HUNK OF PSYCHOSIS, AND SOONER OR LATER HE'S GOING TO FIND YOU. FRANKLY, I DON'T KNOW WHY HE HASN'T ALREADY.
YOU HAVE ONE OF MY BEST STUDENTS IN SOME KIND OF *COMA*. I'M PRETTY SURE I HEARD BROO *CRYING IN HIS ROOM* ON THE WAY OVER HERE.
HERE YOU ARE, CATATONIC, SO DEEP IN YOUR OWN HEAD I CAN'T EVEN SEE YOU. AND YOU HAVE THE *NERVE* TO THROW BLOCKS AT ME?
I KNOW ONE OF US IS SUPPOSED TO BE THE ADULT HERE, AND IT SURE AS HELL ISN'T YOU, BUT I'M NOT GOING TO LAY OFF YOU UNTIL YOU SNAP YOURSELF OUT OF THIS...
...AND TELL ME WHAT THE HELL YOU'VE DONE TO MY FRIENDS!

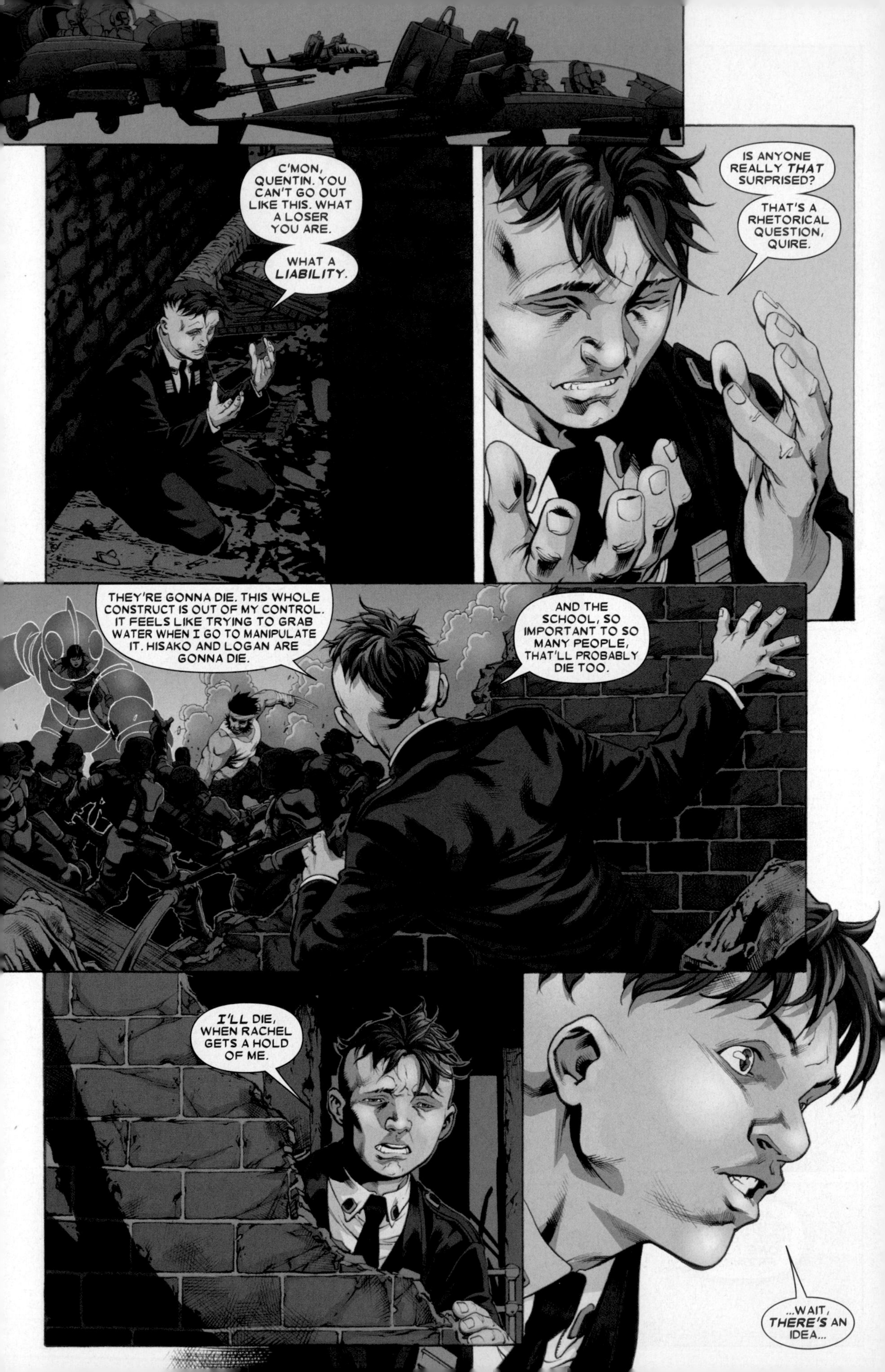
C'MON, QUENTIN. YOU CAN'T GO OUT LIKE THIS. WHAT A LOSER YOU ARE.
WHAT A *LIABILITY*.
IS ANYONE REALLY *THAT* SURPRISED?
THAT'S A RHETORICAL QUESTION, QUIRE.
THEY'RE GONNA DIE. THIS WHOLE CONSTRUCT IS OUT OF MY CONTROL. IT FEELS LIKE TRYING TO GRAB WATER WHEN I GO TO MANIPULATE IT. HISAKO AND LOGAN ARE GONNA DIE.
AND THE SCHOOL, SO IMPORTANT TO SO MANY PEOPLE, THAT'LL PROBABLY DIE TOO.
I'LL DIE, WHEN RACHEL GETS A HOLD OF ME.
...WAIT, *THERE'S* AN IDEA...

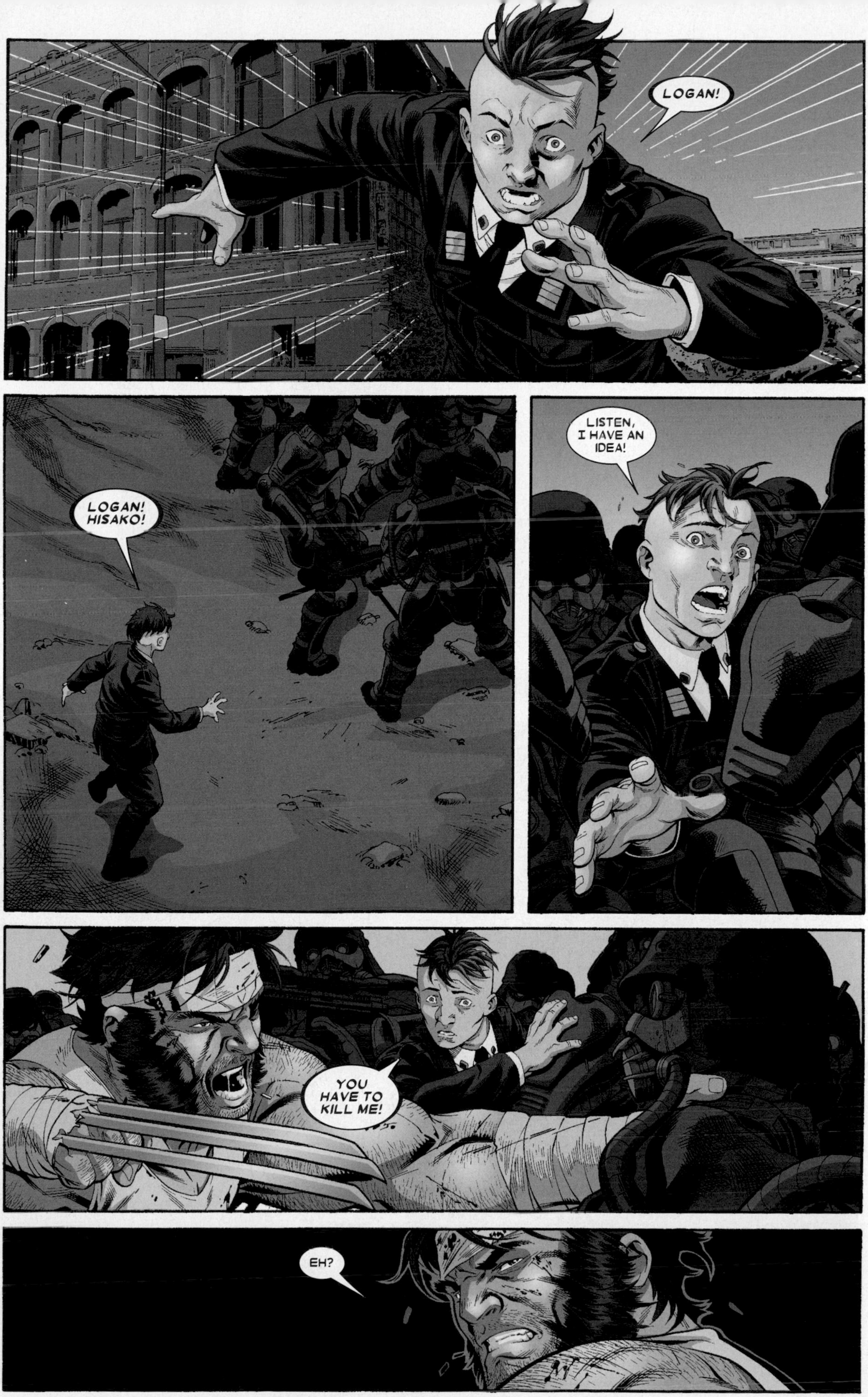
LOGAN!
LOGAN! HISAKO!
LISTEN, I HAVE AN IDEA!
YOU HAVE TO KILL ME!
EH?

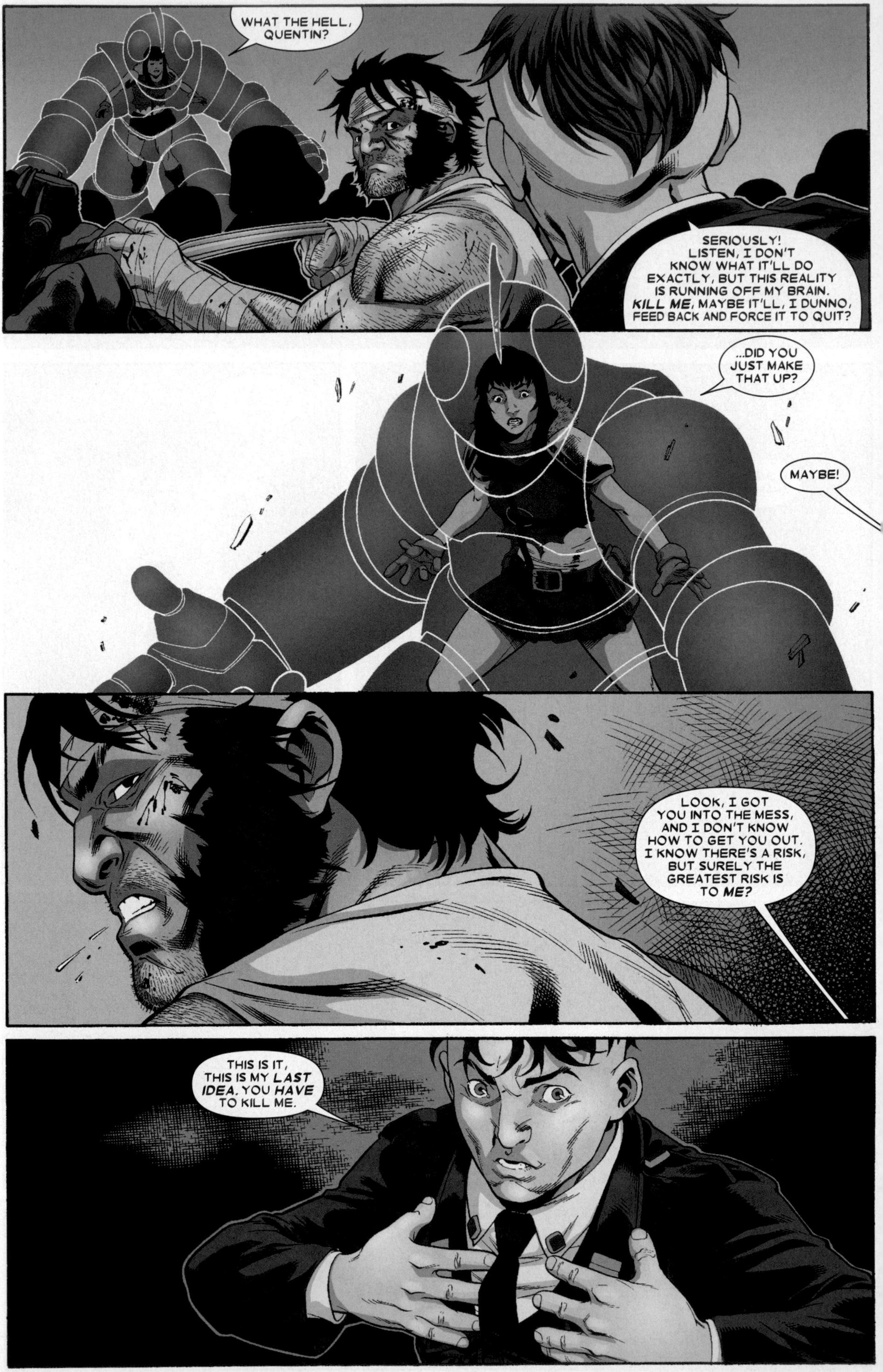
WHAT THE HELL, QUENTIN?
SERIOUSLY! LISTEN, I DON'T KNOW WHAT IT'LL DO EXACTLY, BUT THIS REALITY IS RUNNING OFF MY BRAIN. KILL ME, MAYBE IT'LL, I DUNNO, FEED BACK AND FORCE IT TO QUIT?
...DID YOU JUST MAKE THAT UP?
MAYBE!
LOOK, I GOT YOU INTO THE MESS, AND I DON'T KNOW HOW TO GET YOU OUT. I KNOW THERE'S A RISK, BUT SURELY THE GREATEST RISK IS TO ME?
THIS IS IT, THIS IS MY LAST IDEA. YOU HAVE TO KILL ME.

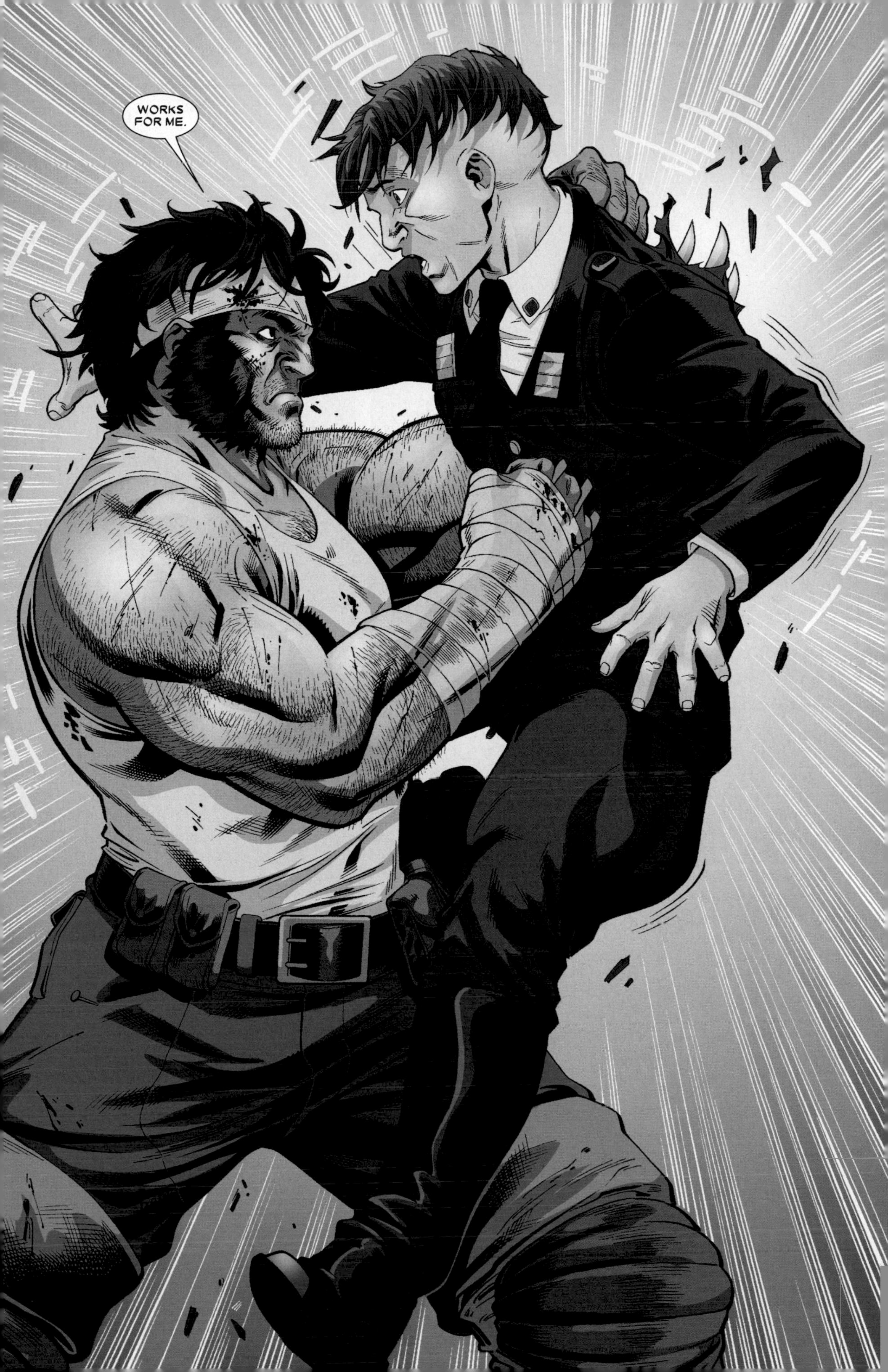
WORKS FOR ME.

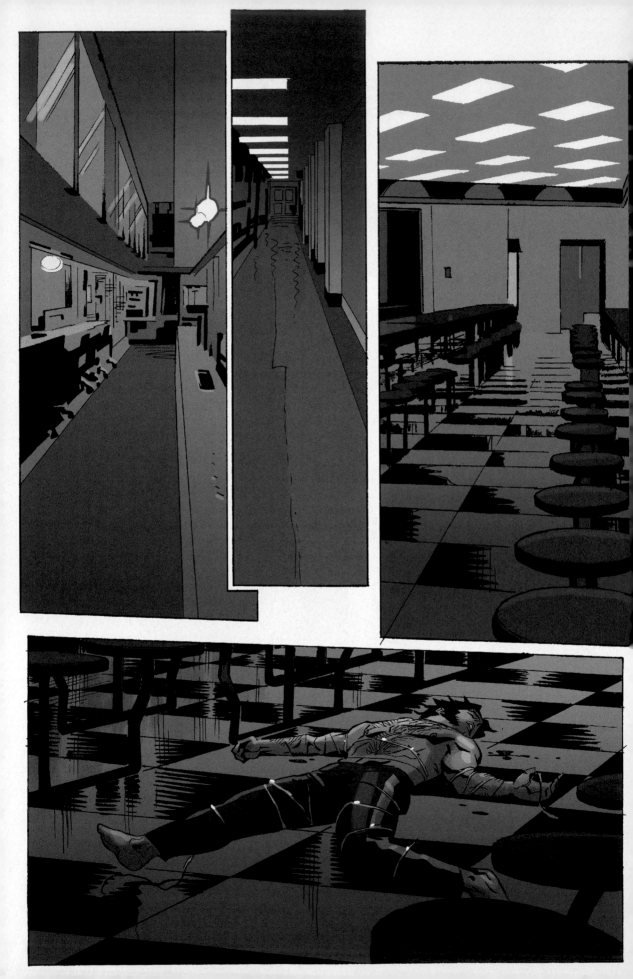

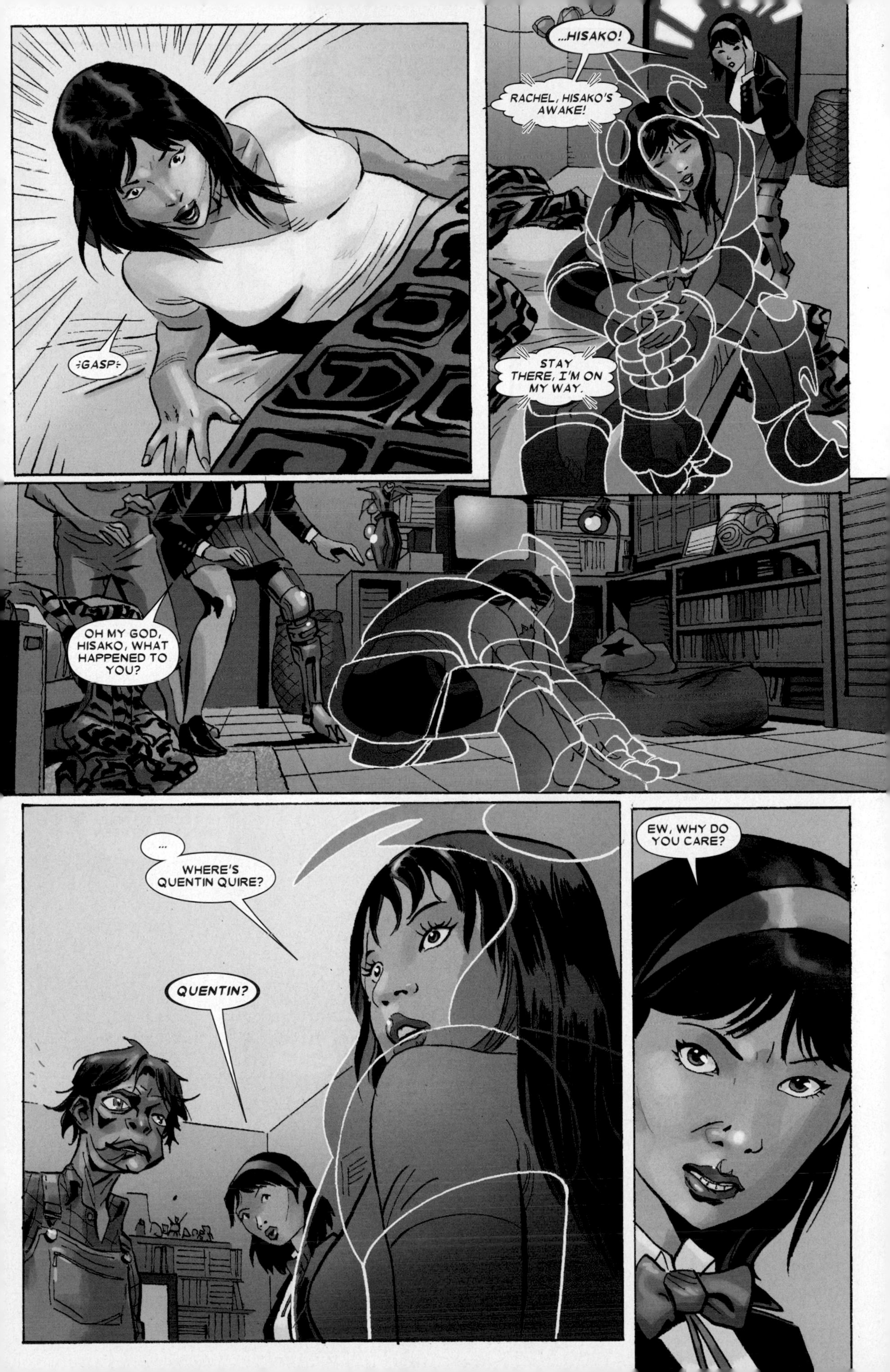

GASP
...HISAKO!
RACHEL, HISAKO'S AWAKE!
STAY THERE, I'M ON MY WAY.
OH MY GOD, HISAKO, WHAT HAPPENED TO YOU?
...
WHERE'S QUENTIN QUIRE?
QUENTIN?
EW, WHY DO YOU CARE?

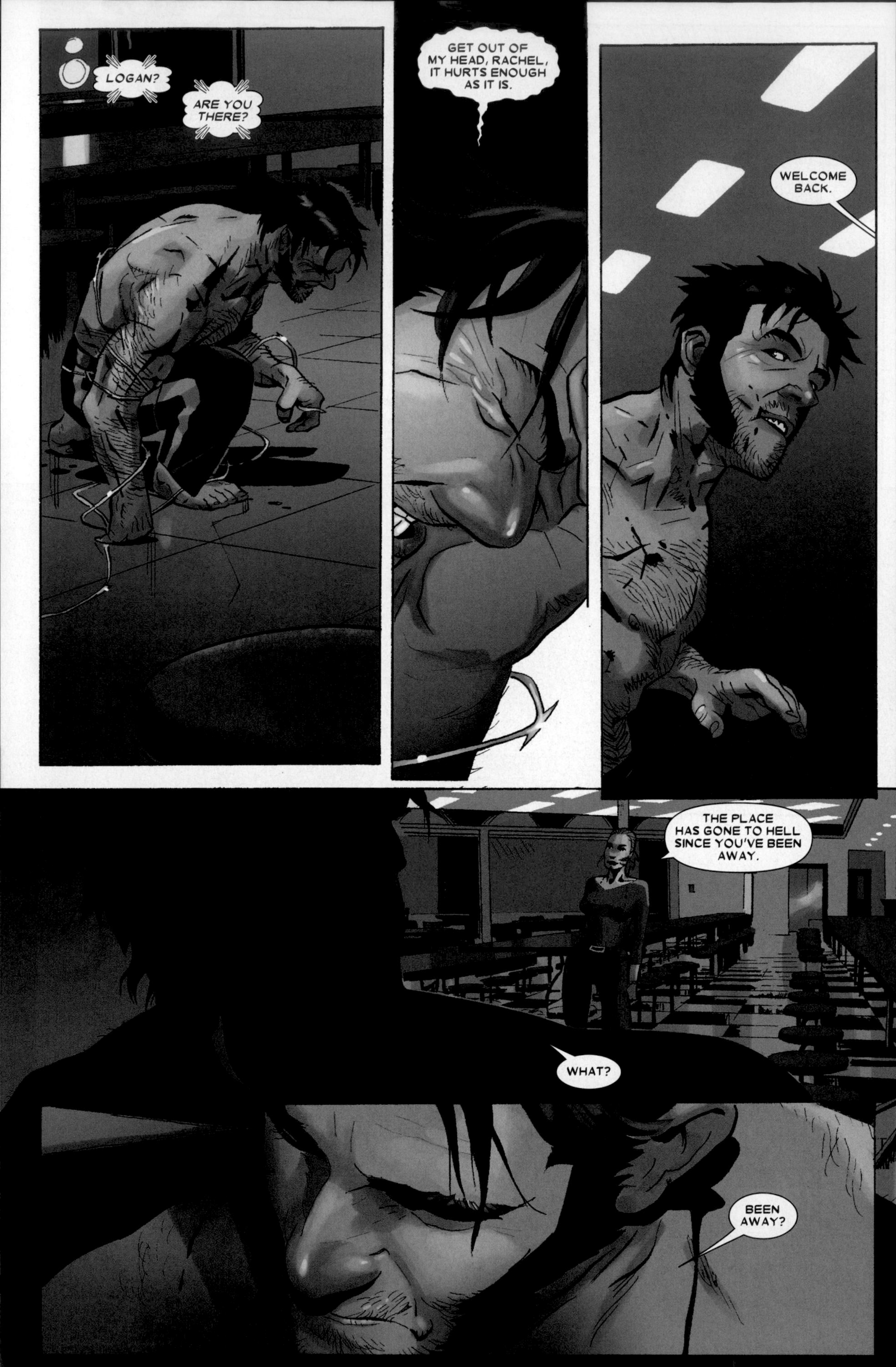
LOGAN?
ARE YOU THERE?
GET OUT OF MY HEAD, RACHEL, IT HURTS ENOUGH AS IT IS.
WELCOME BACK.
THE PLACE HAS GONE TO HELL SINCE YOU'VE BEEN AWAY.
WHAT?
BEEN AWAY?

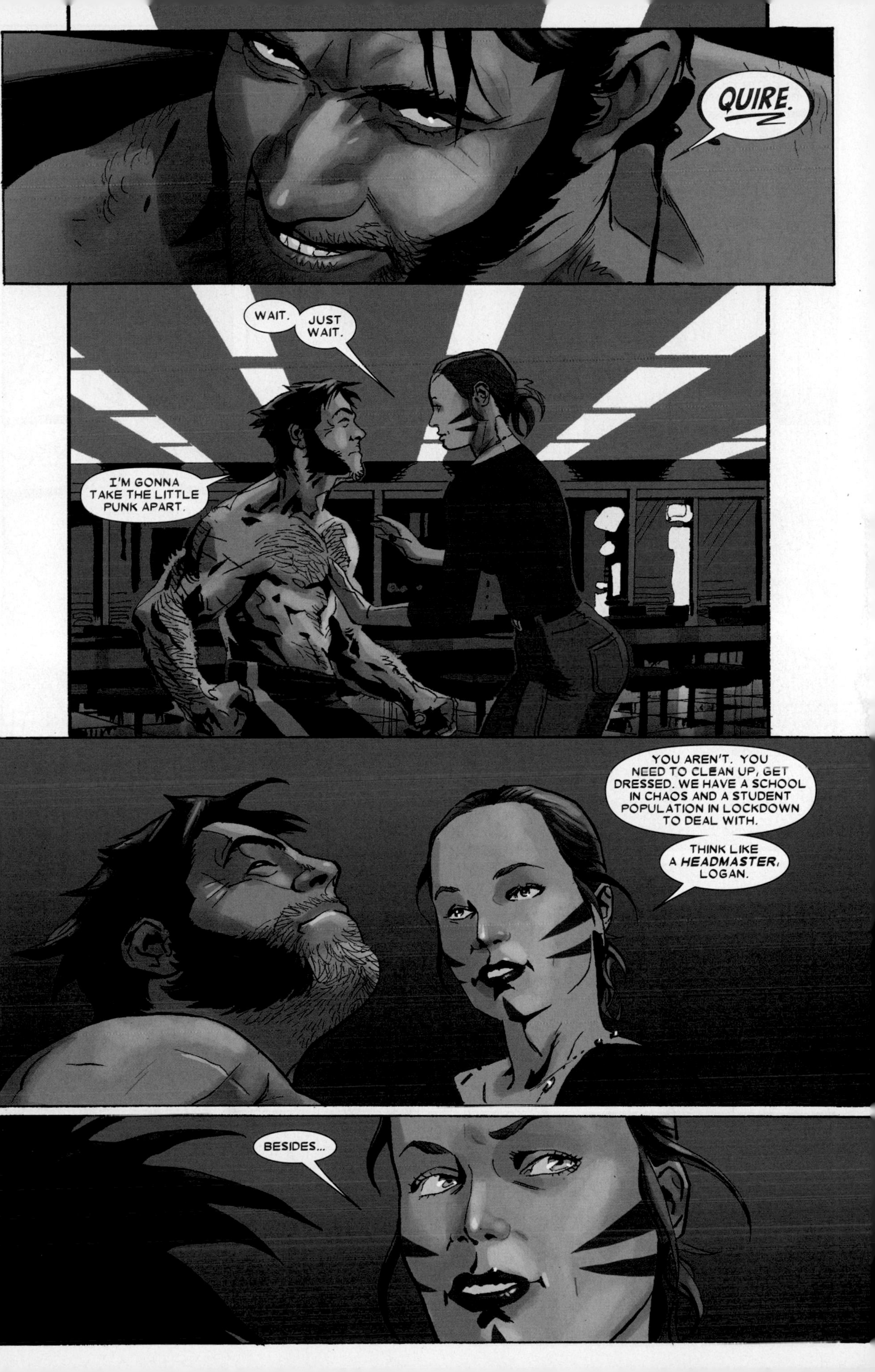

QUIRE.
WAIT.
JUST WAIT.
I'M GONNA TAKE THE LITTLE PUNK APART.
YOU AREN'T. YOU NEED TO CLEAN UP, GET DRESSED. WE HAVE A SCHOOL IN CHAOS AND A STUDENT POPULATION IN LOCKDOWN TO DEAL WITH.
THINK LIKE A *HEADMASTER*, LOGAN.
BESIDES...

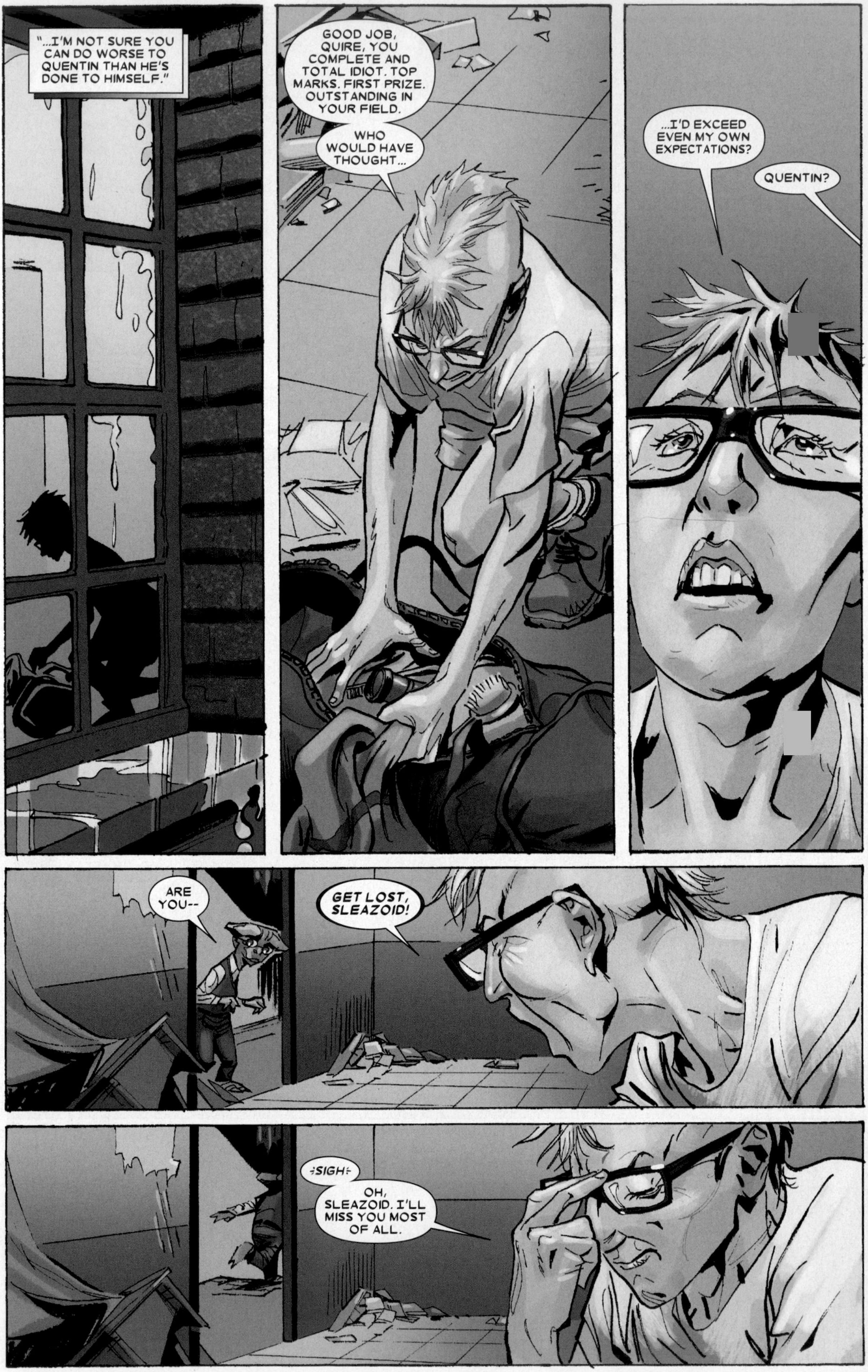
"...I'M NOT SURE YOU CAN DO WORSE TO QUENTIN THAN HE'S DONE TO HIMSELF."
GOOD JOB, QUIRE, YOU COMPLETE AND TOTAL IDIOT. TOP MARKS. FIRST PRIZE. OUTSTANDING IN YOUR FIELD.
WHO WOULD HAVE THOUGHT...
...I'D EXCEED EVEN MY OWN EXPECTATIONS?
QUENTIN?
ARE YOU--
GET LOST, SLEAZOID!
÷SIGH÷
OH, SLEAZOID. I'LL MISS YOU MOST OF ALL.

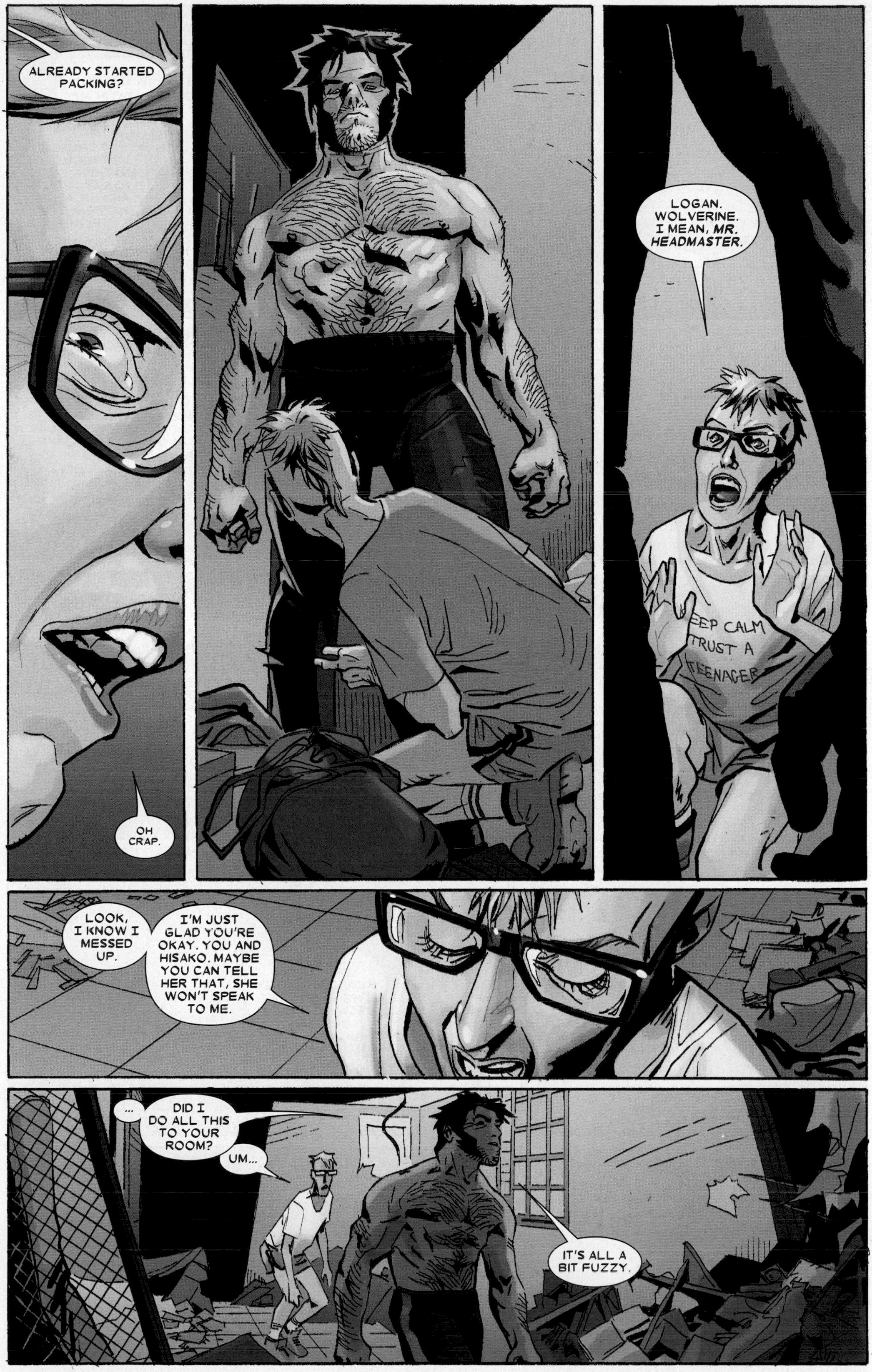
ALREADY STARTED PACKING?
OH CRAP.
LOGAN. WOLVERINE. I MEAN, MR. HEADMASTER.
KEEP CALM TRUST A TEENAGER
LOOK, I KNOW I MESSED UP.
I'M JUST GLAD YOU'RE OKAY. YOU AND HISAKO. MAYBE YOU CAN TELL HER THAT, SHE WON'T SPEAK TO ME.
...
DID I DO ALL THIS TO YOUR ROOM?
UM...
IT'S ALL A BIT FUZZY.

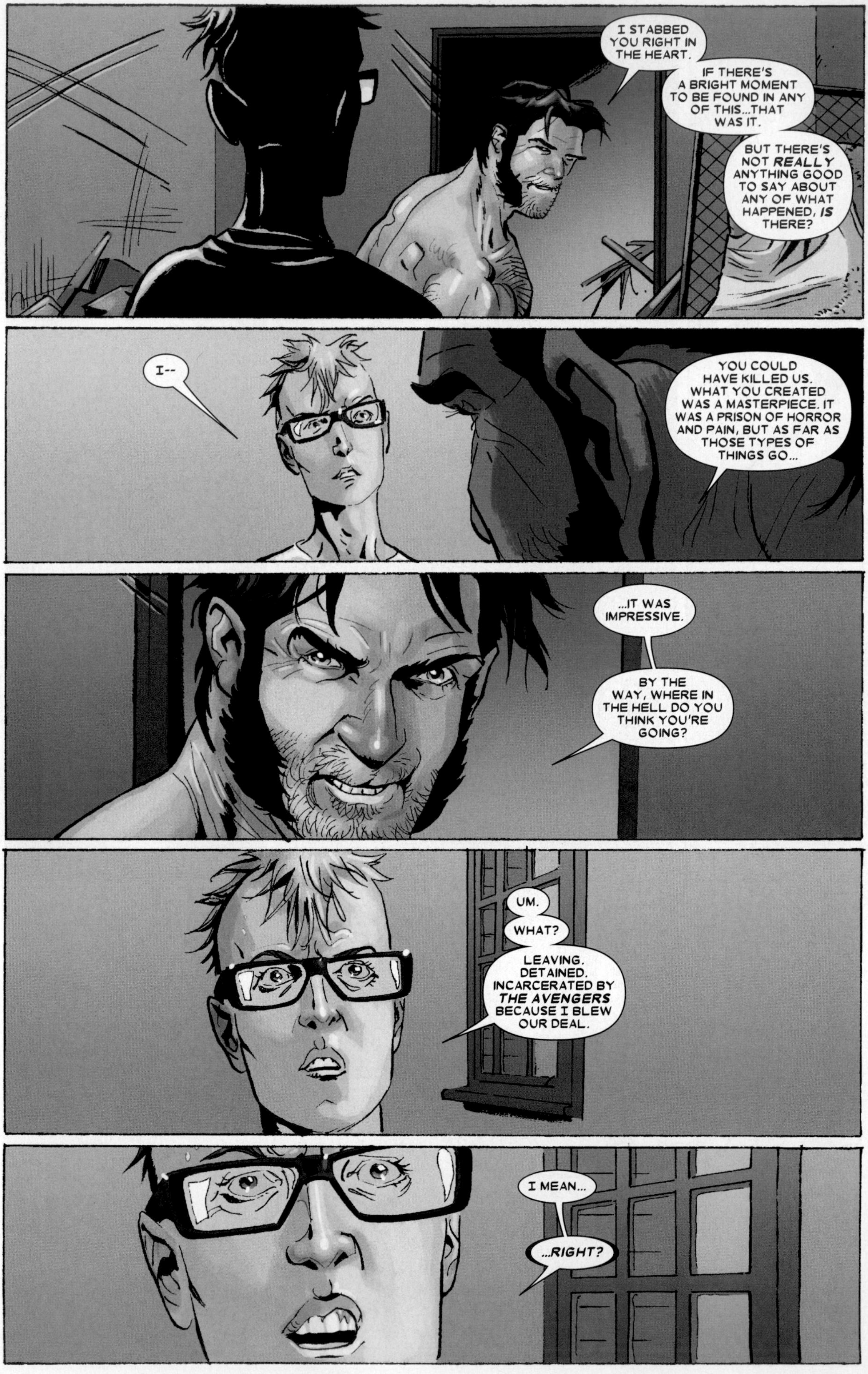

I STABBED YOU RIGHT IN THE HEART.
IF THERE'S A BRIGHT MOMENT TO BE FOUND IN ANY OF THIS...THAT WAS IT.
BUT THERE'S NOT *REALLY* ANYTHING GOOD TO SAY ABOUT ANY OF WHAT HAPPENED, *IS* THERE?
I--
YOU COULD HAVE KILLED US. WHAT YOU CREATED WAS A MASTERPIECE. IT WAS A PRISON OF HORROR AND PAIN, BUT AS FAR AS THOSE TYPES OF THINGS GO...
...IT WAS IMPRESSIVE.
BY THE WAY, WHERE IN THE HELL DO YOU THINK YOU'RE GOING?
UM.
WHAT?
LEAVING. DETAINED. INCARCERATED BY *THE AVENGERS* BECAUSE I BLEW OUR DEAL.
I MEAN...
...*RIGHT?*

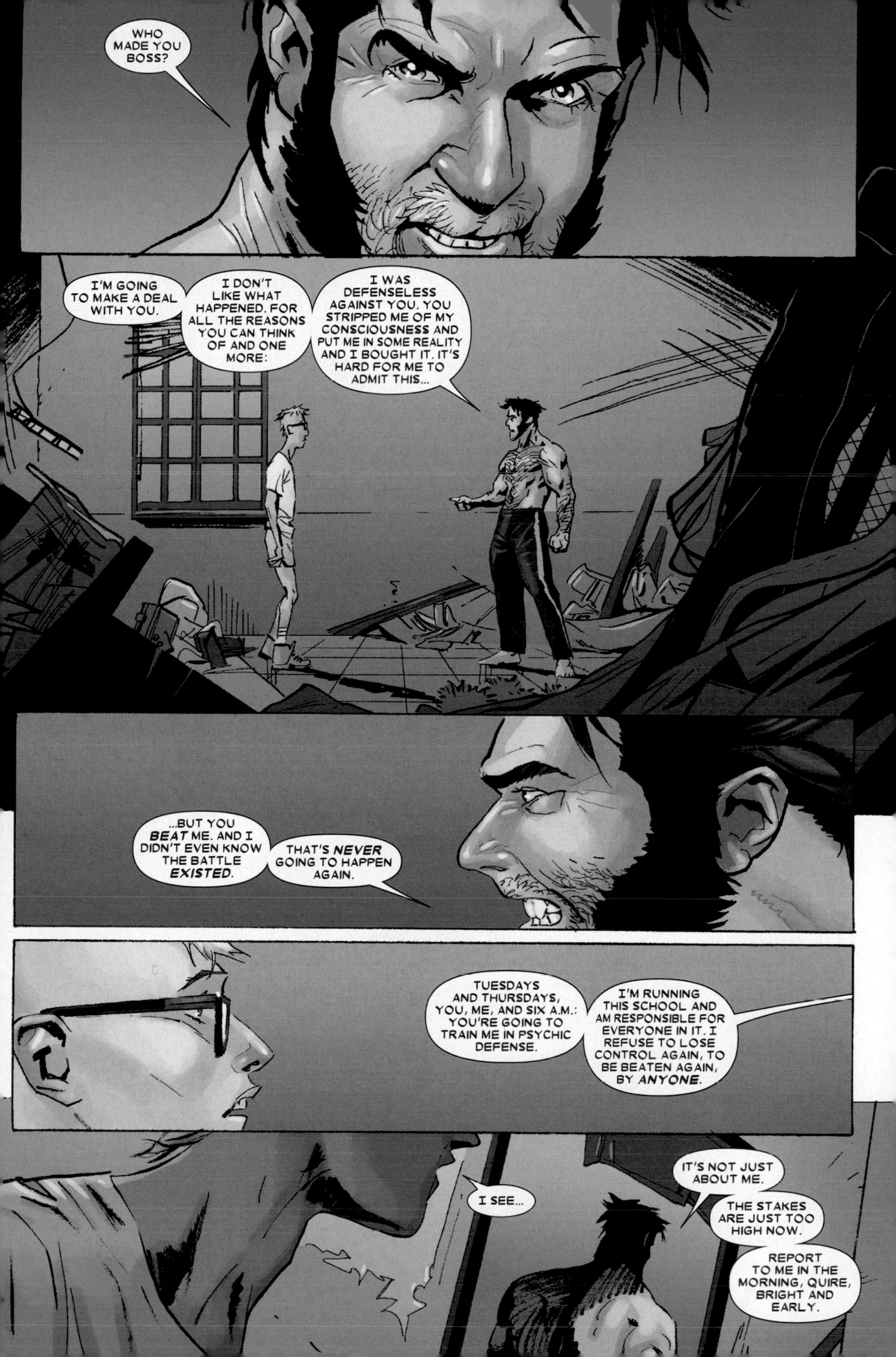
WHO MADE YOU BOSS?
I'M GOING TO MAKE A DEAL WITH YOU.
I DON'T LIKE WHAT HAPPENED. FOR ALL THE REASONS YOU CAN THINK OF AND ONE MORE:
I WAS DEFENSELESS AGAINST YOU. YOU STRIPPED ME OF MY CONSCIOUSNESS AND PUT ME IN SOME REALITY AND I BOUGHT IT. IT'S HARD FOR ME TO ADMIT THIS...
...BUT YOU BEAT ME. AND I DIDN'T EVEN KNOW THE BATTLE EXISTED.
THAT'S NEVER GOING TO HAPPEN AGAIN.
I'M RUNNING THIS SCHOOL AND AM RESPONSIBLE FOR EVERYONE IN IT. I REFUSE TO LOSE CONTROL AGAIN, TO BE BEATEN AGAIN, BY ANYONE.
TUESDAYS AND THURSDAYS, YOU, ME, AND SIX A.M.: YOU'RE GOING TO TRAIN ME IN PSYCHIC DEFENSE.
I SEE...
IT'S NOT JUST ABOUT ME.
THE STAKES ARE JUST TOO HIGH NOW.
REPORT TO ME IN THE MORNING, QUIRE, BRIGHT AND EARLY.

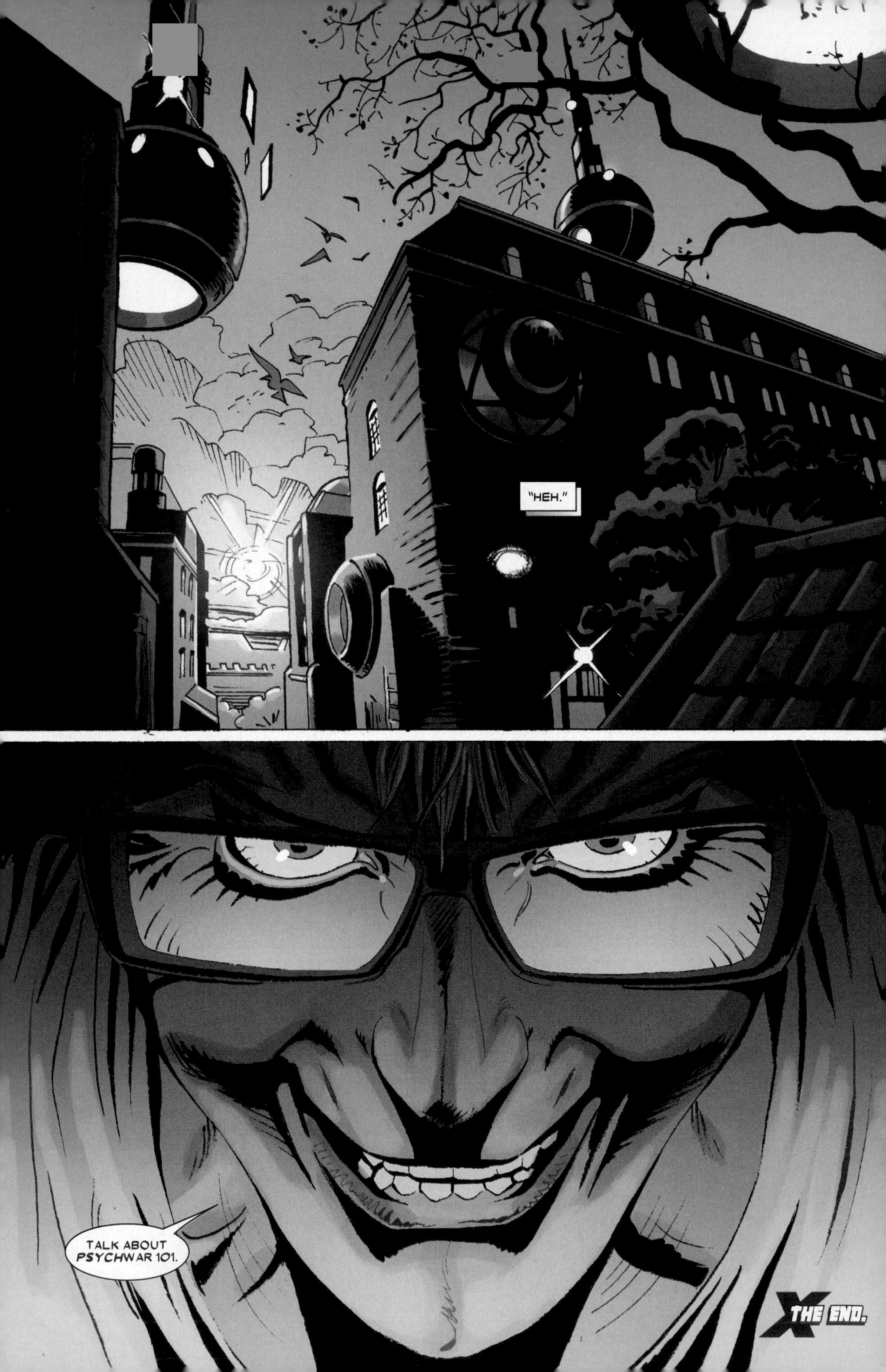
"HEH."
TALK ABOUT PSYCHWAR 101.
THE END.

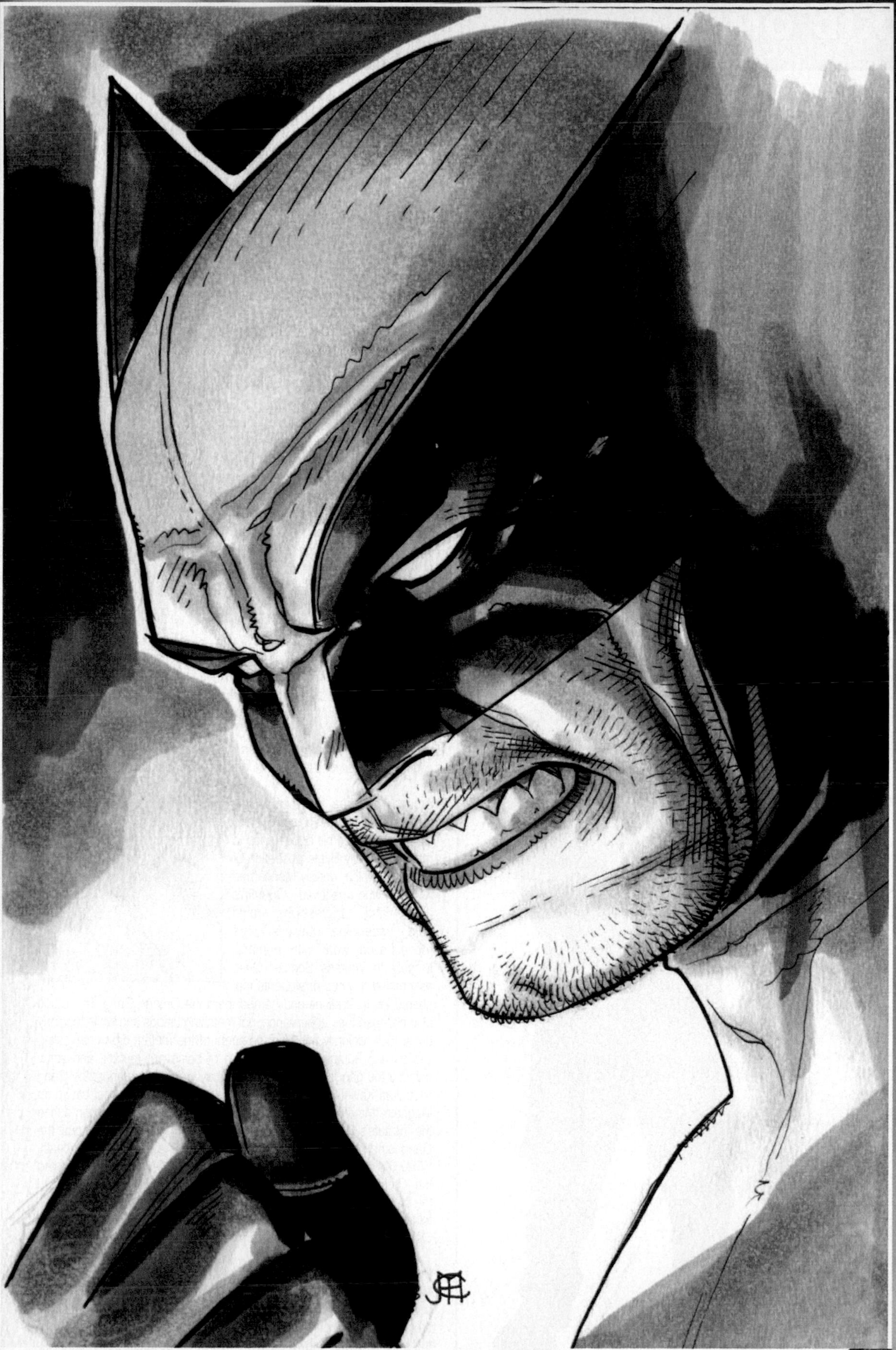

#1 2ND PRINTING VARIANT BY JIM CHEUNG

KID OMEGA

REAL NAME: Quentin Quire
ALIASES: Top Boss
IDENTITY: Publicly known
OCCUPATION: Student, anarchist, terrorist; former gang leader
CITIZENSHIP: USA
PLACE OF BIRTH: Unrevealed
KNOWN RELATIVES: Unidentified adoptive parents
GROUP AFFILIATION: Jean Grey School for Higher Learning student body; formerly Omega Gang, Xavier Institute student body
EDUCATION: Various high school courses at Jean Grey School for Higher Learning and Xavier Institute for Higher Learning
FIRST APPEARANCE: (Photograph) New X-Men #126 (2002); (identified) New X-Men #134 (2003)

HISTORY: Telepathic Quentin Quire was one of the most promising students at the Xavier Institute for Higher Learning, having been inspired by Professor Charles Xavier's dream of peaceful human/mutant integration when he was 13 years old. As a student, Quire created anti-gravity floating devices to grant mobility to the disembodied brain of his fellow student Martha Johansson, longed to be popular and powerful, and became infatuated with fellow student Sophie, one of the telepathic Stepford Cuckoos quintet, hive mind clones of telepathic faculty member Emma Frost. However, the Cuckoos regarded him as a creepy rival for Xavier's attention and rejected all efforts by Quire to gain Sophie's affections. He regularly carried the front page of a Daily Bugle newspaper released on the day he was born which featured an article on the emergence of mutantkind and an accompanying illustration that depicted mutants as striped shirt-wearing, whip wielding masters of humanity, an image Quire came to regard as a pop-art masterpiece.

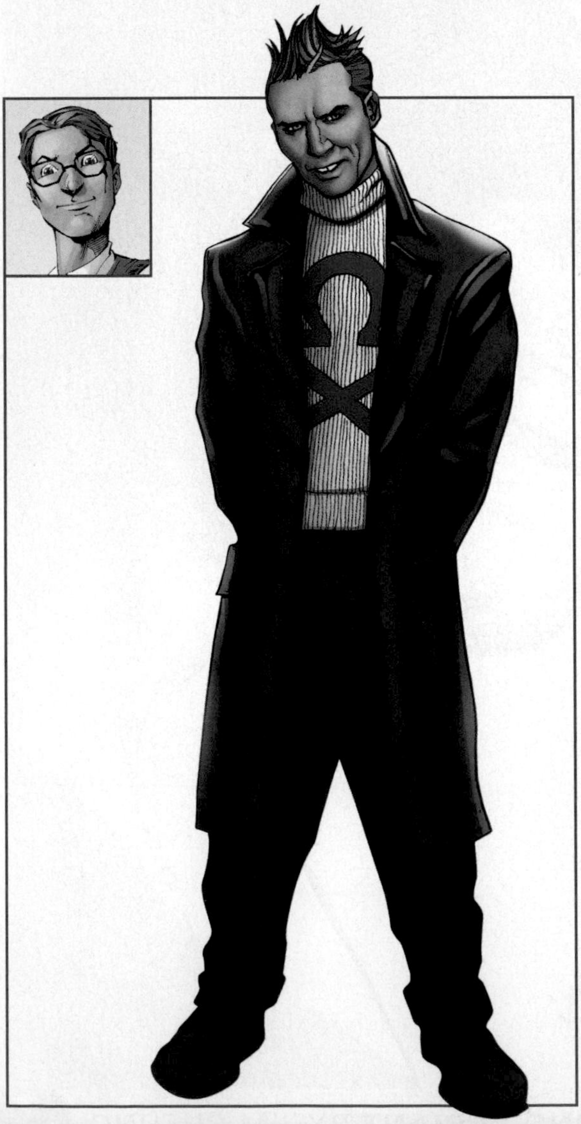

Art by Frank Cho with Keron Grant (inset)

WITH OMEGA GANG

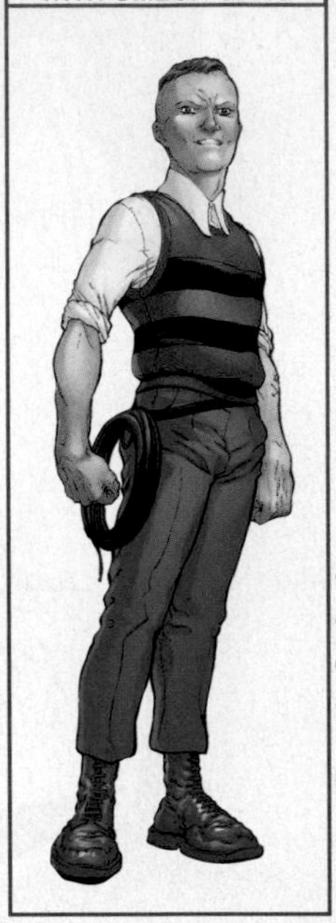

Art by Frank Quitely

Devastated by learning that he was adopted, and haunted by both the extermination of 16 million mutants in the mutant nation of Genosha and the murder of renowned mutant fashion designer and nightclub entrepreneur Jumbo Carnation during an apparent anti-mutant hate crime, Quire began to doubt Xavier's teachings, and developed a more negative and hostile view of the world and of humankind; Quire was unaware Carnation actually died from a self-administered dose of neuro-toxic designer drug Hypercortisone D (aka "Kick"), which increased superhuman mutant powers but also altered the brain's metabolism, greatly enhancing intellectual capacity and imagination but also apparently disengaging inhibitions and rationale. In his frustration at not being able to avenge Carnation, during a musical performance benefit for Carnation Quire disrupted the illusion supposedly handsome and charismatic student Slick (Quincy Marrow) created to hide his misshapen true form, humiliating him in front of the student body, an event that disturbed Xavier. Simultaneously, when blood work revealed Quire's brain was burning sugar at fifteen times faster than normal, the Institute staff became concerned Quire was experiencing a secondary mutation.

OMEGA GANG SYMBOL/TATTOO

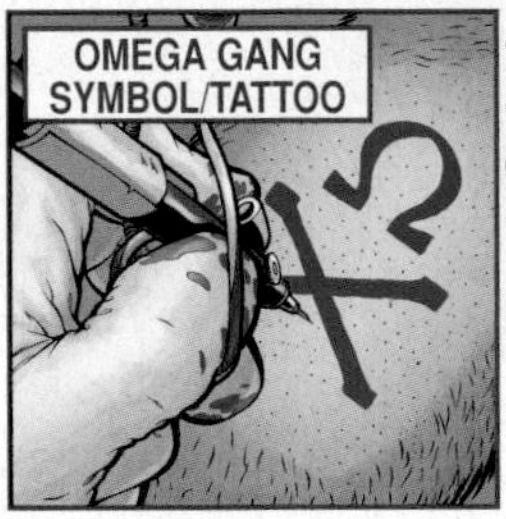

Art by Frank Quitely

Around this time, an increasingly arrogant Quire began using Kick and drastically altered his appearance to match the Daily Bugle illustration of mutants, which greatly concerned Xavier, who believed Quentin's attire and aggression would help undermine Xavier's life's reconciliation work with humans. Largely to impress Sophie, Quire assembled a group of students that shared his frustrations and named them the Omega Gang. This group also changed their appearance, got matching tattoos and while regularly using Kick, violently attacked members of the mutant organ-harvesting U-Men and humans they suspected of being anti-mutant, and spray painting the gang's symbol wherever they went. On campus, the Gang assaulted Xavier and rendered him powerless with a helmet based on Magneto (Max Eisenhardt)'s telepathy resistant technology, then during the Institute's Open Day, an event welcoming humans on campus, the Gang fomented a student riot that resulted in at least one student death. While Xavier's mutant emergency response X-Men easily defeated the Omega Gang, Sophie consumed a dose of "Kick" and utilized the X-Men's psychic-enhancement technology to magnify her sisters' telepathic powers to a level higher than Quire's. Though they defeated Quire, Sophie apparently died from the strain.

Possibly triggered by his Kick use, Quire's physical form underwent his secondary mutation and discorporated, leaving him a disembodied consciousness in a containment unit while the remaining members of the Omega Gang were incarcerated in human prisons. Later, when the cosmic avatar known as the Phoenix Force returned to Earth, its

DISEMBODIED STATE
Subject: Quentin Quire
Art by Greg Land

presence influenced Quire to reconstitute himself in a new physical form, but Quire became distraught when he recalled Sophie's death. He exhumed her corpse and sought out the Phoenix Force to help resurrect her, opposing the X-Men, who sought to contain the dangerous Force to prevent potential destruction it could cause. During the ensuing clash, the Force granted Quire's wish by resurrecting Sophie. However, upon seeing Quire, a disgusted Sophie chose instead to return to death; a heartbroken Quire resumed his disembodied state. When the Institute was destroyed and the X-Men relocated their operations to San Francisco, California, Quire's containment unit was also taken there.

SCHOOL UNIFORM
Art by Chris Bachalo

Quire's consciousness later learned of the X-Men's establishment of an informal mutant nation on the artificial island of Utopia. Believing the idea was originally his, Quire sought to destroy Utopia, but was prevented from doing so by telepaths Martha Johansson and the Stepford Cuckoos. Later, would-be mogul and pre-teen genius Kade Kilgore, while seeking to obtain business for his weapons manufacturing holdings by stoking humanity's fear of mutants, secretly freed Quire from his containment unit and enabled his assault on an international arms control conference in Switzerland, where X-Men leader Cyclops (Scott Summers) was presenting a speech on the danger of mutant-hunting Sentinel technology. Continuing to seek mutant revolution, Quire mentally forced numerous attending world leaders to confess their corrupt or unethical behaviors on live television then publicly claimed credit for his actions; the resulting arms sales greatly pleased Kilgore, but caused anti-mutant chaos worldwide. When arrogantly seeking asylum on Utopia after becoming Earth's most wanted mutant, Quire was detained by the X-Men, and following a philosophical schism that divided the X-Men, Quire was forced by Wolverine (Logan/James Howlett) to attend his newly opened Jean Grey School for Higher Education on the site of the destroyed Xavier Institute in New York state. Despite vocal opposition to Quire's freedom voiced by the Director of US superhuman affairs Captain America (Steve Rogers), Wolverine was allowed to retain Quire in one last effort to reform him on the conditions that Wolverine file weekly updates of Quire's progress, that Quire was monitored by psychic X-Man Marvel Girl (Rachel Grey) and at the first sign of trouble, the Avengers, Earth's premier superhumans, take him into custody.

On the first day of school, during the New York State Department of Education's inspection of the campus, Quire was placed on detention and guarded by headmistress Kitty Pryde's friend Lockheed the dragon to prevent him from causing problems in front of the inspectors. However, to protect his interests in having humankind hate mutantkind, Kilgore and his allies attempted to destroy the school to prevent students from learning peaceful methods of cohabitation. During the attack, Quire secretly used his telepathy to calm Kilgore's genetic duplicate of the X-Men's sentient island foe Krakoa; discovering the Krakoa duplicate was as lonely and misunderstood as Quire himself privately felt, he encouraged it to request becoming the school's grounds and a member of the X-Men. Within the first week of school, Quire attempted at least 14 militant uprisings, including a small riot in the lunchroom over "draconian dietary restrictions regarding tater-tots," and his lack of personal hygiene and his acidic personality further alienated him from the student body, resulting in his further lashing out at his fellow students.

AS TOP BOSS
Art by Mark Brooks

Later, seeking revenge on Wolverine for forcing him to attend the school, Quire extracted his favorite parts from video games he had played and movies he had seen to create a hyper-detailed imaginary world within his brain called the Construct. After he trapped Wolverine's and fellow student Armor (Hisako Ichicki)'s consciousnesses within this world, Quire bragged about it to other students to gain their respect, but he was rejected. However, bereft of Wolverine's psyche, which was living the life of a black market runner that had fallen in his employer's bad graces within the Construct, Wolverine's body was taken over by the animalistic bloodlust that was usually restrained by Wolverine's conscious efforts and went on a rampage within the school while hunting Quire. Realizing his subconscious was helping the Construct take on a life of its own while he slept, Quire entered the Construct and installed himself as the Top Boss of this world while seeking a way to discontinue it from within. As the Boss, Quire convinced Wolverine and Armor to work with him in battling his subconscious, but when all efforts to shut the Construct down failed, Quire realized he had to die to end the program and directed Wolverine to stab him in the heart, a sacrificial act that restored their consciousnesses to their rightful bodies. Following this, a remorseful Quire planned to leave the school to be incarcerated by the Avengers, but impressed by what Quire accomplished with the Construct, Wolverine refused to let him leave and scheduled weekly psychic training sessions with Quire to train Wolverine how to prevent being defeated by similar psychic attacks.

HEIGHT: 5'8" **EYES:** Brown
WEIGHT: 129 lbs. **HAIR:** Brown (often dyed pink)

ABILITIES/ACCESSORIES: Quentin Quire is an Omega-level telepath who can form and organize thoughts at the rate of ten million per second. Among his array of mental talents, Quire can communicate telepathically over long distances, read the minds and manipulate the thoughts and bodily functions of others, shield his mind against telepathic probes, remove the consciousnesses of others from their minds, and create entire worlds within his own brain. Quire has demonstrated some telekinetic abilities and has used his vast intellect to create a variety of devices including anti-gravity technology and a telepathy-inhibiting helmet. Quire is proficient in the use of a bullwhip, is a capable ice skater, an avid video game player and wears corrective lenses.

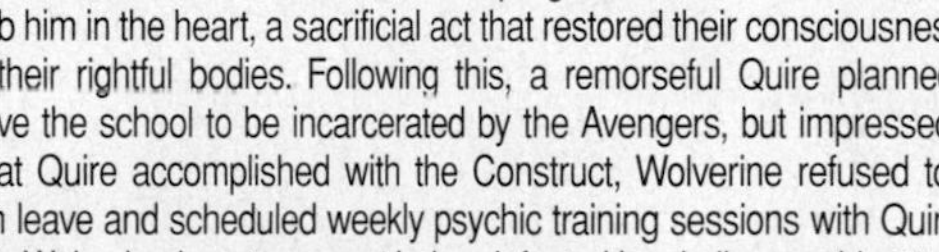

POWER GRID
1 2 3 4 5 6 7
INTELLIGENCE
STRENGTH
SPEED
DURABILITY
ENERGY PROJECTION
FIGHTING SKILLS

Art by Mike O'Sullivan

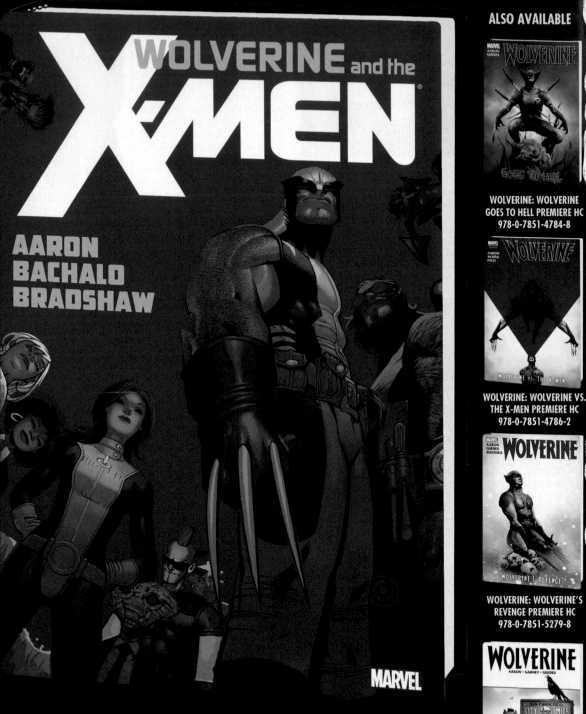